Werner Erhard

Books by William Warren Bartley, III

The Retreat to Commitment
Morality and Religion
Wittgenstein
Lewis Carroll's Symbolic Logic

Werner Erhard

The transformation of a man:
The founding of *est*

By
William Warren Bartley, III

Clarkson N. Potter, Inc./Publishers   *New York*

Distributed by Crown Publishers

Inquiries should be addressed to Clarkson N. Potter, Inc., One Park Avenue,
New York, N.Y. 10016
Printed in the United States of America
Published simultaneously in Canada by General Publishing Company Limited
First edition

Designed by Robert Bull

Library of Congress Cataloging in Publication Data

Bartley, William Warren, 1934–
    Werner Erhard: the transformation of a man, the founding of *est*

    1. Erhard, Werner, 1935–   2. Erhard seminars training.
3. Psychologists—United States—Biography. RC489.E7B37 158 [B]
RC489.E7B37   158 [B]   78-8990
ISBN 0-517-53502-5

Third Printing, November, 1978

For Robert Larzelere, M.D.

Contents

Foreword

BY WERNER ERHARD

This book tells the story of my life. Much of it is in my words, and in the words of my family and friends and close associates in *est*, as they talked with the author, my friend Bill Bartley.

As he explains, I don't think that the story of my life, my personal drama, is very important. The painter Georgia O'Keeffe put it perfectly when she said, "Where I was born and where and how I have lived are unimportant. It is what I have done with where I have been that should be of interest."

While I have a past, I am not my past. I recognize, however, that people are interested, and since a story will eventually be written, I want to support its being presented accurately.

I am particularly pleased that Bill wanted to write this story. I had read his biography of the philosopher Ludwig Wittgenstein, and knew that he was able to weave together the story of a life and the abstractions in terms of which a life takes place.

As I read through the manuscript, I was struck by the quotation from Kierkegaard that Bill uses to open the fifth chapter. It seems to pierce to the heart of what happened: "What our age needs is education. And so this is what happened: God chose a man who also needed to be educated, and educated him *privatissime*, so that he might be able to teach others from his own experience."

I truly did need to be educated. And God did take me and educate me—unconventionally, and *very* privately: for a long time no one, including myself, knew that anything was happening.

This is what did happen.

Introduction

Convictions and ideas came to him, so to speak, from the subsoil. He had a prophetic sympathy with the dawning sentiments of the age, with the mood of the dumb majority. . . . His way of thinking and feeling represented the true America, and represented in a measure the whole ultra-modern, radical world.
— *George Santayana (on William James)*

I first heard about *est* on a rainy afternoon in March 1972, in the office of a medical doctor in Berkeley. I was at that time living in Pennsylvania, was visiting in California for a few months, and had sought out the doctor on the advice of a friend. My complaint was simple. I had had insomnia for nine years, and had been taking sleeping pills and tranquilizers daily since the spring of 1963. One becomes habituated to these drugs—their effect wears off—and it was time for a change. I asked the doctor, an attentive vibrantly youthful man in middle age, to prescribe a new sleeping pill for me. His eyes sparkled with amusement.

He told me that he would be happy to prescribe some sleeping pills for me *if that was what I wanted.* "You don't have to take sleeping pills. You don't have to have insomnia." he told me. What I could do, he explained, was to take a training course in San Francisco. It lasted two weekends; it cost only a few hundred dollars. And on completing it I would no longer have insomnia.

What the doctor said sounded preposterous. I had already taken my insomnia to psychoanalysts. I had had a Freudian analysis, and also a Jungian analysis. Both had benefited me, and neither had touched the insomnia. During my Freudian analysis I explored my childhood memories and my sexuality. And at night when I could not sleep I thought about sex. During my Jungian analysis I explored archetype and symbol in my own existence. And at night when I could not sleep I would think about archetype and symbol. I had spent thousands on these analyses, far more than the comparatively modest cost of this training.

I enrolled immediately, by telephone, from the doctor's office. There was no reason in what I did: I was desperate. To be dependent on tranquilizers and sleeping pills is a living death. I would have done anything for a good night's sleep and—more important—for a day free from the stupor of these pills. I would have tried anything to free myself from the *pretense* into which these drugs forced me. I was a professional philosopher. My job was the life of reason; it was my vocation to be alert. Yet the theme of my life had become the concealment of my stupor—the appearance, not the reality, of alertness.

Two weeks later I began the first weekend of the *est* training. By the end of the second weekend I no longer had insomnia. I no longer take pills of any kind.

est is a training program in the expansion and transformation of consciousness which was founded by Werner Erhard in California in 1971.

From the beginning it has appeared to be a curious and original, indigenously American blend of Asian and European themes—of Zen and Gestalt and a dozen other paths. Unlike most programs and disciplines with which it can readily be compared, it was never a cult or cultish, and has always aimed at the widest possible audience. In this, it has been eminently successful: at the beginning of 1978, 132,000 persons had graduated from the *est* training; by the end of that year, another 41,000 will have completed it; by the end of 1979, these numbers will grow by yet another 50,000.

It is successful. But is it serious? Is it a fad? Or something of more enduring value?

In 1974, when *est* began to come to national attention, it was often seen as another pop psychology California fad, a kind of psychological Barnum and Bailey, catering to the affluent and narcissistic radical-chic residents of West Coast spas and suburbs: it was a circus that came calling on the freak show. By late 1976, as enrollment climbed, *est* centers opened throughout the country—in the Midwest and in the South as well as on the two coasts. Symbolizing *est's* growing reputability, the former chancellor of the University of California's medical campus in San Francisco now sat as chairman of the *est* Advisory Board. *est* itself came to be appreciated more broadly as a consciousness training program of wide value, at least comparable to the old Dale Carnegie courses, and perhaps more powerful. Almost everyone knew someone—aunt, cousin, brother, co-worker, friend—who had taken the *est* training for one reason or another: to shed weight, shyness, phobia; to improve energy, self-image, appearance, love life; to attain what was called, with open-eyed simplicity and innocence, "aliveness."

As I write this, something more is emerging: not something new, for it was there from the beginning; but something that has not been much noticed before. I have in mind *est's* program for "transforming" social institutions. The *est* people have always had a sense of humor—and they started with prisons. *est* has trained prisoners in five prisons with sufficient success that the federal government is funding a major study of the results of the training in federal correctional institutions. Moving to the other end of that spectrum, *est* has started to give trainings to the administrators of city governments.

Prisons and city administrations appear to be only the beginning. For Werner Erhard, the founder of *est* and the subject of this book, is unambiguous about his aim: his aim is "to have a world that works," through the "transformation" of individuals, relationships, institutions, and society. However impractical and unrealistic this may sound, it is not just rhetoric. Erhard's chief difference from virtually every other consciousness leader—from Gurdjieff to Baba Ram Dass—can be summed up in a sentence. Erhard is a pioneer not so much in consciousness as in the *ecology* of consciousness. Individual transformation—whether conceived as "enlightenment" or "consciousness raising" or in other terms—cannot, in his view, readily be sustained in an untransformed environment, amidst untransformed relationships and groups. Thus his program focuses not only on individuals but also on the relationships, institutions, and social issues that provide the environment for individual consciousness.

Nor are the conditions for transformation present, in his view, when people are hungry. Thus Erhard has launched a program whose goal is the eradication, within twenty years, of death by starvation on this globe.

It might be thought that our question—whether *est* matters?—has been answered. Any group with so large and rapidly growing a constituency, and with such ambitious goals, has to be taken seriously. Werner Erhard's influence is obviously considerable.

But that is not really the question. When people ask, as they often do, whether *est* is "for real," it is not its practical impact or potential as a social phenomenon that concerns them. They may even hold that against it. The question, rather, is how *est* compares with other programs, disciplines, and religions in the charting of the human spirit. Is it a legitimate theoretical contribution? Is it a practical, technical innovation? Is it a new religion? What does it have to say about the human condition? What does it do to inspire, transfigure, or at least explain human behavior? And what kinds of measures, what criteria, can one fairly bring to bear in evaluating it?

These are legitimate questions, and they came tumbling into my own mind in April 1972, as I sat through my own *est* training.

The *est* training of April 1972 began in the ballroom of a hotel on Market Street, in downtown San Francisco, and was presided over by a strange man with the unlikely name of Werner Erhard. Werner—as everyone soon began to call him—baffled me. I could not place him—socially or intellectually. For one thing, he came without trappings, without white coat, long flowing robe, or three-piece suit. He was dressed simply and informally in an open shirt and plain dark trousers. Clean shaven and neatly groomed, he wore an ordinary pair of brown loafers. His trousers were sharply pressed, and his shoes were brightly polished; apart from that, there was nothing distinctive about his dress. He could have been Jewish, yet neither his speech nor his mannerisms suggested that. Intellectually, he was even more puzzling. His grammar was peculiar; he repeatedly said "different than" and he used first-person pronouns as the objects of prepositions, mistakes that a formally educated person would not make.

Yet by the time of our first break, about four hours after he had begun to talk, it was clear that we were in the presence of a man of great resources. He seemed to move among the two hundred and fifty people seated in that hotel ballroom with a repertoire of emotions, arguments, and responses that fitted no pattern yet was always on target. He exuded power yet had an unerring sensitivity to everyone in his vicinity. With every person who presented him- or herself to him, he dealt differently. There was no "routine," no set technique or response. At times he seemed callous—as with a woman who was wallowing in self-pity. To those who jumped to her defense, he observed that giving her sympathy was like giving alcohol to an alcoholic. With those who used argument and intellectual structures as protection against their feelings, he displayed brilliance. He had, as it turned out, immense stores of information, and juggled with abstract ideas of physics and philosophy as if they were toys. He would puncture reason and logic with reason and logic—and then stand back to mock the process. To those who tried to please or impress him or to catch his attention, he was politely indifferent—meanwhile leading them into their own special trap. At other times, as some of the group began to "get off it," to emerge from the network of self-deception in their lives, he became gentle and compassionate, even mothering.

He punctured illusions. He unmasked motives. He probed rationalizations. He laughed at hypocrisy. As he worked with us he discerned character, motive, even life story almost instantaneously. He appeared to know what one was *going* to say and immediately understood what one *did* say. He seemed, moreover, to be able to say almost anything to anybody: there was no domination in his unmasking of façades.

Sometimes, what he said seemed calculated to evoke pained or shocked or surprised reactions from the group. As we reacted, he pointed out how easy it was to "push our buttons." Yet nothing anyone could do to "get back" at him seemed to work. Trainees would yell, curse, weep, protest, become indignant, sulk—and he would, chuckling, lay bare the "pay-offs" in these reactions. In his actions and observations there was a combination of warmth, self-control, and spontaneity not to be acquired through sheer discipline, repetition, or imitation.

He stood in front of us—this tall, slender, immaculately dressed blue-eyed man—in full view, for sixteen hours each day, two successive days in a row. Not once did he leave the room for food or rest. Not once did his attention or concentration slack. He had virtually total recall of anything said to him by a trainee and would refer back to things said earlier with minute accuracy. He remembered why each of us had enrolled; and he knew what we thought our problems were.

At midnight he seemed as clean and well pressed, and as fresh, as he had been at eight o'clock that morning. Like most things he did, this was also a kind of . . . demonstration.

Werner was young—he was thirty-six then—yet he seemed at once a child and, Merlin-like, an immensely old and wise man who had experienced everything and seen through everyone. In that hotel ballroom he created a complex psychological space, in which I sensed a roominess that I had not previously experienced.

I was not simply *impressed* by this man Werner Erhard and his *est* training. I was moved. On the second day, to my astonishment, he seated one of us on the stage beside him and, in front of the other two hundred and forty-nine of us, led him back, step by painful step, through his birth trauma. To do this he used a technique which he called the "truth process," probing deeper and deeper into the bodily sensations, emotions, attitudes, states of mind, and memories of this individual. This was a most powerful thing; gradually there was displayed before us the truth about this trainee's life. And as the truth was told, the problem vanished. Another man got rid of—Werner would say "disappeared"—a backache from which he had suffered for fifteen years. A young woman was relieved, at least temporarily, of her chronic asthma.

To mention these incidents may make the training seem medical or psychotherapeutic. That would be mistaken. Werner was training us, as he had said he would, to master problems. These particular physical problems happen to be among the most dramatic and easily describable. Nor had Werner cured anyone. He had not cured my insomnia, nor a backache, nor a case of asthma. Rather, he created a situation—he would call it a "context" or a "space"—in which we could deal with our own ills.

So far so good.

But what I witnessed and experienced during the four days of the *est* training also disturbed me. I had no framework to explain or interpret what was going on. I could hardly believe that all was as it purported to be. What Werner was saying seemed a mixture of the deep, the obvious, and the ridiculous.

The only metaphors and images that I had at my disposal to describe what I was witnessing were religious. I recalled the Bible stories about the healings at the Pool of Bethesda and at Capernaum. Yet the greater part of the training was philosophical, not religious, in character. As a historian and philosopher, I could see "influences." But these had nothing to do with it, really. This man Werner Erhard spoke "as one having authority and not as the scribes." He was a "man of knowledge." *Or was he?* My world began to bristle with question marks. Contradictory questions bombarded me. How could this be happening? Was I the victim of mass hypnosis? Did this man's power lie in my own naïveté? How could it be that I had never heard of anything like this before? Is this fraud? How could such a person be doing what he seemed to be doing? Was he a charlatan? If this was real, it was incredibly important. And if it was a fraud, how could I be falling for it? Who was this most improbable person, this Johnny Appleseed of consciousness, this "transformer"?

As the two weekends of the training went by, I gradually began to pick up bits and pieces of information about him. First about esoteric disciplines that he had studied. Then someone told me that he was a former car salesman. An esoteric discipline indeed! Later, toward the end of the second weekend, I heard that his real name was Jack Rosenberg, and that he was from Philadelphia. I heard tales about his past, "thick with wives and nefarious deeds." Finally I was told that he had become enlightened while driving one day on a California freeway. *A California freeway!*

And what, for that matter, about those disciplines, so-called, that had educated, molded, shaped him during a most peculiar spiritual odyssey: Maxwell Maltz and Carl Rogers, Zen, Subud, Scientology, hypnosis, Gestalt, encounter. What a combination! Can any of it really be taken seriously?

Most of these questions, I found, could be given straightforward answers. Yet there are some obstacles in the way of adequate answers to questions about Werner Erhard and about *est*. Many of these obstacles stem from our own gentility. They cluster in the contrast, identified long ago by the great American philosopher George Santayana, between the "genteel tradition" in American philosophy and the spirt of "aggressive enterprise."[1] As Santayana puts it, "The American Will inhabits the skyscraper; the American Intellect inhabits the colonial mansion." The genteel tradition and the colonial mansion represent the polite yet censorious, conventional yet pretentious, terribly earnest, sterile, and unhappy American intellect and its agonized conscience. Few American philosophers have been able to wrench themselves free from this tradition, which Santayana sees as the chief enemy of vigor and imagination in cultural life. Thus Erhard, and his philosophical education, held particular fascination for me as a philosopher and educator. For I was a genteel philosopher, and his was vital and living philosophy, philosophy in the raw.

Werner Erhard is, indeed, anything but genteel. In the whole *est* approach, not just in the training, there is a mocking, an irreverence, a satire, a humor, reminiscent of Lenny Bruce. Everybody and everything is up for question: those who are trying to be "hip" are challenged just as much as those who are "straight." The trainer "works close to the material." Genteel American comedians such as Bob Hope maintained a distance from the things at which they poked fun; they did not intrude. They released anxiety but did not come close enough to the bone to generate more. The *est* training is not at all Bob Hope: it is very much Lenny Bruce—highly intrusive, and very "down."

Erhard is also the very embodiment of American Will. Intrusive and aggressively enterprising, his philosophy has been called one of "final cause," in which worlds are created and governed by intention, goals, and purposes; in which an idea is the most powerful thing in the universe. If the genteel tradition has never really understood American Will, how readily can it comprehend or analyze a meeting—such as Werner Erhard is—between American Will and *Oriental* Intellect?

To answer all these questions in terms of the known quantities of the genteel tradition is, then, far from easy. This man and these disciplines are, for the genteel tradition, unknown quantities, and are therefore mysteries. Where there is mystery there is fantasy; and where there is fantasy there is belief. Hence such questions tend to be answered in terms of competing beliefs: some believe that Erhard is a saint; others, that he is the most blatant fraud.

Erhard, however, does not believe in belief.

This book aims to penetrate belief by presenting that experience which is captured in a life story. It tells the story of a rogue genius and American original whose person, life, education, program, are all at issue. It is the story of Erhard's life, education, and transformation, and tells how a poor boy from Philadelphia, a car salesman named Jack Rosenberg, a liar, an impostor, and a wife-deserter, got to that California freeway: how he became a man of integrity and compassion. It is also a universal story of the search for true identity and for Self.

W. W. Bartley, III
Piedmont Pines
Montclair-Oakland
California

Werner Erhard

PART I Shadow Play

On all matters of fact I am perfectly honest: I can state dates, acts of treason, . . . etc., with absolute veracity. But once I start confessing the why-and-wherefore of my behaviour (as one is expected to do in a book), I become so entertained by the personal drama of it all that everything I put down has a wonderful ring of truth: I feel myself growing from a particular person into a universal design.
—*Nigel Dennis,* Cards of Identity

ONE Donning the Mask

Like Oedipus, we live in ignorance of the desires that offend morality, the desires that nature has forced upon us, and after their unveiling we may prefer to avert our gaze from the scenes of childhood.
—Sigmund Freud

IN SEARCH OF WHO ONE REALLY IS

This is a story about true and false identity, and about who each of us really is. It is couched in the form of the life history of someone named Werner Erhard, an impostor by destiny and by choice, who went on a fateful journey of self-discovery.

An impostor is someone with a fictitious past. The first thing to learn on the road to one's own true self is that one is not who one thinks one is. Each person, without exception, has a fictitious past; each of us is, precisely, an impostor.

In setting off in search of true identity, one steps into a labyrinth, a maze, a tunnel of love, a hall of mirrors, a derelict graveyard, a long-neglected archeological site. Whatever metaphor one uses, part of the task is to uncover and to confront one's accumulated masks, distorted images, multiple false identities at cross-purposes. One must peel away not only the masks one knows so well, those that one thinks one is wearing now, but a host of other masks—those thought of and those never considered, never even imagined—that one wears in the course of life. Most of the masks we wear have been there longer than we can remember; we became impostors in childhood. And we continue to wear them throughout our lives. Paradoxically, although we bequeath our masks liberally to our children, we also wear them firmly to our graves.

Among those obstacles lying in the way of who we really are, preventing us from exposing our false identities and uncovering our true identity, is a sentimental and romantic notion about the past, in particular, about childhood, that time when the most intractable, the most unyielding of all false identifications—identifications with our own parents—were laid down in our psyches. Underneath those sentimental childhood scenes, those old anecdotes seemingly so unimportant and insignificant in themselves, is the drama of the donning of the mask.

JOE AND DOROTHY AND THEIR BOY

"Man is vile, but people are wonderful." This thought fluttered through my mind as I was sitting with Joe and Dorothy Rosenberg around their dining-room table in Plymouth Meeting, a suburb of Philadelphia. I had been talking with them, first separately, then together, for a week. In front of us on the table was a pile of photographs that Dorothy had rooted out of several albums and drawers. Now the story was coming back again, as Dorothy or Joe identified each photograph and the memory that went with it.

As she picked up another photo of a smiling baby with blond curls, playing at the beach, Dorothy continued her story of Werner's birth. *Werner's* birth. Since 1972, Dorothy and Joe Rosenberg have got used to calling their eldest son "Werner." But the baby that was born at 11:25 that Thursday night, September 5, 1935, in Jefferson Hospital in Philadelphia, was named simply Jack Rosenberg, after a deceased brother of his father.

The account of Jack's—or Werner's—childhood that Joe and Dorothy gave me was such a nice story. It was the sort of story that my own parents—and their parents, and their parents' parents—would have remembered too. Even Jocasta, the mother of Oedipus, would have treasured such memories. Their account—like all such accounts—was sunny and lyrical, evoking domestic sentiment, warm summer afternoons and crisp bright winter days, snug apartments and scrupulous cleanliness, good food and hearty loving relationships. In the foreground lay the little land of counterpane; in the background,

Brahms's lullaby played softly. It was a homey story of proud father and doting mother, and of baby, of a world where the only tragedy was a lost or broken toy; the only smells, those of Christmas cookies and fir trees . . . and lox and bagels.

Joe and Dorothy were young in 1935: both were twenty-five. Joe was tall, slender, and strikingly good-looking, with dark hair and a broad smile. "Joe was a very well-dressed, even suave individual," his nephew Norman Danoff had told me. "He used to wear spats and a derby. And he drove his mother crazy. She still took care of his clothes—the shirts had to be done just so and repairs were not permitted. He looked exactly like Werner does today and a million women were after him. From time to time he would get on the train and go down to Pimlico or somewhere to the racetrack. Nothing to it. They couldn't afford it. But shoot a hundred dollars, that was Joe."

Dorothy was simply beautiful. She was intelligent, and she was determined. She was the sort of woman that other women do not particularly care for and that men often have trouble with—and the sort of woman who commands intense loyalty. She knew instinctively that one cannot reason a person out of a position that he has not been reasoned into. And she used this truth with strength and savvy.

Joe and Dorothy were also independent and hardworking. Living during the Great Depression in one of the nation's most depressed cities, both had jobs in the management side of the restaurant business. Their courtship, in 1933, had been a stormy and romantic, and independent, affair. And the parents on both sides had worried over it.

Joe was a Jew, the son of an immigrant tailor. Joe's father and mother, Nathan Rosenberg and Clara Kaufmann, had both been born in Russia. Joe was their fourth child: the first two children had been born in Russia; the remaining four children, including Joe, were born in the United States.

Dorothy, on the other hand, was an Episcopalian, of English and Swedish extraction, a Daughter of the American Revolution, related on her mother's side to Ethan Allen, the colonial American philosopher. Dorothy's father, William E. Clauson, had graduated from Williston Preparatory School in Easthampton, Massachusetts, and studied for a time at Yale. Her mother, Bessie George, had been a French teacher. The various branches of the Clauson and George families were Unitarian, Lutheran, and Episcopalian.

To get past his parents' initial opposition, Joe introduced

Dorothy to them as a "Swedish Jewess." They quickly learned the truth, and embraced her into the family anyway. The Clausons were a little slower. "When I started going out with Joe," Dorothy explained, "my mother warned me that this wasn't going to work out. But I was determined that it would."

They were married on August 20, 1933. By early 1934, the marriage was in trouble, and Joe and Dorothy separated for a year. Eventually they were reconciled and Dorothy became pregnant. That terminated talk of divorce, and the marriage survived.

Dorothy and Joe had been married by a rabbi in a synagogue, and Dorothy began domestic life as the mistress of a kosher kitchen. As part of an agreement with Joe, she returned from her separation to a kitchen that was no longer kosher, and to a household where religion was for a time to remain an open question. When Dorothy and Joe brought their infant son home to their apartment on Chestnut Street in West Philadelphia, in September 1935, they agreed that he should not be baptized until he was old enough to choose for himself.

So the matter continued for the next three years, undefined, until the spring of 1938, when Joe did the utterly unexpected. He suddenly got old-time religion, and became a fundamentalist Christian. If Dorothy would not become a Jew, Joe would be the one to change. It happened like this.

Joe was managing an all-night restaurant, at 52nd and Baltimore in West Philadelphia, where he worked from eleven o'clock at night until seven in the morning. Near dawn one morning, around the time when the milkman and the drunks came in, a man at Joe's counter exclaimed over his newspaper: "Those damn Jews. I can't stand them. I hate them." Another man, an Italian, looked over and replied quietly: "Well, I don't hate them. I love them. My savior was a Jew." Joe began talking with him, and finally accepted his invitation to go the following Friday evening to a Baptist Mission "to hear a Jew preach Christ."

By Friday evening, Joe had cold feet. Dorothy was out for the evening, and her sister Barbara was baby-sitting. Joe was asleep, and Barbara was instructed to tell any callers that he was out. Little two-year-old Werner, however, had been listening. When the Christian arrived at seven o'clock, Werner scrambled out of his crib, ran to the head of the stairs, looked down, and shouted: "Daddy *is* here. He's in bed asleep."

Werner had given away his father's whereabouts, and Joe had to get up, and did go to the Mission, a dimly lighted hall, a storefront mission, across from the Philadelphia Savings Fund Society on Walnut Street. In the makeshift pulpit, a young man read from the Beatitudes. "I listened," Joe reports, "and I was enthralled. What he said hit me like a sledgehammer. I lowered my head and said, 'If what this man is saying is the truth, Lord, give me a little bit of it.' "

Shortly afterward, Joe met another Jew turned Christian, a preacher named Abraham Moses Zegel, who became the most important spiritual influence in his life. Zegel had been trained in Poland to be a rabbi, and had become a Christian. Trapped on a visit to England when Hitler marched on Poland, Zegel had emigrated to the United States by way of Canada. For years afterward, Joe Rosenberg supported him financially, contributed to his rent, fed him and clothed him. Joe went around with him preaching salvation and the forgiveness of sins from street corners, and in prisons and churches.

"Joe made Billy Graham sound like he was sitting crocheting," reports Norm Danoff. "When Joe was a Baptist, there wasn't a soul within a mile who didn't hear about it. He had an incredibly large voice. And he would talk for hours on end." Zegel formed a group, the Christian Testimony to the Jew, sponsored by the Baptist Church. Joe Rosenberg participated in this group, and served on its Board of Directors for many years.

Dorothy was surprised—and not entirely pleased—by Joe's conversion. Joe had come round to her position in a very *irritating* way. "When Joe became a Baptist," Dorothy recalls, "there was no more smoking, drinking, or going to the movies." Dorothy attended mission meetings with Joe from time to time in those early days, but would not consider Baptist immersion for herself. She held to the Episcopal Church, where she taught Sunday School. (In the early fifties, Joe would become an Episcopalian too, joining his wife and children. He remains a conservative Christian today.)

So it was that Werner Erhard—though by descent half Jewish—did not receive a Jewish upbringing. Before Joe's conversion, the boy went regularly to Episcopal Sunday School; afterward, Bible reading and Christian prayer became part of the household routine. Werner continued to attend the Episcopal Church regularly, was baptized John Paul Rosenberg, was confirmed, and served for eight years as an acolyte at the altar.

"Werner was fond of his Jewish grandparents," Dorothy said. "We used to spend Passover at their house. But he never had a Bar Mitzvah, or anything like that. The belief that Christ was the savior was with us all the way through."

"I taught him Bible stories," Joe recalls. "I spoke to him about these things every time I had a chance. I was on fire with religion. Zegel and I would sit in the living room talking about religion and the Bible, and Werner would watch us like a hawk. Zegel, who was childless, loved Werner, and called him his own child."

The Rosenbergs moved from the endless row houses and unchanging rooftops of West Philadelphia to the neighboring suburb of Bala Cynwyd in 1940, when Werner was five years old. Bala Cynwyd was at the time a small place with a population of about three thousand, the nearest of the Main Line communities to the Philadelphia border. They took a second-floor apartment on City Line Avenue, at the corner of Bala Avenue, only a few minutes' walk from the restaurant where Dorothy was working. Joe's restaurant was a fifteen-minute commute on the number 70 trolley into West Philadelphia. Here they lived for the next ten years.

Werner staked out a territory for himself in Bala. There was a driveway behind the apartment, a small hill beyond it, and then a large lot. Beyond the vacant lot was the house of a boy named Henry Tooke, who became his best childhood friend. Apart from his dog, Maizie, who was born when Werner was six and who lived for eighteen years, Werner had two close friends and constant companions. One was Henry Tooke; the other was Don Clauson, Werner's cousin, who lived with his grandparents in Germantown.

Werner was close to his mother. "We would be in the kitchen together most of the time," Dorothy remembers. "If we weren't in the kitchen, we'd be in his room, where I would read to him, or where he would read to himself before going to bed. He would bring me the things he made in school—I still have a demitasse spoon holder that he made for me," she said, pointing to the dining-room wall.

The relationship of son to mother indeed seemed idyllic. "I remember how, from time to time, Dorothy would walk me to kindergarten," Werner told me. "It was a long walk, it would take about an hour. I remember one autumn morning vividly. It was beautiful, crisp and clear. The leaves had fallen from the trees and lay along the ground. They would crunch and crackle underfoot. As we walked along, we passed a stream that ran partway along the road. Ducks were swimming in it. We stopped, I fed them, we talked about them.

"Dorothy was wonderful to me. She gave me credit for being able to communicate and to learn. She answered my questions, she wasn't condescending. We had conversations in which my opinion counted. In the space she gave me I truly expanded. She was really my guru, almost a Zen master. Her affection was mediated by a lot of discipline and training. She expected and demanded a lot from me. And I had great respect for her."

WERNER AS OEDIPUS

This idyllic setting had a grimmer, darker side. Beginning in 1938 when Werner was three—not long after Joe's conversion to Christianity—Werner met with a series of violent accidents.

Dorothy had gone into the kitchen one evening, after waking from a nap, to prepare dinner. She was still wearing pyjamas. "I had a paring knife in my hands and some spinach," she told me. "Just outside the kitchen there was a fire escape landing, where I had a bushel full of potting soil. Werner ran out there so quickly that I couldn't stop him and started trying to hammer nails into the bushel basket. I was terrified, but didn't want to alarm him, lest he turn and fall. We were three stories up and it was an open fire escape, with iron railings, which didn't provide much protection for a small boy. I thought to take him by the hand, but before I could move there was a small dull sound, and he was gone. He had dropped his hammer over the railing, leaned over to see where it went, and fell down.

"I rushed out and saw him lying on the concrete. I thought he was dead. I don't know how I got down those two flights of stairs. When I reached him, there was no blood streaming, but there was heavy clotted blood in his ears. He was lifeless and without color. I picked him up and ran to the front of the building. I had to get him to the hospital fast. I was standing on the pavement, holding a child I thought was dead, just hoping a car would pass by. We had no car at the time. Joe had worked all night and he was asleep. I yelled to my younger brother, Eddie, who was going to baby-sit for me that evening, to wake Joe up.

"Fortunately a car came by, and stopped, and drove us to the hospital. I thought Werner was dead, but then I heard him groan. When we got to the hospital, they took him into the emergency room and cut his clothes away. I heard him groan again. Meanwhile Joe arrived. He saw that Werner wasn't breathing, called the doctor, and they forced air into his lungs and got him breathing again."

Werner remembered the episode. "Oddly enough," he said, "I remember what the room looked like, and I can see the doctor's face before me now. I actually died then. My body had been shoved off to the side. It was an intern, not the regular attending physician, who gave me the mouth-to-mouth resuscitation."

Dorothy continued her story. "Even though he was now breathing, I didn't know whether he would survive. I ran after the doctor and asked him whether they shouldn't get a specialist. 'Madam,' he said, 'I am a specialist. According to medical science this child has no business living. You should say your prayers.'

"I started to pace the hospital hall, unaware that I was still in my pyjamas. As I walked down the hall I saw a painting of Jesus with the little children all around. I prayed: 'Please God, let me have him to raise.' Then I knew he was going to live, and I was suddenly aware of my pyjamas, and I went home. I dressed, and then went back and asked to be with him when he came to. They didn't want me there, but said that I could stay since it was a borderline case. They told me that he would have a terrible headache when he came to, and might be incoherent. They were anticipating serious brain damage.

"The doctors shaved off his blond curls, and made two incisions, one on either side of his skull. That was all. There was no further surgery. His skull was cracked like an egg, but the doctor said that if he were to touch him he might kill him. 'Just let him be,' he said."

Werner recovered, and after several months returned home, where he had to learn to walk all over again. During the next two years he met one accident after another. As the months went by, he ran a ruler down his throat; he was badly scalded; and he fractured his skull again in an automobile accident. Altogether, during this time, he spent over a year in the hospital. When he was nearly five, the accidents stopped for a time, as suddenly as they had begun. Two years passed quietly by.

Then, in 1942, when Werner was six years old, Joe was drafted into the army. Late the following spring, Joe was badly injured on an obstacle course, and spent six months in the hospital. In the early summer of 1943, Dorothy and Werner, who had remained together in Philadelphia, journeyed to visit Joe, traveling on wartime railroads from Philadelphia to Fort Custer, Michigan, where he was being rehabilitated.

During their visit, they went swimming in a lake. Werner dived into deep water, and nearly drowned. "I was bobbing up and down," he said, "shouting instead of taking in air when I surfaced. Struggling not to drown was terrifying. Once I lost that and couldn't get to the surface anymore and gave in to dying, it was all right. Then I just drowned. I had an experience of dying there. It wasn't bad to die." Werner lost consciousness. The lifeguard reached him in time, towed him to the dock, and he was saved.

Many years later, in the *est* training, Werner was to maintain that most accidents, even trivial ones, are psychologically motivated. The behavior of children, no less than of adults, he would maintain, is shaped by unconscious patterns and dramatic structures. Held in place and triggered into action by powerful repressed memories of painful and threatening content, these patterns come into play in the first few years of life and relate for the most part to one's parents.

An accident can serve, unconsciously, to attract attention to oneself; it can also act as a form of self-punishment. It is a common unconscious mechanism for dealing with feelings of guilt and with the experienced threat of punishment. One punishes oneself so as—with one and the same stroke—to enact the punishment and to obviate the need for it.

Why would Werner need to punish himself?

One possible explanation comes from the writings of Sigmund Freud. According to Freud, preeminent among the dramas of childhood are the battle with the father for the love of the mother. Seeing this as the key to understanding the psyche, Freud described the Oedipus complex. Each child, Freud teaches, is foreordained to reenact Sophocles's drama of the king who unwittingly killed his father and took his mother to wife. The psychologist C. G. Jung contested the Freudian account. Drawing, like Freud, on mythological sources, Jung saw the family romance of childhood in less sexual terms, and as less important causally. It represented, he thought, a heroic dragon fight with the First Parents, an archaic struggle with the archetypal Great Mother and Terrible Father, not with the personal parents.

Whatever the larger interpretation, there is little doubt that virtually every small boy does grow up in a battle-scarred and emotion-charged setting; that he is entwined emotionally with his mother; and that he unconsciously harbors competitive, even murderous, feelings toward the so much larger, threatening, fear-inspiring father-rival who seems to block his way, preventing his desire. So much transpires from the logic of the ordinary situation alone, quite apart from the instinctual and archetypal frameworks that Freud and Jung provide.

This family romance, so Freud and Jung agree, reaches a peak of intensity in the third and fourth years, and by the end of the fifth year goes underground. The boy moves into a latency period, wherein the strivings of the earlier period persist only in a repressed state. With the onset of puberty, the family romance is revivified and charged with the energy of adolescence.

What concerns us here is not the eventual adolescent resolution of the family romance, but the childhood experience of it. Competitiveness and lust erupt into the idyllic "innocence" of childhood. All this takes place, however, below the surface of a consciousness that is itself just surfacing. The child never quite knows what is happening; its parents rarely do.

The whole drama is aggravated by the psychological phenomenon of projection (the casting onto the external environment of unconscious states, feelings, thoughts, that are in fact internal to oneself). Thus may one people one's surroundings with one's own worst aspect. For instance, a boy who is *unconsciously* aggressive toward his father will, by the mechanism of projection, experience his father as being aggressive *toward him*, regardless of the real feelings of the father.

How is the small boy to deal with his unconscious fear of his father? One way is provided through the mechanism of *identification*. The boy unconsciously identifies with his father. *He becomes his father.* He makes internal his father's image, values, viewpoint. This is a survival stratagem to fend off the father's disapproval: the father would not, it is presumed, attack his own viewpoint.

Out of this internalization of parental images, there distills what is commonly called conscience. It may be a stern taskmaster, a repository of harsh commandments, severe out of all proportion to the severity of the real parents—and also irrational and inconsistent. It commands both "You ought to act like your father," and "You ought *not* to act like your father—at least in matters relating to the mother."

Does the Freudian account explain Werner's childhood accidents? I asked him.

"As a child," he replied, "I was never consciously afraid of my father. Nor was there any reason to be. Nontheless, my accidents are suspicious—particularly in their timing. Coinciding as they did with the appearance and passing of the Oedipus complex, they may well have been ways to deal with the unconscious pressures on me, particularly to punish my competitiveness with Joe, and to catch Dorothy's attention."

The same explanation, Werner pointed out, could interpret the near-drowning. Joe's departure into the army and removal from Philadelphia would have given Werner—through no act of his own, but by the grace of God, as it were—precisely what he wanted: sole possession of his mother. Then Joe met with *his* accident, leading Dorothy to travel to his side and lavish attention on him. From a Freudian viewpoint, the scene of the reunited family could have been intolerable for the child. His long-repressed competitiveness with Joe would emerge again—and, again, be punished. "An eye for an eye, and a tooth for a tooth." If one wishes another dead, an appropriate punishment is to be, oneself, dead. To wish death on a person with whom one is unconsciously identified is to order, in the unconscious, one's own execution.

And so it *may* have been with Werner. Whatever the real explanation may be, little Jack Rosenberg was quite unconscious of all these things, and it would be up to Werner Erhard, many years later, to discover the patterns in his past, and to complete his relationship with it. When he did do so, he would choose patterns of analysis and explanation that differed from Freud's.

Meanwhile, Werner and Dorothy returned together from Fort Custer to Philadelphia. Over two years would pass before Joe would return there permanently. Meanwhile, life was indeed peaceful and idyllic. Life was splendid. For a long time Werner would have no accidents.

AN INTERIOR DIALOGUE BEGINS

During these years in Bala Cynwyd with Dorothy, Werner began an interior dialogue, a private conversation that he did not reveal to others for many years.

We talked about this one sunny afternoon in Tiburon, a peninsula at the end of Marin County, stretching southward into the San Francisco Bay. We had just sailed across the bay from San Francisco, past the Golden Gate, past Angel Island and Belvedere, and into the Tiburon dock. We tied up our boat and came ashore for lunch. Werner began to talk about the place of religion in his childhood.

"I was very religious as a child," he recalled. "I usually spent the weekends with my grandparents, particularly during the war, because my mother worked full-time then, managing a restaurant. So the church in which I grew up was not Saint Asaph's, our proper parish church that was quite close to our apartment in Bala Cynwyd. Saint Asaph's was low church. I really grew up in a high Episcopal church, with confession and incense and all that. This was the Church of the Holy Nativity, the Episcopal church in Germantown where my grandparents lived. I was an altar boy there for eight years, and of course learned the ritual and the liturgy very well. I would light the candles, and ring the bell, and march in procession. The priest was a friend of my grandparents and would come to dinner on Sunday evenings from time to time.

"It was at this time that I first began to learn something of Eastern religious thought, too. This wasn't originally out of any desire for spiritual attainment. It was only later, in studying spiritual disciplines, that I heard about spiritual attainment." Werner paused, adding, "Incidentally, there is no such thing as attainment when it comes to being spiritual.

"I remember how I first got into yoga. I had taken the train downtown for my drum lesson. I was eleven or twelve. I had just begun to go downtown by myself. I got out of the lesson early, and was walking toward the train station. I stopped in a bookstore near Market Street, and found an old used book on Hatha Yoga. I took it home, and did all the exercises and practices, the breathing and postures, all of that."

I asked Werner whether he had instruction in yoga or talked with anyone about it. "Oh no, I did this on my own. There was nobody with whom I could have discussed it. This was an internal dialogue, one without external expression. Well, I suppose that there was *some* external expression, but no one would have known what I was doing: I can remember walking down City Line Avenue trying to walk without expending energy. I got one leg to float along without effort. I could never get both legs to work. I remember the elation I had at achieving that effortless motion with one leg.

"It wasn't just physical disciplines that I went into," Werner said. "I also had conversations about God with myself.

"Like a lot of kids, I remember puzzling over the questions that came up in confirmation classes. I wondered whether there really was a God, what all that I was taught to believe in really meant. I wondered why God made it so bad? Why did he make war and famine? I also asked whether I was really responsible. I don't think I put it that way then. I would have said: Can you get away with breaking the rules? Why do you have to keep the rules?

"I thought to myself that if God already knows everything I'm going to do, it doesn't matter: I might as well do anything. But that didn't seem to work either. Because I could only do what I'm going to do because God already knows I'm going to do it. I got so mind boggled that eventually I just gave up and tried to find some other principle in terms of which to live.

"That wasn't the first time I got tangled in philosophical questions," Werner added. "I was around six years old when I first tried to figure out how far out space goes. I began to watch myself watching myself. And then I would watch myself watching myself watching myself. And then I would watch myself watching myself watching myself watching myself. There was no end, and I realized that there was none. I remember going through all of that out in the field, lying in the tall grass, in the warm sunlight. There was a feeling of space, of infinity. It was a sort of meditative trance."

TWO Son and Mother

What all should we say about that particular human being who was called mother? . . . Whatever we say will always be too much, too false, too inadequate, and even too misleading. . . . But one who understands can no longer put such an enormous load of significance, or responsibility and duty, the weight of all heaven and hell, upon the weak and erring human being in need of love, care, understanding and forgiveness, who was our mother.
—C. G. Jung

A CHIP OFF THE OLD BLOCK

In the autumn of 1945, shortly following the Japanese surrender, Joe returned from the army. The ten-year-old child who greeted him was beginning to look—and to act—more and more like him. Werner's voice was not yet breaking, but it was already booming loudly like Joe's. Like his father, he was opinionated, even bossy; and he too loved to talk—and to persuade. He even puckered his lips as Joe did when savoring a point. He would correct his mother's handling of the household chores; and—drawing on his reading from the newspaper and his school books—he would roundly criticize the opinions of his father and uncles when they gathered each week for the "great family debates."

The Rosenbergs and the Clausons would get together on weekends and stay up half the night in heated discussion about practically anything: economics, politics, religion, family relationships, whatever. The whole family would take part—grandparents, uncles, aunts, everyone.

"It was the kind of family that would sit around the living room and talk and eat, talk and eat, until two o'clock in the morning," Werner's cousin Norm Danoff told me. "Remember, these are working people. A lot of them had to get up at five o'clock in the morning to go to work. The houses were small, and everything took place right there in the living and dining rooms. There wasn't any getting away from them.

"The conversation wasn't deep philosophical discussion," Norm said. "But it sure was wide ranging. My father used to get into politics. Joe would talk about religion, and Al Rosenberg would talk about business. Frank was the comedian of the family. He had thousands of stories to tell and he would tell them all night. Max was the audience. He didn't talk a lot. He laughed. People used to say, 'The Rosenbergs are still up! I went to work this morning and the lights were still on and everybody was sitting around the table eating.' "

Werner would pitch into these meetings with fervor. "I remember one of those late night conversations, when I was squared off against my Uncle Al Rosenberg," Werner told me. "It was just after the war, and we were arguing about socialism and communism and capitalism. I had come out for selfishness. Al talked in such a way that I began to sense how intimately my own well-being was related to that of others."

There was some point in the intensity of that conversation. After the bleak years of depression and war, a mood of anticipation and hope was in the air. Joe, for instance, was finally going to be able to go to college—under the GI bill. "Joe used to complain a lot," Norm Danoff told me. "He would say, 'I could have been a lawyer, a doctor, you name it. Instead, here I am slicing salami.' " So Joe entered Temple University, to work for a degree in food sciences and management. He entered an intensive program, aimed at cramming a four-year course into two and a half years; and he threw himself into student activities, becoming president of his college class and also of the veterans' association. He was rarely at home during the days. Dorothy, meanwhile, continued to work full time at the restaurant, and to care for Werner at home.

THE LACROSSE ACCIDENT

As he was growing up, Werner had often wondered why he had no brothers and sisters. "He couldn't understand it," Dorothy told me. "He wanted to know whether God didn't like him." But it had always been . . . an academic question.

In the late summer of 1947, when Werner was twelve, Dorothy became pregnant. Shortly after Werner learned of his mother's pregnancy, there was another accident.

It happened one afternoon in late November 1947. Werner had been playing lacrosse, and had broken his nose. Covered with blood, he raced home. "I was lying in bed with an infrared light on my shoulder," Dorothy recalls. "I had a bad case of bursitis. When he burst into the room, there was blood all over his face and down his front. I took one look and resolved not to get upset. I was following that old wives' tale that says that if you get upset while pregnant you will mark the child. So when he demanded, 'Aren't you going to *do* anything?', I just replied, very quietly, 'You know where the doctor is. Why don't you go to the doctor yourself?'"

Werner gave Dorothy a look that was grim and hopeless and a little absurd. This was for him a moment of shocking loss. He sees it as a turning point in his life. It was one of those moments when an identity is forged out of a situation and a relationship. He experienced a sudden loss of support, and also the unwelcome realization of his own independence. From this moment, his relations with Dorothy deteriorated. Communication and mutual admiration diminished, hostilities arose. They quarreled—shouting loudly, crying, slamming doors, throwing toys—about everything: his friends, his studies, his clothes, the places he went, the hours he kept. The world grew darker. The world was anguished. The lyrical quality went out of life.

Dorothy gave me an account of that time. "This was a more difficult time for me than Werner could have known," she said. "The pregnancy wasn't an easy one. And shortly after my daughter Joan's birth, in May, I went into a depression. The doctor put me on tranquilizers, but these just knocked me out. As they began to wear off, I would start crying. I didn't know what I was crying about, so I just invented things.

"I was on that drug only for about six weeks. But the whole episode made a lasting impression on Werner. This was a time when I felt embattled on all sides. I was having a hard time with Joe that Werner knew nothing about. I had a crying baby, and a teen-age son who wanted attention. Things were in turmoil, and the household itself became upsetting. It wasn't just that I was having tantrums. My own mother thought that I was having a nervous breakdown.

"When I realized the effect the medicine was having on me, I stopped taking it. Yet in the aftermath of all that, I didn't have the resources to stand back from the situation to discover what was happening. The close communication that Werner and I had enjoyed for so long just seemed to evaporate. I lost touch with him."

During these months Joe—who was in the middle of his final year at college—was on the verge of failing a chemistry course that was required for graduation. Werner had been helping his father with his studies all along, and had even coached him on Shakespeare and Plato. Now he rushed in to save him at chemistry.

"This was my chance," Werner told me. "I remember vividly what a problem my father's difficulty with chemistry was. It was interfering with something that he and my mother had invested so much in: his going to college. They were going to begin a whole new life from there. Helping him was a way for me to make an important contribution in a household where I felt increasingly worthless."

Werner read the books, did the exercises, tutored Joe on the material, and waited nervously for the results. But his tutoring was in vain. Joe failed the chemistry examination, and shortly thereafter had to drop out of college. When Dorothy stopped working to have their baby, Joe took over her job at the restaurant on City Line Avenue. Every member of the family felt defeated. "The horror of my life at this time," Werner told me, "was that—very suddenly—there no longer seemed to be any way for me to contribute to my family."

For years Dorothy had been to her son his *femme inspiratrice*, his source of creativity and ambition, his muse. Nor was the relationship one-sided. Nothing more affects the child than the unlived life of his parents; and Dorothy, dissatisfied and disappointed in her marriage, depended on her son for her own development, for companionship, for relatedness. Then, just at a time which is, in any case, critical, when the boy was reaching puberty, when such a relationship must perforce change, everything was complicated by the appearance, for the first time, of siblings. Such much younger siblings give no cause for ordinary sibling rivalry. What is resented—bitterly—is not so much the sibling as the loss of the mother—who doesn't seem to need *him* anymore. Just at the moment when he is beginning to sense that there is a limit to their relationship, that he cannot be her lover, the son learns that neither can he remain her child.

Matters with his father were no better. By giving Dorothy *other* children, Joe demonstrated his superiority over his son twicefold. On the other hand, Joe's shortcomings—as in his weakness in school-work—now became evident to his son for the first time. Werner's only hope, as it were, was to exploit this weakness, and to make his father—and thereby Dorothy—dependent on him. By collaborating with Joe in a common enterprise, the well-being of the family, he would at one stroke propitiate both mother and father. When this did not succeed, the boy failed not only as his father's rival but even as his ally.

Werner now felt worthless, useless, redundant, superfluous. During the war years, life in the apartment at Bala Cynwyd had seemed to revolve around him. Now he felt that there was no longer any reason for him to be there at all, that he was intruding. He was, at least from his own point of view, cast out and outcast. To him it seemed that nothing that he would do would ever be acknowledged; that he could no longer do anything right. And so, in a kind of retaliation, he began to do everything wrong.

DEPENDENCE AND INDEPENDENCE

When I brought up these matters with Werner, for the first time in our conversations, for no more than a flicker of a moment, he looked sad. We were sitting in his den, on the second floor of Franklin House in San Francisco. Across from us, on the wall, mounted against an African wool rug, hung color photographs of each member of his family: his mother and father, his first and second wife, his seven children. Slowly he began to open up that solemn moment of concentrated emotion. "Certainly this was the unhappiest time of my life," Werner said. "Yet I can't tell you what *really* happened. All I can do is tell you about my experience *then*. My experience was entangled in my will to avoid my mother's domination and to show her that I was right.

"In talking about this period I want to stress that this is only how matters *seemed* to me then. None of these old events has anything to do with my mother as she *is* or with my basic experience of her."

Having emphasized the subjective aspect of his account, Werner began to analyze the story in terms that he now uses in the *est* training.

"My mother's refusal to react, to take me to the doctor when I broke my nose was, on one level, trivial. But an incident is more than its outer manifestation, and the point is what I made out of it. I saw it as a kind of ejection from childhood.

"Virtually everyone, while he or she is growing up, has an experience which is conceptualized as a sharp, sudden loss of support," Werner observed. "What I mean by 'support' is the implicit agreement that my parents would take care of me—with all the childish love, care, protection that a state of dependence implies.

"I don't mean that parents necessarily *really do* withdraw their support at some particular time. A child *sees* them as having done so: he takes the incident and conceptualizes it to *mean* that.

"After the lacrosse incident, a pattern of conflict was established in my life in which three things battled one another: my anguish over the loss of my mother's support, my resistance to her domination, and my struggle to prove myself. It was a conflict among three expressions—'I want your love and support,' 'You can't dominate me,' 'I'll show you.'

"Like many teen-agers, I was unable to communicate my love for my family because I became stuck in proving myself. To have communicated my love would have made me—in *my* eyes—more vulnerable, less independent.

"Thus, after this incident, every critical observation that my mother made, her every attempt to correct me, I interpreted as a further rebuff. Every attempt she made to be conciliatory, I interpreted as a ploy to bring me back under her domination. The situation deteriorated accordingly."

Werner chuckled. "As I speak of this, it sounds as if I carefully figured out what to do. Of course I didn't. The patterns behind my behavior were unconscious to me then.

"It may sound crazy. It was, in fact, insane. As a child, I had unconsciously formed the point of view that my survival depended on my mother's controlling, determining, dominating my environment and my functioning within it. Now, as I moved into adolescence, a conflicting point of view was laid on top of this. The conflicting point of view was that my survival depended on being independent of her.

"These two inconsistent points of view lay there together, festering in my unconscious. They produced the command: 'In order to survive, I must be dependent on my mother, but in order to survive I must be independent of my mother.' This reduces to: 'In order to be dependent I must be independent, and in order to be independent I must be dependent.'

"Incidentally," Werner commented, "such nonsensical, self-contradictory, and destructive commands are found in the control mechanisms of virtually everyone. Behavior is at the mercy of unconscious commands like: 'I have to be bad in order to be good,' 'I have to get people to hate me in order to get people to love me,' and 'I have to be unhappy in order to be happy.'

"Such internal commands are so illogical that we can hardly get close to them, to confront them, when they begin to show. Since they do not fit into any system, and are therefore unthinkable, they are unavailable for examination.

"Yet just such commands shape the selection of our environments and our behavior within them. Not only does the past influence the present; it does so in a contradictory, dichotomous way. At best this produces ambivalence; at worst, schizophrenia.

"One can manipulate, change, try to fix one's life, without dealing with such commands. But no mastery, no wholeness or satisfaction, is possible that way. To attain mastery, you must penetrate to the *source* of the trouble—to the commands themselves. You must observe them, and transcend them."

Werner reflected for a moment. "Actually," he said, "another pattern was at work here too, reinforcing the others. I mean the old 'victim' number. I saw myself as Dorothy's victim. I saw Dorothy as the winner—the successful, the strong, the right, the dominator; and I perceived myself in relationship to Dorothy as the loser, the weak, the wrong, the struggler-with-overpowering-circumstances, her victim.

"I even saw her as cutting me off from participating in our family. It was as if she didn't like me anymore and had decided to destroy our relationship. I tried to recruit the other members of the family, my grandparents and my uncles and aunts, and our priest, to agree that she was to blame. But they all explained how she was going through a difficult period, and how I needed to be understanding. So almost everybody presented me with the notion that *I* was to blame for the upset in the family. Not only was I Dorothy's victim! She covered things over so that I would look worse in everybody else's sight! She became for me the enemy."

Werner paused and smiled. "Even my language displays what a victim I was," he said. "Of course I made what I call a 'racket' out of the victim's role: internally, I got Dorothy to take the rap for my life. For years I set up my life so it would appear, at least in my own mind, that my mother victimized me. My life came to revolve around my protest that I wanted to be free from her. Eventually I actually acted out getting away from her."

Werner shook his head. "I was so involved in establishing my independence that I lost my power. Had I had true independence, I could easily have dealt with my mother. I would simply have let her be. I would have stopped resisting her. That would not have been submission. It would have been transcending that stupid game.

"Resistance and the need to dominate and be right destroy your ability to allow things to be. When you have no ability to allow things to be, you have no ability to be responsible for them as they are. When you cannot be responsible for the way things are, you have no space. When you have no space, you have no ability to create. It is in creating that you establish true independence.

"So these patterns cut me off not only from my mother, but also from my own creative ability. This impoverished my life, and touched everything I did."

Werner reflected. "To focus on these patterns doesn't mean that this is the only way to illuminate what happened. A Freudian, for example, would point out how I was going through puberty. Freud says that all growing boys are attracted sexually to their mothers. Unquestionably this was happening to me. It wasn't overt of course. It was unconscious.

"Neither of us could acknowledge what was going on. She may have had certain considerations about what she could and couldn't feel; what she could and couldn't say. We couldn't communicate. So we became nutty about our relationship. My mother handled this by shoving me out. I handled it by pushing back in—while protesting all the while that I wanted out.

"In any case, the explanation you choose is almost irrelevant. The fact is, I was trapped in my story, in the way I conceived my life. My story came to define who I was. Had I been able to let Dorothy be, I might have found out earlier who I *really* was.

"Then it could have been different. My mother's tremendous energy, and her unexpressed capacity for emotion, could have come out as love, and could have been wonderfully nurturing. Unfortunately, I was not at that time able to turn our relationship around. This was an absolute failure for me."

For three years the battle raged. For three years Werner railed against his situation, seeking to win back his mother's attention in any way he could. And then . . . it was as if he realized that his guru had given up on him. And he gave up.

This happened around the time the family moved away from Bala Cynwyd. The apartment had rapidly been growing too small. Another child, Harry, was born in Janaury 1950; and a third, Nathan, was born two years later. In the summer of 1951, Joe and Dorothy bought a house in the new suburb of Plymouth Meeting, near Norristown. At the beginning of his junior year, Werner had to leave Lower Merion High School to enter Norristown High School. Having lost his mentor, he must now move away from his childhood friends and companions. Something went out of him then, as his misery seemed to cast its shadow permanently across his future. At Lower Merion he had earned straight A's, and had talked of winning a scholarship to M.I.T. At Norristown, his grades plummeted.

In the summer of 1952, he made a first, abortive attempt to escape. He had worked that summer as a lifeguard at Green Valley Country Club. At summer's end, he signed up for the Marines.

Dorothy recalls, "I was washing diapers one afternoon when he came in to announce that he was enlisted. He had already taken the physical! He was under age, and of course Joe and I refused to sign." A bitter struggle followed; but Joe and Dorothy held out, and Werner returned to Norristown High to complete his senior year.

Although tolerably successful in conventional terms, that year was, for one of Werner's talents, a time of passivity and drifting. He engaged in sports: he rode, and played lacrosse, and went swimming. He was on the staff of the school newspaper, and was a member of the Press Club and the Creative Writing Club. He assisted in the direction of the senior play, and played the role of the basketball player in a performance of "Our Miss Brooks." His fellow students knew him as "the brain." He became fascinated by Shakespeare's play *Hamlet*, a story of a young prince and his parents, of usurpation and betrayal. He memorized it from beginning to end, and frequently quoted parts of it aloud. And he won the English Award. Except for his English and physics classes, however, he was no longer much interested in school. His attention was elsewhere.

THREE Gregarious and Alone

The religious leader . . . . extends the problem of his identity to the borders of existence in the known universe; other human beings bend all their efforts to adopt and fulfill the departmentalized identities which they find prepared in their communities. . . . No wonder that he is something of an old man (a philosophus, *and a sad one) when his age-mates are young, or that he remains something of a child when they age with finality.*
    —Erik H. Erikson

QUIET DESPERATION

His attention was within. Outwardly, he became detached and aloof.

"These outward things were almost incidental," Werner told me. "I had begun to detach myself from my surroundings—from my family, my friends, my teachers. What was going on within removed me from the world around me. Nor was there anyone with whom I could talk about it.

"As I grew older, and went into high school, this lack of anyone with whom I could share what was most important to me became increasingly significant. I became very much alone—and very lonely.

"By this time I was becoming aware of my intelligence. But my family put me on edge about it. They would not let it be, but acclaimed it, and praised and embarrassed me when I let it show, and berated me when I put it away. This offended my sense of appropriateness, and I began to be intellectual only in private.

"It seemed to me that my family could not really respond to my intelligence. At discussion on the level of opinion, they were good; but on the level of abstraction, they were uneasy. They were not probing or reflective. They did not try out ideas; they pronounced upon them. In those family conversations or debates, valuable for me as they were, there was little process of dissection, analysis, synthesis. Whereas I was by now dissecting everything that I encountered: a novel, a book on how to survive in the woods, a treatise on mountain climbing, a dialogue of Plato's—whatever.

"The same was true of my teachers and friends. My old relationship with my friend Henry was virtually gone. My relationship with my cousin Don dissolved as he went into the navy and left town. One of the few people whom I eventually came to be able to talk with was my cousin Norm Danoff. But by now, essentially I had no friend, no true comrade. It was not only the form of our interaction that set me apart from these people, not only the fact that they did not have the habit of intellect. It was also a matter of content. Barriers were set up as to what could be discussed. People had forbidden themselves to talk about things that were to me most important.

"I was interested in the problems of human existence, human relationship, love, sex, the purpose of it all, values, ethics, integrity. I could not discuss such things with my family, school friends, or teachers. It seems that an adult could not readily talk about such things with a teen-ager without somehow making the relationship suspect. This was even true of my best teacher. He admired the things that I wrote for him, and he supported me subtly. But we couldn't really talk about it. We had to keep some distance. It was all right to write about such things, but not to talk about them. That was forbidden intimacy.

"I falsely generalized my perception, and set myself even more apart, concluding that most other people did not experience deeply. I saw people as shallow. This was foolish as I now know, but I took their absence of expression as a sign of the absence of depth of experience.

"Whereas, I thought that I was gaining from my reading the very depth of experience. Thus I was a true sophomore, thinking that I had discovered life.

"I knew that there *were* people, living and dead, who had penetrated deeply into these matters. But no one whom I knew. The only place where I could find both intellect and depth of experience was in books.

"On another level, I was almost gregarious," Werner said, smiling wryly. "I arranged a group for myself with which I could have hearty but superficial relationships, one that I could enter and withdraw from as I chose, a group to which I was not deeply attached. On this level, I participated with my school friends, most of whom were athletes. While certainly not being hell-bent to be part of the group, I even engaged in some conventional struggle for teen-age social position. But when push came to shove, learning—by which I don't mean schoolwork—was more important to me than my social life. That's why I needed a group from which I could retreat.

"As I detached from all these groups, from family, friends, social life, I began to observe them. I began to develop an almost Proustian interest in the world of manners and morals. I began to see that most people had given up, that they got no satisfaction from life, and led lives riven with hypocrisy. Underneath a thin veneer, I saw desperation.

"There was one kid at school with whom I could talk," Werner said. "He was a brilliant fellow named Bill, competent in mathematics and science, who became a nautical engineer. He was not the inventor type. He had a more abstract kind of intellect. From time to time I would drop out of my social set and spend time with him. He didn't belong to any social set. He was independent. Yet somehow we never established a real relationship.

"It was my senior English teacher who most helped me to express myself during this time. He taught me what education could be potentially.

"His name was Donald W. Shaffer. His class was open by invitation alone, and was restricted to able students. It was college English. In fact, the man wasn't teaching English; he was teaching learning. He didn't do teacher stuff. He didn't coach any teams. And he went to as few faculty meetings as he could. I won an award for the work I did in his class. My mother went up to thank him at graduation. She told him that I couldn't have done it without him. He said, 'Yes, that's right,' and walked away. It *was* right, and he knew it. He was not at all personal in his relationships.

"The first thing he did was to ask us to write something. Everyone went home and worked like hell trying to please him. When the papers came in, he put them in a pile, and then shoved them off his desk into the wastebasket—without looking at any of them. He said that he knew that they were not what he wanted. We had, he said, written stories: stuff we had made up, had figured out, had dreamt up. He said he didn't wany any *authors* in there. What he wanted is what really happened. He wanted us to write from our experience."

Werner beamed. "I got it! I got exactly what he said, and I sat down and wrote it just as it was. I didn't try to make it look good. I wrote stuff that surprised him. He would read the papers aloud sometimes. He would start reading mine, and halfway down the first page he would stop and continue reading to himself. He would say that this was too adult to read aloud. Writing became the only medium in which I could express myself. Shaffer provided the space in which I could do this, and he appreciated, and quietly acknowledged, what I was doing.

"Eventually, he called me a one-cylinder James Joyce—James Joyce himself being an eight-cylinder James Joyce.

"Most of the time I wrote short stories. But he also taught us essay writing. And we had to expand our vocabularies.

"He had a great grading system. One grammatical error was B, two was C, three was D, four and you failed. He said he didn't like to grade papers, and if he could find four mistakes quickly he didn't have to read the rest of the paper. He got annoyed one day because people weren't punctuating correctly. He said we had been through eleven years of school, still hadn't learned to punctuate, and were now going to take one day out of class and learn once and for all. And we did.

"We studied literature too," Werner said. "I got turned on to Shakespeare and to Plato, some of whose works I had read earlier. What interested me about Shakespeare was not Shakespeare the playwright. I was interested in his philosophy. I wanted to understand life and other people and myself. It was here that I came to see that some people knew powerfully and insightfully. They didn't just have a pile of knowledge; they could pierce into the pile. I also remember reading e.e. cummings, Theodore Dreiser, and Thomas Wolfe. I was especially impressed by James Joyce, particularly by *A Portrait of the Artist as a Young Man*.

"As a result of what I was reading, I concluded that reality was a back alley. Many people must go through a dark period as teen-agers where reality is dirty and down.

"I began to see the sham in life; that reality is not on the surface, that it is dark and dirty in the sense of being hidden. I don't mean 'dirty' in the conventional middle-class sense. Under the influence of the novelists, the conventional sense of 'dirty' became irrelevant, even meaningless for me. What was dirty was lack of integrity, not earthiness. That is what makes people drab. People had dirty little secrets. Earthiness, by contrast, began to be appealing and allowable. It at least was real.

"Again I perceived that what was real was not spoken about. People did not discuss what was really going on with them. Yet their dirty little secrets were dirty only because they were held as secrets—and indeed secrets which they held to be dirty. People demeaned their own experience.

"Several plays supported me in this experience," Werner went on, "particularly Tennessee Williams's *The Glass Menagerie* and *A Streetcar Named Desire*. *The Glass Menagerie*, more than anything else, stated the quiet desperation underlying life. I identified with its hero, Tom. Tom feels trapped by his family—his nagging mother and his crippled sister. Finally, he runs away from home.

"I would stay up all night to read," Werner told me. "I would study until the sun came up. I would go to sleep for an hour or two and then wake up, but I often couldn't get awake enough to go to school. I spent my last year in school this way."

"It was terrible," Dorothy told me. "I kept nagging him, trying to get him out of bed for school. The kids would make bets about whether he was going to make the school bus. He would come tearing around the corner at the last minute to catch it. One morning the school principal called and threatened to expel him if he didn't come on time.

"Werner was still sleeping, so I woke Joe and told him, and asked him to get Werner out of bed. Joe stormed into his room, picked him up bodily, right out of bed, and stood him on his feet. Then he punched him in the eye. Werner flew across the room.

"I was upset," Dorothy said. "I had not meant for Joe to hit him. But Joe was annoyed. He had worked all night, and had only been asleep for about an hour. I had pulled him out of bed too. Werner didn't get to school at all that day. He had to bandage his eye and he wouldn't let me help him with it. He went off to Germantown to stay with his grandmother. From that time on, he ran his own life."

This was no accident. This was *real* punishment. I spoke to Werner about the confluence of forces entering into this incident.

"I had always thought that my father saw things the way I did," Werner said. "Having identified with him, I would naturally assume that he agreed with *me!* This was so even though I saw him as taking a lot of nonsense from my mother.

"When he punched me, he shifted—at least from my point of view—from his normal position, which I saw at worst as relatively neutral, as simply going along with my mother. Instead, he actively took her position. Instead of being a fellow traveler with me, he became the enemy too.

"That blow confirmed all my worst feelings. What it said to me was, 'Get out of here. You are not wanted around here anymore.' "

PAT

Werner did not want to return home, and would have stayed in Germantown with his grandparents had that not been too far away from his girl friend, Pat. For he was also in the throes of his first grown-up romance: grown-up, but with all the unbearable, panting, doglike ardor of adolescence.

"I'll never forget the day I met him," Pat Campbell told me. We sat talking in the living room of her apartment in San Francisco, where she is a member of the *est* staff. (She still carries the name of her second husband, from whom she is divorced. Her maiden name is Pat Fry.) Pat is an attractive, cheerful, and vulnerable blonde woman, with a keen sense of humor. She was obviously amused by her story. From time to time her voice pealed with laughter. She was also at times on the verge of tears.

"The first time he walked through our homeroom door at Norristown High School, at the beginning of our junior year, I took one look at him," she told me, "and something magical happened. I cannot put it into words. I knew that I was going to be married to him and that he was going to be famous and successful. 'Things are going to be great!' I thought to myself."

They were in several classes together; and around the end of November they went out for the first time.

"When I first fell for him, my friends thought I was crazy. He was new at school and seemed arrogant. He was very outspoken," Pat said. "But for me he had what it was going to take for whatever he was going to do in life."

Pat lived close to the high school and, as the year wore on, Werner began to spend more and more time with her. He would go home with her after school and stay for dinner. "My mother used to say she thought he would never go home," Pat said. "But we were in love."

They also spent weekends together, going around with two friends who later married. They went to movies, to basketball games, to swimming meets, and to the football games, where Pat was a drum majorette. They went to the playhouse in the park and to a teen-age hangout for hamburgers and milk shakes. They would drive over from time to time to Lower Merion for parties with Werner's old friends. Later they attended the junior and senior proms and the school banquets. Several times they played hookey from school, going to the seashore or to Valley Forge Park.

In the densely packed and ardent experiential time of an adolescent girl and boy they drew very close. For his writing class, Werner wrote a poem, referring to Pat, called "Sunrise."

Summer sunrise is a honey-haired girl
Wriggling her toes,
Crouched on the moss-soft blue haze of a hill;
The hair-thin, golden strands speckled with shimmering
 dewdrops.

No morning herald,
This child of laboring night,
Matured morning in a moment;
Belongs to a diamond-flecked carbon night.

Ringing, bleary-eyed morning,
Dazzles full, heavy.
Sweat-soaked sticking sheets,
Cry five more minutes.

Heavy, oppressive air standing stark,
Like a cornered animal—frightened, ponderous, premonitious.
Black-green grass billowing in quivering fear,
Under fleeting gray-black, hazed fury,
Still—quiet still—ponderous still.

Pat and Werner had been going together for nearly a year before she met his family. In the fall of 1952, on her birthday, he took her to the house in Plymouth Meeting for dinner. Shortly afterward, he began to introduce her to his wider family. He took her to see Helene, one of his favorite cousins, Joe's niece, the daughter of his brother Frank. Helene, alone among the members of the family, had supported him when he had wanted to go into the Marines. Helene remembers Werner at this time as "searching." "I don't think it is romanticizing to say that he has real depth. I felt it then, and I feel it now. But I don't think that there was any definite direction to his search yet. He was trying to find out where he fit in, where he was going, and what he was going to do. He knew a lot of English literature, and it was fun to talk with him. Pat didn't say much when we were together, but she obviously adored him."

Werner would talk with Helene about writing. "He wrote well, but he had gotten into trouble over it with Dorothy. He had written some things that were supposed to be advanced sexually for the time." Helene was referring to "Sunrise" and to an essay entitled "His Presence," set in a church confessional, which Werner had written for his English class. The essay speaks of sin and temptation, and of the paradoxes of destiny and freedom:

> The door scraped closed behind me. I knelt down quietly on the red velvet cushion and slid my arms to the sides of the stand.
> In the Name of the Father and of the Son. . . . The air in my lungs pushed against my chest because in speaking so softly, I didn't use it fast enough.
>
> . . . and of the Holy Ghost. Amen.
>
> Bless me, Father, for I have sinned. I twirled the thumbtack that holds the prayer card in place and when the priest's voice dropped I went on.
>
> I confess to Almighty God, to Blessed Mary Ever-Virgin, to all the Saints, and to you, Father, that I have sinned very much in thought. . . .
>
> *The Saint Swithin's Prayer Book* was opened to the list of sins and I went down it rattling them off, except that one I could never bring myself to tell this man who was my friend as well as my priest and who knew me by the sound of my voice. It wasn't really a sin, for I always judged by asking myself if I would do this thing if Jesus were standing in front of me. I loved her and anything that happened was good and happened only because of love.
>
> As the priest talked I thought of the smile that my confession might bring to God's face. Of course, all that I do and am to do was written in the books long before I was born, but still you couldn't say the devil with it and do as you really pleased. Well, I guess you couldn't say it because it was written that you wouldn't. Funny, you can do what you want but there is only one thing to do, so you do it.

This time I wasn't going to do anything wrong: I said that many times before, but this time I meant it. Damn it, nothing was going to make me sin.

In June 1953 Werner graduated from high school. Almost immediately afterward, he went to New York City for a holiday. Then he returned home, where for several weeks he lay brooding about the house, temporizing, marking time. What was he to do now?

For a while, he escaped from his thoughts by playing with the children.

"One of the things that they used to sell in Times Square is turtles," Werner said. "They have the Empire State Building painted on the back of them, or they print your name, or whatever. I got my sister Joan one of these. I had the man write Joan on the back of the turtle and had it mailed back to the house in Plymouth Meeting.

"A few weeks later I went home. I was sitting in the living room and my sister came in crying. With those great big racking sobs that only a five-year-old is capable of, giant alligator tears rolling down her cheeks. I put my arms around her and pulled her up onto my lap and held her. After a while she calmed down a bit and I asked her what was the matter. And she said, 'The turtle died,' and started to cry all over again. If you're five years old you can make a best friend out of a turtle.

"My little three-year-old brother, Harry, was standing in front of the chair like a bird dog honoring the point. It wasn't his turtle, so the tragedy didn't really touch him. But he was solemn for the occasion. Then I said, 'Well, I guess we'll have to bury the turtle.' Joan stopped crying a little, so I knew I was on the right track. I kept going. I said, 'Yeah, we'll get a matchbox, and we'll line the matchbox and we'll make a gravestone, and we'll have a whole funeral.' By this time there was no more crying. There were matches spilled from the matchbox all over the kitchen floor, and Harry brought the spade. I led everybody outside. We lined the casket with tinfoil and dug the grave and made a headstone. We were ready. I said, 'Well, Joan, we have to get the turtle. Where is it?' She said, 'It's in the den.' So we went back in the house and into the den, and no turtle was there. I got down on my hands and knees and was looking around under the furniture for the turtle. Sure enough, under one of the sofas, there was the turtle, walking along.

"So I said, 'Joan, Joan, we don't have to have the funeral, the turtle's alive.' She looked outraged, and said, 'Kill it! Kill it! Kill it!' "

Such distractions were only temporary. Werner's thoughts turned again and again to the question of what to do. It was a delicate question. His life was overcome with inertia, passivity, indecision.

He wasn't working, and had no real plans to get a job. Of course it was assumed that he would go to college, but he hadn't even applied, let alone taken admission tests. "Things were loose-ended," he said. "I just let things slide. I was relying on Dorothy to tell me to apply for college. I told myself that if she didn't care I didn't care either. And I didn't think she cared."

But Dorothy was not nagging him any longer; nor was their relationship so intense. "She had become more ordinary for me," Werner said. "I felt that she was done with me now that I had finished high school, that she expected me to leave the house."

None of the opportunities that now presented themselves seemed to lead any place that he wanted to go, and some pointed in directions that he did not want to pursue. This was true even of college. "I would have liked to continue to do the things that I had done on my own and in my English class during my senior year," he said. "But I didn't see school as a place to pursue ideas." He wrote a poem about his future:

What's in the Cards

What's in the cards?
Teachers say college.
The man in the blue-dyed army clothes,
who eats his dinner in the drugstore,
says you'll find a home in the army.

What's in the cards?
Girls say two can live as cheaply as one.
The black-suited man with the hollow mouth,
who drinks his tea and reads the paper,
doesn't say anything.

What's in the cards?
The ditchdigger says make a mint,
learn a trade, son.
The ads in the magazine say:
"$1,000 minimum a month—Greenland, Africa, Brazil,"
and I say life.

"Life." An admirable sentiment—and unspecific. So Werner went off to the beach to sort things out with himself and to talk the whole thing over with his cousins Norm and Anita Danoff, who lived in Atlantic City.

Norm and Anita, who were brother and sister, were working, and Werner was alone during the day. One morning, shortly after arriving, he went to the beach by himself and lay still in the sun for a long time. "It was so hot that day that I could barely move," he told me. "It was quiet, in the sense that few people were around making noise. Yet I was surrounded by, immersed in, sound: the sound of the waves and the rhythmic beating of the surf, the jangling sounds of the boardwalk. I just lay there, doing nothing, being bathed in that sound, that white noise. As I lay there I began to have the most extraordinary experience. I just detached from everything. I hate to call it an out-of-body experience, but I transcended myself as a personality there. With my eyes closed, I could see what was happening there on the beach, how others were moving, how I myself was lying there. And then I could see everything and everywhere. I experienced a oneness with the universe. I lost the kind of consciousness that locates one in a place. *I became the universe!*"

Werner looked up, his eyes twinkling. "I never did anything with that experience," he said. "It just happened. I didn't have the slightest idea how to deal with it."

In the hot summer evenings he would talk with Norm for hours. As if by premonition, he avoided discussing the future. Instead, they talked philosophy. The question of what he was to do was, after all, connected to the question of who he was. He was not the universe; so who then was he? He talked with Norm about Christianity, how it had affected him, what it meant to him.

His philosophizing and lack of direction came to a sudden and dramatic halt late on a Friday afternoon in early August:

"We were planning to go swimming that evening," Norm told me. "We were sitting together at my place talking, and then Werner excused himself to telephone Pat. He talked with her—I couldn't hear what they were saying—then hung up the phone and came back into the room. He was absolutely white. I asked what was the matter, and he said, 'Pat is pregnant.' "

Werner had had another "accident." It had happened a few months earlier, shortly after that bitter morning in Plymouth Meeting, when Joe had pulled him roughly out of bed and struck him in the eye.

Norm continued his account. "When I asked Werner what he was going to do about Pat, he replied that he didn't know. He had just asked her, over the phone, whether she wanted to get married.

"I tried to talk him out of that. He was only seventeen years old. I told him not to rush headlong into a marriage, and offered to give him the money for an abortion. I was going with a nurse at the time and I thought I could arrange it. But he said to me emphatically, 'I don't want to do that.' "

Werner returned to Philadelphia immediately. "We discussed the whole matter carefully then," Pat told me. "There was no need for us to get married. I could have put the baby out for adoption. We didn't think of it as a catastrophe. We went over all the pros and cons and decided that we really wanted to get married. We were in love."

No one else was so sure. The idea of an abortion came up again and again. Werner's uncle Jim Clauson and other friends also volunteered to help arrange one. But Werner rejected the idea flatly—as did Dorothy. The idea was never mentioned to Pat.

Dorothy was terribly upset. "When Werner came home and said that he was going to marry Pat, it was like a death notice to me," Dorothy said. "I had put so much into him, and planned for him to go to college. I saw that great potential going down the drain. Even the priest at my mother's church said to me, 'Dorothy, you know they don't have to get married.' Even the priest was not in favor of it! I replied that as I saw it he did indeed have to get married. That was exactly what had to be done."

Opportunity had become obligation. Werner and Pat were married in Pat's church, Trinity Evangelical and Reformed Church, on September 26, 1953, just three weeks after his eighteenth birthday.

FOUR Derailed

Needles and pins, needles and pins,
When a man marries his trouble begins.
    —*Mother Goose*

His nature was not remorseless, but to escape from a trap he has to act
without pity.
    —*Tennessee Williams*

DOING THE RIGHT THING

By custom and tradition in our society the several years after graduation from high school are designated, at least for young men of talent
and ambition, as a time of liberal and professional education, as a time
to separate from the family and choose a wider set of associates, a time
to firm up talents, confirm skills, widen horizons, and stake a claim to
freedom. These years are also sometimes called a moratorium, a time
to delay momentous life decisions about who one is and what one is
to become.

  With his marriage to Pat, Werner lost his chance for such a moratorium. He was now to enmesh himself, becoming more and more
deeply overcommitted to what he was not. He had nowhere to come
from and nowhere to go. It was the "holocaust of one's experience on

the altar of conformity."[1] He had "done the right thing" about his marriage. He and Pat had produced no bastard and no abortion. It was an expensive sort of righteousness, a costly honor. Though he did not see it then, the sacrifice involved was almost heroic.

Discussing various misuses to which the Christian doctrine of sacrifice may be put, an eminent theologian has written: "To sacrifice ourselves is, it is said, to realize the image of the crucified, whereas the self-sacrificing may simply be mutilating himself, purposively destroying the sweetness of existence in the name of illusion, in order to make himself a hero in his own eyes. . . . The ethic of sacrifice indeed provides a symbolism under which all sorts of cruelties may be perpetrated, not so much upon the weak as upon those who have been deceived by a false image of goodness."[2]

Such heroism, such pride, such sacrifice, is the stuff of soap opera. What is soap opera? American television or radio drama is a shrine to unconscious conventions, to established cultural norms. It embraces death, pity, avarice, and lust, and established ways of dealing with them. There is little room in it for true tragedy, or comedy, or irony. All these involve some attempt on the part of the individual to transcend the norm; and such attempts involve at least a flicker of conscious awareness. A soap opera crisis is, then, an attack on convention from within the framework of convention. It may test the framework, but may not transcend it. Its chief question is, "Who can get away with what?" Its chief assumption is that he who flouts convention must come to grief.

Werner was about to become the villain in his own soap opera. Each party in the drama must, for a time, play from his own position. Comedy, tragedy, and irony abandon this scene.

A FAMILY MAN

After visiting Norm and Anita in Atlantic City, Werner found a job with an employment agency that specialized in hiring and training derelicts. By late August he found a better-paying job in the refrigerator of a meat-packing firm. On Saturday, September 26, he and Pat were married, and went away for a brief honeymoon at Mount Airy Lodge, in the Poconos.

Shortly afterward, they nestled into an apartment on Washington Lane, in the Germantown section of Philadelphia. On March 13, 1954, a daughter, Clare, was born.

Initially, Pat was happy with her new role. "I was ready to settle down into married life and all that goes with it," she told me. She particularly liked her new family. "It was a big warm happy family.

Everybody would converge on the grandparents for dinner on Sundays and holidays. We had great times. I was never close to my own family in that way."

But Werner was not happy. The domesticity bored him. "He was never satisfied," Pat said.

"He used to say that there was more to life than marriage. I don't think that he knew what he was looking for, but he kept buying books to read and search in." She pointed to the bookshelves on one wall of her apartment.

The first casualty of their marriage was their further education. Although she abandoned her own plans to study nursing at the University of Pennsylvania, Pat encouraged—indeed, nagged—Werner to attend night classes. "He was wasting his time at the sort of work he was doing," she said. He was, however, prepared to go to college only on his own terms, on a regular daytime basis, paying his own way. He would not consider applying for a scholarship. Werner was to have no alma mater, no "bounteous mother."

Yet the inner education, the search, the interior dialogue, continued. He read widely at home each night. He would get books and essays—Archibald MacLeish's essay on poetry and the press is one that he remembers particularly—and take them apart sentence by sentence. He also began to read Freud. "The parts of my life were sharply separated," he told me. "There was the world of making it, in which one earned a living and raised a family. Then there was that private world that made the other tolerable." He had no one, including Pat, with whom he could or would share his private world. There was no meaningful connection between the way he saw himself and the way those around him perceived him. "Search as he would, he could not find himself anywhere in this shell. Somewhere along the way what he had meant to be had been mislaid."[3]

"Marriage was for me," Werner said, "truly a burden. To say that I intended to 'make the best of it' is true but overstated. I submitted to it. I made up my mind to do something positive within the circumstances. But my perspective—seeing life as suffering—provided the context for my marriage, and for whatever happened within it, whether positive or negative. That perspective came from my observation of my family—not just Joe and Dorothy but also several uncles. It seemed to be the common experience that all of life, like my marriage, was something that you were stuck with, and that you put up with—decently. This view, with all its false 'nobility,' is the perspective of someone who is at the mercy of circumstances, who is not the author of his own life. This is how it was for me."

During the first year and a half of the marriage, Werner held a number of different jobs. A few months after the marriage, he left the meat-packing plant and took a job briefly at the restaurant and health club where Joe was working. Next, for nearly a year, he worked as a salesman for a heating and plumbing contracting company, which had just branched into the remodeling business. Werner learned estimating. And he got his first taste of sales success.

In February 1955, a few weeks before the birth of their second child, Werner and Pat moved from Germantown, to live for six months with Pat's parents in Norristown. Their second daughter, Lynn, was born there in March 1955. Werner was now working in construction, supervising subcontractors for another firm.

While living with Pat's parents, Werner and Pat began to quarrel. They would fight about almost any little thing. About which relative was to buy which gifts for the children. About the way in which the children were to be disciplined. "Life with Werner was either great or it was hell," Pat sighed. "At this point it began to be sheer hell. Living with my parents wasn't good for any of us, including my parents." So they moved again.

SELLING CARS

They found a house on a farm in the northern section of Norristown, near North Wales, Pennsylvania, and remained there for three years. During the first year, Werner managed a medium-duty industrial equipment firm. The business had been nearly defunct, and under his management became successful again. Werner quit this job to become an automobile salesman, and for the next five years he worked at a succession of dealerships. First he sold Fords at a dealership under the general management of Lee Iacocco, who later became president of the Ford Motor Company. Later he worked for a Mercury dealership; still later, he sold Chevrolets.

In 1958, after he had been in the automobile business for over three years, Werner joined a Lincoln Mercury business owned by a man named Irvin Green. At this time Werner adopted the name Jack Frost, and continued to use it in business for the next two years.

It has occasionally been suggested in magazines that Werner changed his name at this time in order to hide the Jewish name Rosenberg. But Werner was working for a Jew with a Jewish name; the automobile dealership was located on Roosevelt Boulevard in a part of the northeast section of Philadelphia that was predominantly Jewish; and most of his customers were Jewish. The name Jack Frost was an introductory gimmick, Werner told me. "By the time someone bought a car from me he knew that my real name was Jack Rosenberg. I wanted to give customers a name that was easy to remember while they were out shopping for a car."

Werner was successful as a car salesman. "He could sell you City Hall," Dorothy told me. Werner's Aunt Edith Rosenberg was more emphatic: "Not only would he sell you City Hall. You would think you got it all tied up in a ribbon. Werner sold something to you graciously." He quickly became the top salesman in the dealerships for which he worked. "He developed great friendships with the fellows that he worked with," Norm Danoff said. "He would take half a dozen guys to lunch and pick up the tab. He would buy everybody drinks. Making money was important to him, not keeping it. It was funny to see him in that company. Here was a kid only a couple of years out of high school. He had never gone with anyone seriously except for Pat, and he had two kids. There he was, twenty-one years old, in with a bunch of car dealers, men who were high livers and constantly running off to Atlantic City or Wildwood for the weekend to shack up or whatever. Werner had never done any of these things, and he had all the obligations of an old married man."

At this time Werner started running around with other women. "It wasn't obvious at first," Pat said. "But later I began to find evidence. He would go off and say he would be right back, and not come home for hours. I didn't bring this up with him then, and things just got worse. When I think of all that should have been said and never was, I get discouraged. It got to the point where I wouldn't say anything because I didn't want a fight to start."

VICTOR/VICTIM

Everyone else in his environment, Werner charmed. Pat, however, became his "victim." She was the wife of a car salesman, but had no car and could not drive. She was "stuck at home with the children." Werner's worst aspect was reserved for her. It was almost as if he needed to have her around to victimize. Apart from their quarrels, communication between them withered away into the exchange of information. When Werner was home, he would ignore her, preferring to read or watch television. He would reprimand the children occasionally, but apart from that played increasingly little part in their upbringing.

I asked Werner about his relationship with Pat. We were at Stanford University for the weekend, where he was leading a workshop.

During the lunch break, we found a secluded patio where we could sit in the hot sun and talk. There Werner treated me to a dispassionate account of his first marriage.

"This part of my life," he said, "was one long disaster. I messed up almost everything I touched. You could go down a list: my relationship with my parents, my academic record in high school, my applications for college, getting Pat pregnant. And then—after I was once involved in a teen-age marriage—having two children in rapid succession.

"We could go over each event in this period, look at the circumstances, and discuss the rationale behind it. But that would be boring soap opera, and would get nowhere near the *source* of behavior like that.

"Let me give you an example. What Pat said about our lack of communication is accurate; yet the source of the trouble was not lack of communication. It is true that I never called on her to interact with me intellectually or emotionally; I took my failure to share with her to cruel lengths. But this was a by-product, not the source of our problems.

"There's another obvious explanation of what was happening to us that also *doesn't* reach source. It would be easy—and, again, accurate—to say that Pat's parameters—her expectations, ambitions, and fantasies about the future—were more conventional than mine. Although she hadn't planned an early marriage, it was a natural, if arduous, development for her. She was thinking in terms of being a housewife and mother. That was a world that she had bargained for. Whereas for me, conventional relationships were much more in question. It wasn't that I hadn't been thinking of marrying Pat: I hadn't been thinking about marrying anyone. Having a family at that early stage conflicted with the process that had been going on within me. For me the marriage was a dead end."

"Yet the source of the problem had nothing to do with Pat, and little to do with the situation. It had to do with the way that my mind was patterned in the course of my childhood interactions with my mother—Dorothy.

"Earlier, I told you how much I resisted my mother as a teenager. Well, it is a law of the Mind that *you become what you resist*. Just as, when a small child, I had identified with my father, later I began increasingly to operate in my mother's identity. Having resisted my mother, and lost my mother, I *became* my mother. *I became Dorothy*.

"So, in order to understand how I would behave in any

situation—such as with Pat—you have to ask how I perceived Dorothy.

"Remember that although my mother was the victor in her relationships with me, and with my father, she too perceived herself—and was perceived by me—as the victim of circumstances in her marriage. But she was the *dominant victim.* She dominated the other victims. You might call Dorothy's identity, as I perceived it, that of the 'dominant victim of circumstances,' an utterly hopeless position in which even the winner *must* lose. So in becoming Dorothy, this is what I became: the dominant victim of circumstances.

"With Pat, I unconsciously acted out Dorothy's identity. From this position, I dominated Pat. Thus Pat had to play to me the role that my father and I had played to my mother. And I played Dorothy's role. To work within this crazy pattern, I truly needed someone like Pat to dominate; and I also needed to be the victim of overwhelming circumstances myself. So I kept creating circumstances to be the victim of—I would keep getting Pat pregnant, and so on.

"So there was no problem with Pat. I always appreciated her. When I was blaming someone, I blamed Dorothy for getting me trapped in those circumstances. All this of course was reinforced by my *other* identification, my identification with Joe. Dorothy dominated my father; and I dominated Pat.

"Only much later, when I became aware of the unconscious patterns and identifications that were at the source of my behavior, only then did they lose their power over me."

Werner paused. "As we talk about these things, you may feel uncomfortable. You may feel that we are talking about puppets, not about people. The fact is, until people are transformed, until they transcend their minds, they *are* simply puppets—perhaps anguished, hurting, strongly feeling puppets, but ones nonetheless limited to a fixed repertoire of responses. And that is what *karma* is all about. There really is no mystery about karma. In retrospect—only in retrospect—it is . . . obvious."

Eighteen years earlier, in Philadelphia, the unconscious source of Werner's behavior was no more obvious to Pat than it was to him. She took the children to her parents and filed for divorce. When Werner heard this, he drove straight to her parents' house. "He came in and told me that there wasn't going to be a divorce, that things were going to get better, and that he loved me. I told him that we weren't making any headway, that the same thing was going to happen again. I told him I didn't want to live that kind of life."

But she acceded. Proceedings were dropped. Shortly afterward, in the summer of 1958, they moved into an apartment on the second floor of a country house in Riverton, New Jersey, across the Delaware River from northeast Philadelphia. Pat was pregnant again. Their third child, a son, John Paul Rosenberg, Jr., was born in November 1958. For a short time afterward, "everything was great," Pat told me. "Werner had a son and was happy about it." She remembers the scene at the hospital. "He started to come in the door, and the staff tried to stop him. 'Don't tell me that,' he said, 'My wife just had a son.' He came into the room and was really excited.

The good mood lasted only a few weeks.

JACK FROST MEETS JUNE BRYDE
In January 1959, when he was twenty-three, Werner met a tall blonde young woman named June Bryde. She lived in Philadelphia with her parents, and worked for a real-estate agency.

They began to see each other regularly. Although their relationship eventually developed into an affair, it began, and remained for several months, a simple—and not so simple—friendship. Werner found in her at last someone with whom he could share his interests and aspirations, someone to whom he could present his developing philosophy. In her he regained, if only for a moment, his muse. It was exciting to be with her. In her company he could develop; he could take up again the threads of speculation and experience that had stirred him during his final year of high school, and which he had abandoned so abruptly five years earlier. She acknowledged in him the emerging identity that he saw in himself: thinker, talker, poet, artist. They talked of architecture and art, of writing novels and poetry, of travel and the good life.

As their relationship developed into an affair, it became stormy. At one point Werner broke it off, writing: "June, I pray the situation will change, but until it does I can't see you anymore. We will get more involved and later parting will be even worse, if that's possible."

Within two weeks they were back together. By the spring of 1959, Werner had arranged to move back from New Jersey to Philadelphia, to be closer to her.

"He came in one day and told me to have everything together to move in two days," Pat told me. Werner, Pat, and their three children moved to an apartment in Hatboro, Pennsylvania, a town located on the Pennsylvania Turnpike, within easy commuting distance to Plymouth Meeting, Norristown, and June's home in Philadelphia. "It was the first apartment we had that I really liked," Pat said.

By early summer, Werner was under immense pressure—at home, in his relationship with June, and at work, where the dealership for which he worked was just emerging from the economic recession. One afternoon, as he was sitting in his office, closing an automobile sale, his mind went utterly blank. A few days later, as he pulled into the parking lot, he blacked out at the wheel of his car.

Alarmed, he went to his doctor, who advised him that there was nothing physically wrong and suggested that the ailment was psychosomatic. Over the next four months, Werner consulted regularly, several times each week, with a Freudian psychoanalyst. "I was by now worried sick," Werner told me. "I was sick of my marriage, sick of my wife and my mother, and sick of myself. My body began to respond, however, to that psychoanalytic therapy. It would be inaccurate to say that I had a full psychoanalysis. I didn't carry it through to its culmination. But what I learned there, about psychoanalytic theory, and about myself, was invaluable."

During the course of this treatment, relations between Pat and Werner became even worse. "In June or July of 1959, when I was pregnant again," Pat said, "Werner came in and told me that *he* wanted a divorce. I hadn't expected that. When we went through that earlier, he had said we would never get a divorce. I wouldn't argue with him. I was pregnant and had three children. What could I do? I didn't want an upheaval. And I didn't yet know about June."

Dorothy came to Pat's defense. "Dorothy's initial response to the marriage had been not to interfere," Werner told me. "Later, when she saw that I wasn't paying much attention to Pat and the children, she was drawn into our marriage. Pat had an ally in her; they began to form a coalition. That threatened me."

Dorothy had seen the trouble coming long in advance. "One night Werner called me to say that he wanted to stay with us that night. He asked me to leave the door unlocked because he was going to be out late. I said, 'If you can't go home there must be something wrong. What's going on?' He didn't get in until about four o'clock in the morning. He was not out working *that* late. So I woke him early the next morning, and I can still see him standing at the top of the stairs. I said, 'What you're doing is going to get you involved with someone else. Don't you realize that?' He just stood there and told me not to worry. I said, 'You're up to no good.' Pat had told me that he was pushing her around and brushing her off. I felt that she was pretty complacent about it, but there was nothing that I could do about it—at least at first.

"Then the strangest thing happened," Dorothy told me. "I got a bill from my florist. For flowers. I hadn't sent any, so I called them. They told me that Jack Frost had bought the flowers. I asked where they had gone. 'Well, we thought it odd,' they replied, 'that Jack Frost sent flowers to June Bryde.' Both of them sounded like fictitious names. The florist gave me June Bryde's address.

"A few nights later, I saw Werner at my brother Jim's house. After Werner left, I followed him in my car. He lost me but I had June's address and drove there, to the West Oak Lane section of Philadelphia. Sure enough, his car was parked in front of June's house. I knew that I had to do something about it. I shouldn't have gotten into it, but Pat was in a situation where someone had to defend her.

"A few days later, I tried to talk with him. I told him that at one time I would have banked on his integrity, but that I didn't know about that anymore. He stood there and told me, 'Mother, I want you to know that I do have integrity.' I didn't quite get that then."

In early August Werner moved his work to the Mercury dealership in Bethlehem and Allentown, north of Philadelphia. Pat refused to move to Allentown. So he stayed in motels there during the week, returning to Hatboro and Philadelphia on weekends. "Werner would come home just long enough to change his clothes, and then he would leave to spend the weekend with June," Pat said.

Dorothy and Pat decided to confront June. On Saturday morning, August 22, when Werner was away in Allentown, Joe and Dorothy and their three younger children, and Pat and her three children, all got in a car together and drove to Philadelphia to see June Bryde.

"We went into the house," Pat told me. "I was holding my baby in my arms. And I was obviously pregnant. We met Mr. and Mrs. Bryde, June's father and mother and one of her brothers. June wasn't there. Dorothy told her parents that we understood that they couldn't have known that Werner was married. They were very religious people, and they said that they wouldn't let Werner back in the house again. They told us that Werner had said that his family was dead, that he was out in the world by himself. They said June had been engaged once before and had broken off the engagement. Finally, June herself came in.

"I'll never forget my first sight of her," Pat said. "She came in with her hair all up in curlers, and wearing just a bathing suit and dark sunglasses. She was a big girl, very tall. I weighed only about 115 pounds. I really couldn't see the attraction.

"Finally I asked to talk with June alone. She admitted that she knew that he was married and had children. I told her that I wouldn't grant him a divorce. She didn't say much to me while I was there."

Werner had awakened in Allentown that Saturday morning in a strange and apprehensive state. He phoned June. But afterward, as he wrote to her, "I still felt something was wrong. That telephone conversation began running through my mind. I knew it was the first time you were ever evasive with me, and I knew that that meant trouble."

Then Joe telephoned Werner and told him to come to Plymouth Meeting immediately after work. "By his tone, the conversation with you, and what had been running through my mind," Werner wrote, "I was pretty sure what I would hear when I got there."

Werner left work immediately, rushed home to shower and dress, and then drove to his parents' house.

"When I walked up to the door," he wrote to June, "I could see my mother's face through the screen door. From the look on her face I knew my fears were confirmed."

Dorothy told him, in detail, about their visit with June and her parents. Werner attempted to telephone June, but was told by her parents that she didn't wish to speak with him again. Werner stormed out of the house and drove away.

"I kept turning around on the highway," he wrote to June, "not knowing which way to go, and all the time this emptiness, this death. As I calmed down, I began to wonder which way my life would go without what had become the point about which my life revolved.

"Becoming tremendously successful, or rich, or famous, or writing a good novel seemed to be meaningless without you to share it. Nothing, no matter how I tempted my mind with wonderful things to do and accomplish, meant anything. Life had lost all meaning and all reason. . . . I could picture myself as one of those pitiful individuals who let the world around them shape their lives, with no place to go, rooted where they stand."

June received his letter, reconsidered the matter, and found her love for Werner intact. A month passed before the relationship was wholly restored, but by the end of that month they had made definite plans. They decided to go away together, as soon as Pat's baby was born and they had saved some money. When Pat tried to contact June several months later, June's brother told her never to call again. "I don't know what Werner told the Brydes," Pat told me, "but he was back at June's house almost immediately."

During the next four months, letters shuttled back and forth almost every weekday between Allentown and Philadelphia, between

Werner and June. He promised her that he would never again despair
as he had done that weekend in late August. "June," he wrote, "the
whole world seems to be closing in around me and it will probably be
a couple of months before this changes, but you are at least the ray of
light through these encircling walls." Again and again he wrote of
June's "willingness to wait for me." He quoted to her Elizabeth Bar-
rett Browning's poem "How do I love thee? Let me count the ways,"
and told her that she was "the only inspiration I have to be a human
being."

They discussed their future home together. In October, Werner
began to write to June of his ideas about architecture—and continued
to use images of being "hemmed in." "Look about you," he wrote.
"You'll see, no matter where you are, that although the walls protect
you from the elements they close you in and keep the world outside.
Now don't the windows which are merely punched in the walls only
make the walls more prominent, more confining? The floor seems to
hold you up and the ceiling to hold you down. The furniture sitting
on the floor heightens the feeling that the floor holds you up; and the
lighting throws the ceiling—looming down at you—into greater
prominence. Is there really any beauty around you? Do your surroundings inspire you? Does the building you are in or any that you
can think of look as though God had planted it?"

In one exchange they discussed their attitudes to communication, later to become one of Werner's chief concerns. He spoke of the
poverty of communication in his relationship with Pat and with his
parents, and vowed that that must not happen with them. He wrote:
"The one thing that I cannot stand from anyone is an unwillingness to
agree to the truth—an unwillingness to admit a mistake—saying
black is white when you know it is black and stubbornly sticking to it.

A few days later he returned to the subject: "A mistake is no dis-
grace—only the same mistake. . . .

If I care very much about you, I will never say, 'Oh, well, this
doesn't matter, so we won't discuss it any further.'

If we never let anything go by—not even petty annoyances—
they will never get a chance to pile up. Let us then agree not to let
anything be beneath our discussing it. . . .

The statement, 'You *always* question *every* one of my answers' is
not intelligent . . . a statement like that makes it hard to discuss a
thing with much hope of success. . . . It hurts me when you say 'I
only agreed with you so we wouldn't have to discuss it anymore.'
Does that mean that I'm not important enough for you to fight so that
I will know what is right? . . .

June, you and I are going to interest ourselves in a great many things—we're going to get a lot out of life—we're going to delve into things so that we understand them. In the process of studying them we're going to have divergent opinions and we're going to discuss our opinions. You will defend yours and I will defend mine. The thing that will be important will not be that you win or that I win but that we decide together on the right . . ."

In their autumn weekends together, they discussed issues heatedly. They went to plays and jazz concerts. And one cool and windy Sunday morning they drove to New York City. They went to church to hear Norman Vincent Peale; afterward they went to lunch, and wandered through the Museum of Modern Art. Then, as they walked around Manhattan, Werner tried to illustrate to June his ideas about modern architecture.

These weekend hours counterpointed the bitter quarrels and chilling silence that Werner met when he went home to Hatboro. A crisis came at Christmastime.

Werner arrived home on Christmas Eve, spent the night, then went to June's house for Christmas day. Meanwhile, Joe and Dorothy, and Mr. and Mrs. Fry, Pat's parents, arrived in Hatboro for Christmas celebrations and dinner. "My parents didn't yet know what was going on," Pat said. "We had dinner. I got the children into bed. Then I began to go into labor. I was taken to the hospital in Abington, and Debbie was born that evening. Werner heard about it from Dorothy the next day. He had driven directly back to Allentown without even coming home that evening."

The Saturday after Christmas, Werner returned to Hatboro and saw Debbie and Pat in the hospital. On Monday he brought Pat home. "He saw that I had everything that I needed, and then started to leave for Allentown. Before he left I told him that I wanted to get things settled one way or the other. I didn't know what was going to happen. But he wouldn't talk about it. I was up in the air."

"You could tell by looking at him that he was living a double life at this time," Werner's Aunt Kitty Clauson told me. "He became dissipated looking, he showed the strain."

So things continued for another few months. In late March, Werner gave up the job in Allentown. He moved back into the apartment in Hatboro, and sold cars in Philadelphia. Secretly, he also took a room in New Jersey, to establish residency there, and used that address to obtain a New Jersey driver's license under a false name. Back home in Hatboro, his clothes gradually began to disappear from the apartment closet. One night in late April 1960, Pat got up from bed after Werner was asleep. She went through his remaining clothes, and then went outside to search the car. In the glove compartment she found false identity papers—Social Security cards and drivers' licenses, and a checkbook—for both Werner and June.

Pat immediately told Dorothy what she had found. "I was scared to face him alone," Pat told me. The two women arranged to confront Werner together three weeks later, on May 22, when the two youngest children were to be christened. They decided to mention nothing at the church: Dorothy and Joe would follow Werner and Pat home after the ceremony, and confront him there.

"Werner didn't know that Dorothy and Joe would come back to the house," Pat told me. "So he went over to their car and said good-bye to them in the most beautiful way. He was so nice to them. I knew that he was going to leave almost immediately."

Pat and Werner returned to the apartment in Hatboro, followed shortly by Joe and Dorothy. "We presented Werner with what we knew," Pat said. "We told him that if he left he would just be making things worse. He didn't have much to say. At that point I was willing to give him a divorce—conditionally. The condition was that he straighten himself out instead of just making things worse. We went over this again after Joe and Dorothy left."

Pat smiled. "I felt so sorry for him then," she said. "I felt that he was in a hurry to get on with his life, and find himself, and he'd made one mess after another. Here he was with one wife and four kids. And now he was ready to run away with another woman. I hated her. I think that Werner wanted to talk, but he couldn't. You could see that he was in a bind."

The next day—Monday, May 23, 1960—Werner went to Plymouth Meeting to see his brothers and sisters. Joan Rosenberg, Werner's sister, told me of this visit. "Harry and Nathan and I were all at home. I was just twelve, Harry was ten years old, and Nathan had just turned eight. Werner sat us down. There was a sense that something was about to happen. He didn't tell us that he was leaving, but he told us that he loved us. I felt that it was an end to something. It was as if he were getting a picture of us to take away with him."

On Tuesday evening Pat got a telephone call from June's mother saying that her daughter had left home. All her clothes and suitcases were gone. "Suddenly her mother wanted *me* to do something." Pat smiled. "Then her brother came over. Now *he* wanted to talk too. I called Werner at his office, and he came home. June's brother and I talked with him about where June might be." June was in fact waiting in a hotel nearby.

On the following morning—May 25, 1960—Werner's six-year-old daughter Clare watched him closely at breakfast. She recalls thinking that would be the last time that she would see him. After breakfast, he went out, saying to Pat that he would be back. "He didn't say that he was leaving," Pat told me. "He just walked out, but I knew that he was leaving for good."

Pat looked up at me and laughed. "You know," she said, "it seems like such an unhappy story when we sit here and talk about it. But we had some great times in there. The whole seven years were not unhappy. It became most unhappy toward the end."

Werner left a letter for Dorothy. "He wrote that he had to do what he was doing, that he was responsible for his life, that he had to find out the truth for himself. He emphasized that he would fulfill his obligations. The letter was about independence. And that was all. He just disappeared." Werner arranged with a friend, John Croft, to keep an eye on Dorothy and Joe, and Pat and the children, and to report to him regularly concerning their welfare.

As he recalled his departure, Werner told me: "I left Philadelphia in a 'screw-you' mood. I still experienced myself as a victim. That requires that someone must have done it to you. That person is automatically bad and may be punished. As a victim, *you* get to be righteous, and that is all you get. All that any of us were getting there in Philadelphia was a lot of righteousness.

"I came to see it as righteous to get out of a situation where I was trapped. I had to prove myself outside my mother's arena. In her arena I couldn't win. While Dorothy was no longer going to find out what I did, it was as though I got her permanent attention by withdrawing my attention from her."

Werner shook his head. "What a fool I was. How can someone who is Dorothy escape from Dorothy? You cannot do that by traveling in space and time."

PART II Education

FIVE Out to Beat the Game

What our age needs is education. And so this is what happened: God chose a man who also needed to be educated, and educated him privatissime, *so that he might be able to teach others from his own experience.*
—*Søren Kierkegaard*

DOWN AND OUT IN SAINT LOUIS

That morning of May 25, 1960, June Bryde drove to work as usual. She parked her car in front of the office, leaving the keys in the glove compartment. She walked into the office, greeted her colleagues, and then calmly went out the back door into the alleyway, where Werner was waiting in a car.

She got in, and they dashed to the airport in Newark, where she had left her suitcases the previous day. They abandoned the car in the parking lot, and boarded a flight to Indianapolis.

To prevent their families from tracing them, they had decided to assume false identities. But they still had no new names. The false names they had chosen some weeks earlier were discarded unused, since Pat knew them. As the plane flew over Ohio, Werner was browsing through an old copy of *Esquire*, reading an article on West Germany. From the eminent Germans who were featured in it, John

Paul Rosenberg hurriedly picked out the names Werner (from Werner Heisenberg, the physicist and philosopher), Hans (from Bishop Hanns Lilje), and Erhard (from the economics minister, later chancellor, Ludwig Erhard). June Bryde chose two names that she had always liked: Ellen Virginia. Thus John Paul—Jack—Rosenberg and June Bryde ceased to exist. Werner and Ellen Erhard came into being . . . *gradually*.

"We didn't think of these as permanent names," Werner told me. "I suppose a year passed before I realized that I had acquired a more or less permanent name. When we first picked these out, the main criterion was that they provide us with an effective cover. I wanted a really implausible name for myself, one that nobody—particularly not my family—would suppose that I would pick. My mother was persistent, and my uncle (Jim Clauson) had been a captain in the Philadelphia Police Department. I was sure that they would be after us, and was determined to prevent them from tracking us down."

Ellen remembers their airplane descending that afternoon over the Indianapolis 500 racetrack. From the airport they took a bus to the train station. Still covering their tracks, they remained in Indianapolis for only a few hours, and then went on by train to Saint Louis. There they were to live until early the following spring.

The home of the Saint Louis blues was for them a setting for exile, not for a new beginning. The Saint Louis summer is hot, humid, and oppressive. The city's downtown area is like a burning oven; its office buildings and hard pavements reflect heat relentlessly into the surrounding streets. Werner and Ellen had no way to mitigate the harshness of their new setting. Between them, they had only a few hundred dollars; and they were to remain poor for over a year. They had neither friends nor families to turn to, and neither credentials nor references to show to prospective employers.

For a few weeks they lived in a hotel downtown, eating in cheap restaurants and in drugstores, which at least were air-conditioned. Finally they rented an apartment in a rundown area near the park, and spent their remaining cash filling its cupboards with food. The apartment had a foldaway Murphy bed, and there were mice in the drawers of its built-in closets. Directly outside their windows burned a bright streetlight; it was never really dark in the apartment, not even with the blinds drawn all the way.

Werner began looking for a job. Using the new names, he obtained new Social Security cards for himself and Ellen, and a driver's license for himself. But cards of identity do not an identity make. So they also, both of them, supplied themselves—from their imaginations—with rich, full pasts, stories that they could tell to anyone who might inquire about who they were, whence they came, what they had done. Then they taught these to one another, and tried them for consistency.

They each altered their birth dates by several months and days. Ellen subtracted three years from her age, while Werner added three years to his. "I did that to avoid raising questions about not having been drafted," he told me. "I hadn't been able to figure out how to handle that issue otherwise." Werner put his birthplace in Connecticut, and said he had grown up in Philadelphia and New Jersey, and had gone to school in Connecticut. Ellen was to say that she was from Camden, in New Jersey.

"I had been afraid that I would have to give my first employer in Saint Louis some employment references," Werner said, "but as it turned out these stories were never needed. I just walked on to a used car lot and told them that I wanted to go to work. I was told, 'Go ahead, try it out.' That first day I sold three cars, and that was the end of that conversation. After that, they didn't care who I was. The next day they gave me a car to drive."

Werner sometimes earned additional money by playing poker and chess. Ellen stayed home, and began to learn to cook. I asked her about those days. She is a tall, slender blonde woman. Her face is striking, showing the angles of her Danish and Hungarian forebears. Her large blue eyes are penetrating and humorous. At the memory of Saint Louis, she grimaced. "That was an adventure for me," she said. "Particularly during the first several weeks. I had been the eldest child in my family, and had been raised strictly. As a child I was sickly—I was thought to have a heart murmur—and was never permitted to do anything dramatic at all. And here I was, a runaway from home!

"But I was also sad and guilty and uncomfortable, and Saint Louis seemed to heighten that aspect of our life. Our new life, for which we had so much hope, had a very slow beginning. It just dragged on and on. Our apartment was terrible. It was so hot and sticky inside. I would leave it in the morning, and would spend most of the day walking and sitting on the benches in the park. I could listen to the Municipal Light Opera being rehearsed there. I liked that.

"We didn't have much money that summer," Ellen said. "We had enough to get by on, and just enough extra for a little entertainment. We saw *Kismet* at the Civic Light Opera, went to jazz concerts, and even took a trip on a riverboat. But we weren't able to accumulate anything. We were just struggling to keep ahead."

As fall began and their life settled into more of a routine, Werner and Ellen experimented with cooking together. "When I first met her," Werner told me, "Ellen used to burn water. But she soon learned to cook in an inspired way."

"Yes," she recalled. "Later that year, in November, I was ill. On Thanksgiving Day I was in bed. Werner had gone shopping and had bought groceries, and he started to prepare dinner in the kitchen. Every five minutes he would come in and say, 'Ellen, do this, come do that.' I would have to get up, and chop the celery, or some such. It was like a television comedy. By the time the dinner was ready, I could barely move. And then he came walking into the bedroom, holding high a platter with a flaming duck. There we were, with no money, eating an orange duck flambé for Thanksgiving dinner!"

Despite such occasional celebrations Werner Erhard was preoccupied. Had he been asked, at the time, what was puzzling him, he could not have answered accurately. He was fumbling, intuitively, unconsciously, with a problem that he could not define at all, and with a condition that one does not find cataloged in the ordinary reference books of psychology.

The problem, simply stated, was the problem of who he was. The "condition" cannot be put so simply. The "raw material" that he had to work with—still fresh from Philadelphia, as it were—included his body and his unconscious behavior patterns. The latter had not been left behind; unknowingly he had brought along the false identification with his mother, the "dominant victim of circumstances." Onto these he affixed a fake name, false identity papers, and a fictitious past.

He was now at least twice removed from himself—and where was he? Who was he, *really?* In all the more obvious ways, he was living a lie. Yet in his farewell letter to his mother he had written that he must go off to find out the truth for himself. He had to create or find a new identity for himself, one that would go with the fake name and papers, and the fictitious past. But Werner, as yet, didn't really know anything about true identity. What he figured he needed was a *winning self-image.*

He told me how he saw himself on his arrival in Saint Louis. "In escaping from Philadelphia I was gambling," he said. "My gamble was that it was possible to beat the entanglement of life.

"I saw all mankind as being entangled in their own life stories. Every move that anyone made to get free from the story only added a new chapter.

"I don't mean that life circumstances are always bad. Some people put together a good story. Yet, whether the story is good, bad, or indifferent, it remains desperate. The Buddhist notion of suffering, which I learned about several years afterward, relates here. Suffering for the Buddhist is not simply a matter of circumstances; it is the background, the context, for all circumstances.

"One afternoon, in a kind of meditative state, I saw an image— you could call it a vision—of the brutishness of life." Werner looked into the distance, and then began to relate a vision of Hell and its inmates, reminiscent of the paintings of Hieronymus Bosch or the massacres of Tamerlane.

"I saw a huge tower made of stone, impervious to water. In it there was a sea of bodies. One is introduced to the tower at the bottom. And the 'game,' as it were, is to get to the top. It is as nasty as you can imagine. To get to the top you must tread on other people; you must put them down; get over them; have it over them. Each step, each move, defines a pattern.

"Suppose that you do get to the top. So what? The top is the top of the bodies. It is not the top of the tower. Where do you go from there? You are just at the top of a pile of bodies. And you won't even be there very long.

"There are many ways to interpret this image," Werner reflected. "It is easy, for instance, to see the stone tower as a phallus, and its imperviousness to water as a shield against the incestuous drives of the Oedipus complex. As I initially interpreted it, however, this image was archetypal, and symbolized the human condition. It was for me a universal metaphor, in terms of which people unconsciously live their lives. When we were in Saint Louis, I was still caught in the grips of this metaphor myself. Despite the absurdity of the idea, as I now see it, being on the top represented for me at that time a way out of entanglement. I thought that I could beat that entanglement. I thought that by accumulating stuff, a new image, knowledge, respect, position, money, whatever, I could at least compensate for the horror of it all. I could buy a space of calm within the story.

"To hold the circumstances, the suffering, the horror of life at bay, I thought that one needed competence and excellence, that one needed to be 'smart.' I suppose I had in mind the building of a kind of fortress of competence. In Saint Louis I began to build that fortress. Jack Rosenberg had screwed up his life. Werner Erhard was going to do it right."

Werner had confronted horror. American culture is reluctant to acknowledge the existence of horror, let alone to concede that it is ineradicable. Since the horror, being unacknowledged, never becomes part of the culture, the individual who experiences it is the more isolated. "Fortress" is the right word. Werner started to build his fortress of competence, his escape from horror, by reading. He would emancipate himself through knowledge. Trudging back and forth between the apartment and the Saint Louis Public Library, he read book after book on career and success. Early one evening, on the bookrack of a corner drugstore, he found a typically American answer, in the books of Napoleon Hill and Maxwell Maltz on positive thinking and self-image psychology. Hill was the author of *Think and Grow Rich*; Maltz, the author of *Psycho-Cybernetics*.

As Werner remarks, the idea that he could escape horror at all—let alone escape it through Maltz and Hill—was absurd. But at this early point in his education, knowing no better and still limited in experience, he took an archetypally American solution to archetypal horror.

Maltz and Hill exude optimism—and the go-getter energy, good fellowship, and boosterism of the Rotary Club: there is a great day coming; you had better believe it. They represent the supposition of American experience that there is no problem so great, no condition so horrible, that technology cannot solve it. They present a technology of the interior—for tinkering with, managing, engineering human nature itself. And their books are readily available in the most obvious places: the corner drugstore and the supermarket, accessible to the masses who want to get better, to improve themselves, to feel better, and who have no money for such things as psychotherapy and Esalen-style encounter courses.

While searching through these and other books for a new, winning self-image, what Werner actually found was a sort of religion.

"Towards the latter part of our year in Saint Louis," he said, "I got a kind of religion. It was a religion of self-motivation and self-reliance. I'd like to tell you about this because it is badly misunderstood. I know that people make fun of persons like Napoleon Hill and Maxwell Maltz, but if you really look at what they have to say you find integrity and humanity. It is almost a religious philosophy. The core of their work is spiritual. What they say is, admittedly, not deep; but it is not silly either. If you don't master the issues that they are dealing with—personal competence and success—you will never be in a position to go more deeply.

"During those first two years after I left the East Coast, nothing really cleared up in my life. But I did begin to get an education—and a kind of infectious enthusiasm. I found hope for myself in those books."

Having cut himself off from ordinary routes to academic and professional training—and being in touch only with a culture, or sub-culture, whose story has not yet really been told—Werner began to shape a distinctive and indigenously American grass-roots training program of his own. The men and women with whom he later became associated—those who have during the past several decades come to play roles of initiative and leadership within the human potential and transformation movements—have tended to take ordinary routes through the universities and the professions. They have come through psychotherapy, from the medical and paramedical professions, from the arts and humanities, and occasionally from the church.

Werner's route was to be by way of business: unable to attend university, he initially came to the human potential movement through the study and application of motivational techniques. From there he was to go a step further to what he now self-mockingly calls the "business of transformation." If his acquisition of a liberal education within the business world is not surprising, perhaps that is at least in part because methods used to enhance motivation in business are not all that different from those used to develop human potential generally: both refer, for their success, to the true generality and universality of liberal education. This aspect of Werner's life story permits two sharply separated cultures, contexts, ways of life, to be joined together.

During the course of his own training program, Werner Erhard encountered various ideas, theories, techniques, and disciplines on which he drew to remedy his confusion and to give form to his self-definition. "*Intersections*" will, in this book, mark the major crossroads where, on his journey in search of Self, Werner encountered these seminal ideas and practices. They contain background material about his self-education, material which, while outside the narrative, is also crucial to it. The first Intersection treats of motivation and self-image psychology.

Intersection
ONE: *MOTIVATION AND SELF-IMAGE PSYCHOLOGY*

Academic historians . . . have been noticeably snobbish about some of the most potent and significant figures of recent times. And while these academic historians have justified their studies of earlier figures (such as Ralph Waldo Emerson) by elevating publicists into philosophers, finding subtlety where there may have been only ambiguity, they have been much less generous to figures of their own era, especially to those who attained financial and popular success. A good example of this neglect is Dale Carnegie, whose books and programs have reached millions, shaping and expressing dominant attitudes of the age.
—Daniel J. Boorstin[1]

The self-help textbook of success motivation is neither particularly recent nor peculiarly American as a form of literary expression. There are venerable antecedents among the European classics. In France, there is Michel de Montaigne's *Essays* (1571–1580), and in England, Francis Bacon's *Essayes* or *Counsels* (1597) on Riches, Ambition, Fortune, Anger, Vicissitude. Later, there were Lord Chesterfield's *Letters* to his natural son (1774), and Samuel Smiles's essays on self-help and thrift, in his *Lives of the Engineers*

(1861–1862). In America the self-help classics include Benjamin Franklin's *Poor Richard's Almanac*, particularly Father Abraham's speech in it on "The Way to Wealth," and some of the essays of Ralph Waldo Emerson.

These classics are written with wit, humor, urbanity—and more than a touch of world-weariness. They are addressed chiefly to the European gentlemen of bygone days.

The twentieth-century American examples of this genre are written in a different style: they are earnest, humorless, and urgent. And they are addressed not to gentlemen but to the masses. And not just to the American masses! The former premier of Burma, U Nu, is the translator into Burmese of Karl Marx's *Das Kapital*—and of Dale Carnegie's *How to Win Friends and Influence People*. When U Nu came to visit the United States, the person he most wanted to meet was Dale Carnegie. After all, Carnegie's book was outselling Marx's in Burma.

Such books, oddly enough, are mentioned in none of the consciousness literature. Werner Erhard may be the only consciousness leader who has read, let alone studied them. Evidently, for many people, the idea of positive thinking conjures up the image of sugary cheeriness covering over the plain greed and pressure tactics of direct salesmanship and the crude realities of the world in which it functions.

Yet many important notions about consciousness are embedded in these unadorned manuals of self-enrichment and self-improvement. Far from teaching sales techniques, let alone instructions for conning the customer, these books speak with unabashed pleasure and open sincerity about love, happiness, honesty, success. Their authors—themselves often self-taught, self-made men—are full of a robust enthusiasm to share with their fellowmen what they plainly see as the secret to happiness. Successful business tycoons have written some of the most ardent of these texts. *I Dare You!*, by William H. Danforth, the founder of the Ralston Purina Company, of Saint Louis, is a good example.[2] His very chapter headings— "You Can Be Bigger Than You Are," for instance—proclaim his message: that you change yourself into a better, happier, more successful person.

Of the two books to which Werner gives special credit, Napoleon Hill's is older and simpler. *Think and Grow Rich,* his best-known book, comes encrusted by its publishers with glowing testimonials to his methods from politicians, captains of commerce and industry, and of labor, such as William Howard Taft and Woodrow Wilson, F. W. Woolworth, John Wanamaker, George Eastman, and Samuel Gompers. Hill credits the steel industrialist and philanthropist Andrew Carnegie—yet another self-made man—with having inspired his work, and claims that his formula for success is based on Carnegie's own recipe for achievement, disclosed personally to him as a youth.

Hill's book was published during the Great Depression and is directed to those whom it left crushed, fearful, bereft. Echoing Franklin D. Roosevelt's inaugural declaration that "the only thing we have to fear is fear itself," it is presented as a system of self-analysis to uncover fear and inhibitions standing between the reader and the "big money." Hill's aim is to "help you to negotiate your way through life with harmony and understanding."

Underneath the nostrums, the homilies, and the romanticized tales of success in the face of great odds, there lie, plainly articulated by Hill, several basic principles of consciousness. The book is more about thinking than about growing rich.

The first notion of Hill's books is that all achievement, including earned riches, has as its source an idea freely created: with ideas one can create something out of nothing. Hard work and sacrifice are in vain unless accompanied by ideas.

The second basic notion is that ideas have an inherent tendency to transmute themselves into reality. They do this because of the nature of the human being, his mind, and his conscious and subconscious powers. An individual's mind becomes "magnetized" by its dominant thoughts and emotions. This magnetism attracts to him the forces, people, and circumstances that happen to harmonize with his dominant thinking. This brings fate within one's control: the only limitations on success are those erected in one's own mind. "You are," Hill repeats, "the master of your fate and the captain of your soul."

The nature of one's fate, however, depends on *which* thoughts one feeds on. The mind transmutes into its physical equivalent a thought of a negative or destructive nature as readily as it does a positive or constructive thought. Thus, to allow negative and destructive thoughts into one's mind—"tramp thoughts," Hill calls them—is to sow misfortune. By contrast, implanting thoughts of achievement creates the mental conditions for success.

How does one get positive thoughts into the mind and keep negative ones out?

This may be done, Hill urges, through *autosuggestion* directed to the subconscious mind. One eventually comes to believe whatever one repeats to oneself in this manner. In fact, autosuggestion goes on willy-nilly, whether done deliberately or not. And if one neglects to implant positive desires, thoughts, and emotions, the subconscious will feed upon negative thoughts. For it is constantly bombarded by fear, doubt, and unbelief, which exert a hypnotic effect on it. To prevent this, the individual must take the initiative and "feed his subconscious mind on thoughts of a creative nature." These thoughts need not be true: it is permissible to deceive one's subconscious mind when giving it instructions, in the service of a positive goal.

Merely *thinking* positive thoughts does not suffice. Although all thought *tends* to transmute itself into reality, this is strikingly, dramatically, true of thought that has been emotionalized, given feeling, and mixed with faith. To aid this, Hill suggests reinforcing autosuggestive processes with what later came to be called techniques of "active imagination."[3]

The role of the imagination is crucial to Hill's approach. One must make detailed statements of goals, specify what one is prepared to pay in order to reach them, and color them with desire and imagination. One must visualize oneself "on the road to success," taking definite steps toward those goals—and then see oneself as having attained them.

A careful selection of friends and acquaintances also reinforces positive thoughts and emotions, and keeps out negative ones. For, as Hill cautions, people take on the nature, the habits, and the thoughts of those with whom they associate harmoniously.

The subconscious mind further serves to connect one to what Hill calls the forces of Infinite Intelligence, which magnetized minds can attract from the "ether." In this connection, Hill endorses extrasensory perception.

To tap Infinite Intelligence, one's mind must operate with the highest "vibrations." Then one is lifted to a higher point of view and sees beyond ordinary barriers. A high rate of vibration is achieved by *blending* ideas with emotions through the use of what Freud called sublimation and the Hindus call Kundalini: the transmutation of the sex drive. The mind must be switched from thoughts of physical expression to thoughts of some other nature, redirecting energy and imagination that usually go into sexual gratification to higher ends. When done correctly, Hill contends, this produces genius. A genius is one who, by the sublimation of sex, has increased his mental vibrations to the point where he can communicate with sources of knowledge not ordinarily available.

Hill's book is rich in enthusiasm, limited in technology. It reports human achievements and tells how some people explained their success to themselves. Yet it fails to give a specific technology and context to aid someone readily to re-create those achievements. In this respect it resembles enthusiastic reports about great mystics and psychics and gurus—Madam Blavatsky, Gurdjieff, and others. Many of these also report miracles, and relate how those who experienced them interpreted and explained such things to themselves. But they fail to provide a detailed, popularly available, practical technology for attaining these states—any more than Hill's book provides a practical technology for achieving success and riches.

The second book to influence Werner in Saint Louis was Maxwell Maltz's *Psycho-Cybernetics*. Although Werner later outgrew Maltz's thought, it shows a considerable advance on Hill with regard to explanatory power, technique, and applicability.

Although *Psycho-Cybernetics* is a success book, Maltz, unlike Hill, does not conceive of success in terms of the acquisition of money or symbols or prestige. Success for him is oriented not to material things but to "satisfaction, fulfillment, and happiness."

Two ideas lie at the heart of Maltz's account. The first is "self image"; the second has to do with the relatively new science of cybernetics.

As a plastic surgeon, Maltz noticed that altering the facial features—the physical, external self-image—of his patients through plastic surgery often effected, as intended, a remarkable positive change in personality. But not always: in some patients, a positive change in external image—no matter how spectacular—failed to effect any positive psychological effect.

To explain such failures, Maltz postulated an *internal* self-image. Cosmetic correction of external self-image does not work when the internal self-image is distorted. "We act, behave, and feel according to what we consider this self image to be and we do not deviate from this pattern," Maltz writes.[4]

To display the effect of the self-image, and how one might work with it, Maltz uses *cybernetics*.

The science of cybernetics dates from 1942, and was named in 1947 by the mathematician Norbert Wiener and the physicist Arturo Rosenblueth. Wiener and Rosenblueth define it as the "science of control and communication in the animal and the machine."[5] It is based on the fact that both biological organisms and some machines have sensors that measure deviation from a set goal, and signal this back as "feedback" into a coordinating mechanism which then corrects the output or behavior of those same organisms or machines.

A simple example is central heating with a thermostat. To maintain a particular temperature, one sets the thermostatic control accordingly. When the temperature falls below the set temperature, an electrical circuit is activated that triggers an increase in the rate of burning in the heating unit. Should the room grow too hot, the heating unit is turned off or its burning rate is reduced. The heating unit controls the temperature of the room by way of information conveyed by the thermostat. Another example is the "servo-mechanism" that keeps a ship on a steady course by automatically counteracting any deviation from a set course. The word "cybernetics" in fact relates to this example: the Greek *cybernitos* means "helmsman."

Here self-image theory connects with cybernetic theory: internal self-image acts as a thermostat. To change the temperature of the room, one must reset the thermostat; to change behavior or habits, one must alter self-image.

For Maltz, self-image is a "premise, a base, or a foundation upon which your entire personality, your behavior, and even your circumstances are built." It organizes and interprets experience and defines behavior. Depending on whether it is positive or negative, such reinforcement leads either to a beneficent or to a vicious cycle. The self-image is the "real key to personality and behavior." It sets the boundaries of individual accomplishment—of "the possible."

In setting the boundaries of accomplishment, self-image will even explain learning difficulties. It will be hard to learn mathematics, for instance, if doing so is incompatible with self-image. Habits, to take another example, are garments tailored to self-image. "Effort" in trying to change a habit is beside the point: in the face of contrary self-image, effort actually reinforces the habit that one wishes to break. To change a habit one must, hence, first change self-image.

Maltz sees the failure of "positive thinking"—as in Hill's books—in its neglect of self-image and the cybernetic principles in terms of which it works. A patch of positive thinking on an inadequate garment cannot be expected to work; it is impossible to think really positively so long as one's self-image is negative.

The same applies to goals. Human beings are engineered cybernetically as goal-seeking mechanisms, and must have a target at which to shoot. But people may be so inhibited by negative self-images that they cannot express goals—in which case they go around in circles. Only after one has destroyed one's negative self-image, inhibitions, and limiting beliefs about what sorts of goals are appropriate can one form, through imagination, new truly realistic goals.

How *does* one destroy negative self-image, limiting beliefs, and inhibitions?

One must first look carefully at the position one takes in life, Maltz maintains. For there are various "barriers," of a more or less philosophical character, deeply imbued in people in our culture, which tend to reinforce negative self-image.

First of all, people with negative self-images tend to suffer from what Werner calls the "victim's position." In emphasizing this point, Maltz is not only at one with Hill; he has hit on one of the major themes of the consciousness movement. On the victim's interpretation, the environment fully determines behavior as a product: one *is* what the environment has done to one. Whereas— in Maltz's view—feedback from the environment merely guides or corrects or stabilizes a preexisting pattern of behavior.

No one, Maltz maintains, can expect to change his self-image until he recognizes his *responsibility* for it. He created it in the first place through "creative experiencing"—and can change it by the same method: through experiencing it again, and creating a better self-image by the use of imagination. "No longer can you derive sickly comfort," Maltz writes, "from blaming your parents, society, your early experiences, or the injustices of others for your present troubles."

This point, incidentally, marks a difference between Maltz and some Freudians. Maltz rejects the supposition that one must dig out *past* painful—traumatic—experiences in order to effect personal change. Nor does Maltz locate the source of psychological distress in an "unconscious" or "subconscious," at whose mercy one exists. One must, rather, be responsible for the entire cybernetic machinery, including not only past records but also the conscious *thinking* mind.

Other barriers reinforcing negative self-image are *resentment* and *righteousness*. An adequate self-image is impossible, Maltz emphasizes, unless one feels that others are worthy too. The main barrier to this is resentment, which is the "worst aspect of the failure mechanism." Resentment and the self-righteousness that attends it are doubly pernicious: they fixate one in the past, and render one the victim of some other party to whom one attributes causative power.

What has happened, Maltz stresses, *has* happened: there is no point in resisting it. Resentment represents mental resistance to what has happened. It is an emotional rehashing or refighting of some unalterable past event. Like a broken record, one keeps reliving—replaying—past injustices. Such an "engram" (as Maltz calls it, after British biologists and neurophysiologists Sir Charles Sherrington and Sir John Eccles) becomes more potent with each replaying.

What if one's resentment is based on *real* injustices and wrongs? That does not matter. Justified or not, resentment is self-damaging. It hurts one's own cause, prevents one from seeing oneself as self-reliant, and makes one more likely to continue to fail. It is an exceedingly expensive emotion. Without excluding the possibility that resentment *is* based on real wrongs, Maltz concludes: "Whether you 'ought' to forgive, or whether you 'should' forgive, or can reasonably be expected to do it, is a matter which is outside the scope of this book. . . . I can only tell you as a doctor that if you will do it, you will be far happier, healthier and attain more peace of mind."

In sum, resentment puts the individual out of causative control over his own life—victimlike—and surrenders the reins of his life to others who dictate how he shall feel and act. It fixates one in the past, and leads one to look for further injustices to validate one's self-image. Such resentment is inconsistent with creative goal striving, wherein one is not a passive recipient but is actively responsible for one's own success and happiness.

Guilt is another emotion, connected to resentment, which forms part of the failure mechanism of negative self-images. Guilt, for Maltz, is an attempt to make right in the present something one did or thought of as wrong in the past. Since one cannot change the past, guilt is inappropriate. The correct use of emotions is to help one to respond appropriately to present reality. Neither resentment nor guilt do this.

Resentment, righteousness, and guilt work together to create *inhibition*. Inhibition involves excessive monitoring, causing the servo-mechanism to overcorrect. When one is inhibited—shy, timid, self-conscious, hostile, guilty, insomniac, nervous, irritable, unable to get along with others—one cannot express one's true creative self. When inhibited people receive feedback indicating that their manner of expression is somewhat off course, they often jump to the absurd conclusion that self-expression itself is wrong, or that success is wrong for them. Such a personality, as Maltz puts it, "stutters all over."

To overcome inhibition, Maltz suggests practicing forms of "disinhibition": just opening one's mouth and saying something without wondering in advance what one will say; acting, correcting one's actions as one goes along, but not planning them beforehand; avoiding criticizing oneself; making it a habit to speak in a loud voice (inhibited persons are notoriously soft-spoken); letting people know when one likes them.

These various symptoms of a poorly set "thermostat"—resentment, guilt, inhibition—have an important feature in common. Each pulls the individual out of the present. This Maltz sees as the most important underlying emotional problem, and at the root of all dissatisfaction in life. People have either forgotten, or never learned, how to employ their cybernetic machinery so as to control *present* thinking. The thermostat is poorly set, the machinery goes out of control, and the individual is chained to the past. Instead of responding to the present environment, he or she reacts automatically, as if to some past environment, to what Maltz calls a "fiction," an image from the past that exercises iron control over life. Whereas, when functioning at optimum level, cybernetic mechanisms respond appropriately to the present environment and its problems *here and now*. "Full recognition of this," he says, "can frequently bring about an amazingly quick 'cure.' "

Repair of these symptoms goes hand in hand with creating a new positive self-image. The main tools for these tasks are three: physical relaxation, imagination, and hypnosis.

When relaxed, one no longer has to respond automatically to negative beliefs. Maltz instructs his readers how to achieve such a relaxed state, using techniques similar to the "induction" techniques of hypnosis. When learning to relax, he advises, one should create in imagination a "room of the mind," or laboratory of the mind. Into such an imaginary retreat one should resort at least thirty minutes each day. In such a meditative or trance state, one imagines, in vivid detail, new positive goals—taking advantage of the principle that the nervous system cannot distinguish between an actual experience and one vividly imagined. As Maltz writes: "The proper use of the imagination can be equivalent to the beginning of a goal and a belief in this goal. And if this belief is strong enough we hypnotize ourselves with it . . . all our habits, good and bad, are daily forms of self-hypnosis. Belief is a form of creative hypnotism."

Here we reach the heart of Maltz's technique. Whereas Hill referred to hypnosis only obliquely, calling it autosuggestion, Maltz advocates it openly. Hypnosis is for him the key tool—through "creative experiencing"—in the building of a new, positive self-image.

BREAKING DOWN THE FIXED REALITY

These notions, especially that of self-image, struck Werner as exactly what he was searching for. The *external* trappings of a new identity—new cards of identity and a new name—hardly sufficed. He would also need an internal self-image that would expand the range of the possible in his new life, and exclude those things that had led him to fail before. Later, he would come to use the word "Self" in a very different way that goes beyond position and identification. At this moment, however, in Saint Louis, he had as yet little grasp of a higher sense of Self. Werner wanted to bring his life under control; and self-image is a control center, providing a context for the self-construction of one's life. His highest aspiration now became the creation of a better self-image, a better internal position in Maltz's sense.

As the winter months in Saint Louis passed by, Werner spent his days outdoors, on the used car lot. In the evenings, and on weekends, he stayed at home with Ellen. There he worked a kind of spiritual plastic surgery on himself. Following the program of Hill and Maltz in detail, he chipped away at his own resentment toward Dorothy and the other members of his family, and at his guilt about leaving them.

He tried elaborate exercises in active imagination and in autohypnosis on himself, in an effort to bring his own "cybernetic machinery" fully into present time, to set up new goals, and to establish a positive new self-image to fill in his new synthetic identity.

He was already familiar with hypnosis. He had once been hypnotized by a stage magician when he was ten years old, at a cub scout banquet, and had also learned something of it in his early studies of yoga. In high school he tried experiments in hypnotism with some of his classmates. Ellen now became his subject too.

"I turned out to be a good hypnotic subject," Ellen told me. "After hypnotizing me, Werner did the extraordinary 'showman' things that hypnotists can do. For example, he put out a cigarette on my hand without leaving a burn or a mark. He stuck pins in my hands and arms without my experiencing any pain.

"One morning, just before he left for work, he said 'Let's try something,' and then he put me into a hypnotic trance. He instructed me to remember a dream that I had the previous night and to write it down for him, with all the details, and to show it to him when he got home that night. Well, I did sit down after he left, and I did remember every detail of a dream. I can still remember it—and I don't usually remember my dreams.

"That was just the beginning. I would have headaches from time to time. Werner would get me to sit in a chair, and he used a technique involving what he called a 'black velvet curtain.' The headache was gone just like that. So I had to give some credibility to what he was doing. I couldn't say that I wasn't really hypnotized and that I pretended to do all that. It really happened. That baffled me.

"The most fabulous experiment came shortly after we arrived in Saint Louis. We lived between the park and the railroad tracks. I had a thing about train whistles. I hated them. I was asleep one night when a train passed by and let out a shrill whistle. I sat bolt upright in bed in an absolute fright. Werner said:. 'What in the world is the matter with you?' I didn't know. Right there and then he hypnotized me, and in the trance I recalled a memory of a childhood trauma associated with a train whistle when I was four years old. I had completely suppressed that memory—and under hypnosis it came back. I never had any trouble with train whistles after that.

"So we had a bit of fun with it. Werner was careful about it. He never tried anything that he didn't know something about; and he would not offer posthypnotic suggestions that were nutty or odd."

When I asked Werner about these experiments in hypnotism,

and about his attitude toward them, he told me that the technique he had used on Ellen's headache in Saint Louis was a form of "hypnotic block." "I now see such techniques as counterproductive," he added. "The techniques that I have developed since then for eliminating pain are intended to *complete* the pain, not simply to block it."

Werner had been reading widely about hypnotism, he told me, since he was a teen-ager. In those days he bought books on the subject from drugstore stands. "People didn't know much about hypnosis then," he said. "So those books often made wild claims, and were bound to intrigue someone as naïve as I was. I found that I had some facility at doing hypnosis, and I gradually picked up the skill by practicing it with close friends."

His interest in hypnosis had grown out of his interest in yoga, and was the beginning of his interest in "other realities." "Hypnosis was for me," he said, "one of the first things to break up the ordinary fixed reality. Ordinarily, people can learn only what fits into the fixed reality, and this limits them to knowledge of content. Hypnosis got me to begin to look at the structures behind reality, the context of reality, and also at the effect of belief on individuals. Maltz and Hill made me begin to see the *practical* bearing of this.

"Hypnosis is, however, generally misunderstood," Werner observed. "It would be good to begin the whole subject over again with a new definition and a new context. The data that have been reported are generally sound, but the interpretations that accompany them are often unsound."

I ntersection
TWO: HYPNOSIS

Hypnosis is controversial. Nothing that one hears or reads about it, including what is written here, is to be believed or trusted. Perhaps the two most authoritative reference books available to the general reader are the *Encyclopaedia Britannica* and the *Encyclopedia Americana*. Thus we read in the *Americana* that hypnosis is potentially very dangerous, whereas the *Britannica* reports:

> Concerning harmful effects, none have been reported by earnest students of long experience, but the inexperienced and the armchair theorist are often emphatic in affirming such possibilities.[6]

Hypnosis is characterized by an altered state of consciousness—a trance state—induced either by oneself alone or with the assistance of another person. In this state, one can go beyond many ordinary limitations: pain and bleeding can sometimes be controlled so as to obviate the need for anesthesia even in major operations such as amputations; memory and recall of past, long-forgotten experiences are enhanced; control of sensation and motor phenomena is heightened. One may also dramatically reduce stress and tension, with a resulting increased flexibility on almost all levels, physical and emotional. One may also produce vivid auditory and visual images of the type ordinarily associated with dreaming or hallucinating. From the very beginning, powers of healing, clairvoyance, and extrasensory perception have also been reported in connection with the hypnotic trance.

How and where were these states first discovered? The conventional western textbook account of trance states is quite inadequate.

It has become conventional to say that hypnosis was discovered by a maverick Viennese physician, Franz Anton Mesmer, who became famous throughout Europe in the eighteenth century for the spectacular healing that he did. Mesmer himself viewed his results as the effect of a physical force—which he called animal magnetism—akin to electrical magnetism. When it was discovered, in Paris, in 1784—by a blue-ribbon scientific commission including the great chemist Lavoisier and also Benjamin Franklin—that no physical magnetism was in fact present, many dismissed mesmerism, as it had come to be called, as a hoax.

This was in part put right in the early 1840s by an English physician, James Braid, of Manchester, who coined the word "hypnotism." Braid contended that Mesmer was no charlatan, but had simply misunderstood the nature of the phenomena he was dealing with. While Mesmer's *explanation* in terms of magnetism was incorrect, the *phenomena* which he and his followers had reported and demonstrated were quite genuine. Braid reinterpreted hypnotism as a trance state induced by concentration of attention.

This is simply the Western textbook account. Actually, the phenomena connected with hypnotism were known in the West long before Mesmer. And in the Orient, they were not only well known, but had been elaborately investigated. Trance states are mentioned breifly by Plato in the *Phaedrus*, as early as the fourth century B.C., where their connection with prophecy and healing is noted. (Anthropologists report that such states may also be found in shamanistic practices throughout the world. In the religions of the

Orient—in the meditative and yogic practices of Hinduism, Buddhism, and other religions—they were brought to an exceptional height of refinement.)

Thus, in the 1840s, when Braid was only beginning to take an interest in hypnosis and any British physician practiced it at the risk of being denounced as a charlatan, James Esdaile, one of the pioneer British mesmerists, practiced hypnotism in India on a wide scale. Although the British and British-trained medical profession in India was unfriendly to his work, the native Indian administrators—to whom such phenomena were by no means unusual—encouraged him. Between 1845 and 1851, when he left India to return to Scotland, Esdaile performed some three hundred major operations with the use of hypnosis, greatly reducing the number of deaths usually expected following such surgery.[7]

Although hypnosis is often described as a *"special form of trance* developed in Western civilization,"[8] many states reached through hypnosis resemble those reached through meditation and yogic practices. The techniques, the ritual and paraphernalia, and the setting are, to be sure, different: the so-called "induction" or relaxation procedures vary; so, too, the Oriental will use a Sanskrit word for his mantra (the sound associated with trance induction), whereas a Westerner may in its place use a euphonic Western word such as "butterfly." Most of the phenomena attributed to hypnosis in the West are found in the meditative and religious disciplines of East and West.

As knowledge concerning traditional Oriental meditative practices becomes widely available in the West, one may expect a unified theory of altered states of consciousness to emerge.[9] One problem that such a unified account of trance states East and West will have to confront is the whole matter of "suggestion." Thus far, Eastern meditative disciplines have barely discussed suggestion, whereas in the West hypnosis is frequently reduced to manipulative suggestion. In trance states the subject is indeed highly suggestible, as is illustrated by hypnotic stunts. Thus the hypnotist might give his subject a posthypnotic suggestion to perform a particular action after leaving the trance state and not to remember consciously that he had been given such instructions. The subject might be told, say, to take off his wristwatch whenever the hypnotist crossed his arms. He would do so, without consciously knowing why. If challenged, he would invent a reason for so acting.

Western psychologists have reasoned from phenomena like these to the conclusion that hypnosis is *nothing but* suggestion, which has in turn led to fears that some unscrupulous persons might deviously exploit hypnosis to gain control over others. In the East, on the other hand, trance states are cultivated as aids to overcome outside influences and to heighten the freedom of the individual.

A further example of such differences between East and West—and perhaps part of the explanation of them—is the general practice in the West for one person to be hypnotized by another, who might thereby gain control; whereas in the East one typically goes into meditative trance on one's own, without assistance from another, a feat that Westerners such as Napoleon Hill describe as "autohypnosis" or "autosuggestion."

Evidently the trance state is in itself neutral, and can be used either for good or for ill, either for heightened freedom or for imprisonment by oneself or another.

To say that Werner encountered hypnosis at this time is to say that he encountered an altered state of consciousness *called* hypnosis, and that he found his way to it by way of books and techniques favoring a Western terminology, and a limited interpretation of its status and scope, and embedding it in a more or less behavioristic philosophy.

Although Werner made some connection between hypnosis, as he practiced it in Saint Louis, and the yogic practices in which he had disciplined himself as a boy, it was not until several years later, in California, that he made a broader connection between hypnosis and meditation, and reinterpreted both of them.

In his conversations with me, Werner deplored the usual connection between trance and suggestion. "Just as you can be in trance without being under the influence of suggestion," he said, "similarly you can be under the influence of suggestion without a formal hypnotic trance. In fact, the so-called *normal* state of consciousness is something very much like a state of posthypnotic suggestion. This means that you don't need a formal preparation—what hypnotists call 'induction'—in order to be hypnotized. For most people are already prepared. All that is needed is for you to use the circumstances of the· trance that is already present in order to deepen that trance. Thus you can hypnotize people with a single word or action.

"So-called *normal* consciousness is, in any case, not where matters are for me. This just tends to be self-definition by Westerners of what is normal for Westerners. People are already, *normally*, in trance. A good example of this is the very rigid, fixated person. It is hard to hypnotize such a person only because you can hardly get his attention. He is already fully hypnotic.

"Almost any belief, whether an idea uncritically accepted from another, or an idea that one has, through repetition, convinced oneself is true, will have a hypnotic effect on one. Many people lead their lives in servitude to such beliefs and suggestions—and live as if entranced. A young woman, for example, may in a moment of stress say to herself, 'I'll never love anyone again,' or a child may say, 'I'll hate so-and-so forever.' Such a declaration can gain as much unconscious command value as any posthypnotic suggestion made by a professional hypnotist. It can run, and ruin, the life of the person who has made it.

"Those patterns that I described to you earlier—the ones controlling my relationship with my mother and with Pat—are of this type. They had as much power as if they had been formally implanted by a hypnotist. I was definitely entranced by them."

Werner remarked that there are two quite distinct uses of hypnosis and other trance states. "Hypnosis and trance states," he said, "can be used to transcend the Mind, to go beyond it to what I was later to call the Self. They can also be used—as they very often are—to operate simply on Mind.

"In itself, a trance state of Mind is a *state of Mind*, and must not be confused with a state *beyond* Mind.

"When I was first learning about these things, in Saint Louis, I didn't know anything about Self, or about states beyond Mind. I learned then that there was a lot more to life than ordinary consciousness, but I didn't yet sense how *much* more. Nor did I as yet know about metaconsciousness or dimensionality. Maltz and Hill work entirely at the level of Mind. My interest in hypnosis at this time was devoted entirely to tinkering with Mind, to operating with cybernetic machinery. I later saw this as a mistake—or rather, as something of quite limited value.

"You see, there is a danger in the very word 'hypnosis.' If it refers simply to trance states and to the practices used in reaching them, there is no problem. But more often than not, especially in the West, the word 'hypnosis' also means the *theory* of hypnosis. And the usual theoretical account of hypnosis that you find among Western psychologists not only fails to recognize the existence of Self; it *excludes* the possibility of Self. Thus you get into the confusing state where hypnotic trance can be usefully practiced on the route to the Self, but where *hypnosis*, as a theory, doesn't acknowledge the existence of Self.

"Here you find the real difference between hypnosis, as understood in the West, and the meditative and yogic disciplines, as understood in the East. In Eastern religions and disciplines, it is well known that trance states can be used to provide *power* to manipulate the cybernetic machinery of the Mind. But that is not the point of it all; that is just a stage that you pass through. The Eastern disciplines recognize the existence of Self beyond Mind."

"The point is to be *de*hypnotized. That is what an *expanded* state of consciousness actually involves. This is a state of consciousness characterized by freedom, one in which one is not at the effect of suggestions, beliefs, patterns, or any other unconscious or mechanistic forces. On the way to such an expanded state of consciousness, one moves through both the trance of normal states of consciousness and those states formally labeled as trance. It is as legitimate to make use of trance states, as it is to make use of normal states of consciousness. Both normal and trance states are, in and of themselves, neutral states of being."

TO SPOKANE: A NEW BEGINNING IN THE BOOK BUSINESS

The cities swept about me like dead leaves.
   —*Tennessee Williams*, The Glass Menagerie

In the spring of 1961, Werner and Ellen left Saint Louis. Werner became a traveling salesman. He took a job as a traveling "registrar" for a correspondence school that instructed people in the operation of construction equipment. His job was to visit and sign up persons who had written to the school headquarters requesting information and an interview. Those who registered for the course took so many lessons by mail, and then traveled to a center for the final two weeks of the course, during which time they would actually operate equipment.

"Four of us went on the road," Ellen told me. "There was a friend of ours, and his girl friend, and Werner and I. We were traveling in two cars, and drove all over the Midwest. According to the terms of his contract, Werner kept as his commission the usual down payment that people made for the course. So whenever we got a down payment, we could sleep in a motel. Several times we had to sleep in the car."

The car that Werner set off in did not belong to him, and its registration plates had expired. Its owner had asked Werner to sell it for him. Werner wanted to buy it himself, but did not have the money. Without asking for permission, he began to drive it—figuring that he could do so for a month or so without any serious objection from the owner. He allowed mud to accumulate on the license plates, to hide the date, and they drove off into the plains.

Once they were nearly caught. "I was driving," Ellen remembered. "To make things worse, I didn't have a license. I looked up in my mirror, and saw a flashing red light. We pulled over. Werner got out quickly, and told me just to sit there. The policeman ambled up and said to Werner, 'I see you're from Saint Louis.' He told Werner that that was his hometown too. Finally he said that he just wanted to tell us that if another policeman came along, and wasn't from Saint Louis, we would get in trouble—because it was impossible to read our license plates! He asked Werner to wait a minute, returned to the police car, and brought back a can and a polishing rag. The policeman bent down on the road and cleaned our license plates. Then he waved and left!"

Ellen painted a tale of nomadic life on the road in the Midwest: Werner in his best suit, getting stuck in—and covered by—mud and oil next to an oil rig in Kansas; in a barn in Nebraska selling the course to a farmer milking his cow; stopping for the night in the pitch dark under the stars, listening—as they drifted off to sleep—to the crickets chirping in the fields around them.

They kept body and soul together, but not much else. Two months passed. Despite Werner's enthusiasm, they had not been able to save any money. By the middle of May, both Werner and Ellen were ready to abandon the open road and the provisional life. Whatever they had hoped their life together would be, they had not found it in Saint Louis and the Midwest. If you don't make it where you are . . . you can always take your self-image westward.

The head of the correspondence school was located in California, near Los Angeles, and Werner and Ellen decided to drive there, to apply for relocation on the West Coast. They returned briefly to Saint Louis, gathered their meager belongings, and then, like thousands of visionaries and gold-seekers before them, set off on the well-worn westward journey to the promised land. They took route 66, driving through the great American desert to Upland, California.

By now the car that they were driving was no longer "borrowed." It was, in effect, stolen. "I suppose that it wasn't *technically* stolen," Werner told me. "For the owner had turned it over to me. But he didn't know where I was anymore, we had been out of touch for weeks, and as far as *I* was concerned the car was stolen. I hated that. It went right against everything that I had been trying to do with myself in Saint Louis. But we couldn't do without the car; and by now I was afraid to go back to the owner without the money to pay for it. So we moved fast, in the hope that we wouldn't be caught, and could make some money quickly in order to pay for the car."

Almost as soon as they crossed the border into California, they began to feel better, Ellen told me. "We still didn't have any money," she said, "but it felt like we were suddenly going from famine to feast. I remember driving into California with my arm out the car window. The air was warm and dry, and it was so exciting to be there. We were famished, and stopped at a hamburger stand—I think it was one of the first McDonald's—and ate a half-dozen nineteen-cent hamburgers. Then when we arrived in Upland, the head of the school immediately took us out to a superb dinner at an elegant restaurant. What a change!"

To their dismay, they found that they would almost immediately have to leave California. Werner was reassigned to sell the correspondence course in the Northwest. They drove north, first to Seattle, and then to Spokane. It was another world again. The Spokane area is a large one, and an enclosed domain unto itself. Spokane presides over a vast mining, lumbering, and agricultural region of some 80,000 square miles, for which it is the center of culture, transportation, and distribution. This area, between the Cascades and the Rockies, includes—in addition to eastern Washington—the Idaho panhandle, northeastern Oregon, western Montana, and the southern part of British Columbia. Werner was to remain here, traveling within its mountainous limits, for over a year.

Shortly after arriving in Spokane, Werner heard of an opportunity to work for the *Encyclopaedia Britannica*'s Great Books Program, an ambitious publishing and adult education program under the directorship of the philosopher and educator Mortimer Adler. He applied for the job and got it. For two months, Werner worked successfully in Spokane as a salesman for Great Books, and then was promoted to be training manager for the program in the Spokane area.

"The Great Books Program turned out to be my first real chance," Werner told me. I was looking for something to do and that job came along. Once I got into it, I became fascinated not only by the business, but by the product, and by the way in which I could apply in it what I was learning about success and motivation, and about myself and other people."

As a training manager for the program, Werner was to teach salesmen how to sell. He began to implement the ideas of Hill and Maltz. "I saw that the motivational and self-image approaches could be shared," Werner said. "If you could motivate yourself, you could motivate others too. As it turned out, I had no problem turning other people on.

"I also began to share with the people with whom I was working my own basic perception about the way people get entangled in their own life stories. In doing this, I began to know them on an intimate basis. When you go into questions of resentment and guilt with other people—and when you begin to examine the barriers that keep them from succeeding—you get to know their stories. As I got close to the truth about their lives, I saw over and over again the same kind of entanglement that permeated my own life."

After several months, there was an important crisis, when Werner had a disagreement with the manager of the Spokane office. "The man was cheating on the commissions of the men who worked for him," Werner told me. Werner resigned his job in protest, drove to Seattle, and asked the head of the Great Books operation there to give him an office of his own in Montana.

"I know it sounds crazy," Werner said. "Here I was, driving a stolen car, and being self-righteous about someone who was cheating. I was in a funny in-between period. I was *trying* desperately to get better, to be an honest person, to create a new and effective self-image for myself. Meanwhile I had these things in my past—my desertion of my family, and my stolen car—weighing me down, and scrawling 'Hypocrite' in large letters over every good and decent thing I did."

The men who had been working under Werner in Spokane did not know about his past, and they resigned in sympathy with him. Most of them got new jobs with another book operation in Spokane run by Parents' Magazine Cultural Institute, a child development materials division of *Parents' Magazine*. The Parents operation produced and sold materials for preschool and early grade-school children.

The head of the Parents operation for the Northwest was named

Ron Baldwin. The men he had just hired showed, in their handling of their affairs, in their selling, a number of techniques that astonished him. When he asked them where they had learned to do such things, they told him about Werner. As Werner put it, "Ron knew that business was predicated on how many good people you had working for you, and he asked me to come to work for him because he thought I would draw good people."

Meanwhile, Werner had gone to work in Montana, where he was beginning to develop his own operation. He refused Baldwin's offer of a job several times. But Baldwin persisted, and they spent several days together, talking. Finally Ron offered Werner whatever working conditions he wanted. "That hooked me," Werner said. "For I knew exactly what I wanted. I told him that I would work for him for two weeks. I set the amount that I wanted him to pay me—a lot of money in those days—and asked him to guarantee that to me. I told him that if I didn't *earn* more than I was paid in that two-week period, I was to be fired. And if I earned more than that, I would tell him then what I really wanted.

"But the main thing about Ron was that I suddenly had someone to talk with. I immediately sensed that I could be honest and open with him—and that I couldn't be any less than that. To my own astonishment, I began to tell him about my past, and to tell him that I couldn't come to work for him unless he knew all about me. I told him about the family in Philadelphia, and about the stolen car. This was a tremendous relief."

There was nothing that could be done immediately about the family in Philadelphia, but Ron insisted on dealing at once with the car from Saint Louis. Werner now had enough money to pay the owner for it. Ron took him to his attorney; the attorney contacted the owner; and the matter was settled amicably, with more being paid for the automobile than it was worth. Werner then set off on his trial sales run.

"The two-week trial run in Montana," Werner told me, "was, compared to what I was used to, like shooting fish in a barrel. I was simply telling people about materials for their children. For months I had been selling Great Books to tough lawyers, doctors, and businessmen. They had been full of resistance. With these people from Montana I didn't get any of that. They simply wanted good educational materials for their children. I sold so much that I was afraid I would get fired. I was sure that everyone would back out and disclaim the orders. It had been too easy. I could handle resistance—I trained people to handle resistance—but nobody resisted!"

Werner looked for a moment astonished, as if he still couldn't believe how easy it had been. "Anyway," he said, "the two weeks were over, and I had earned a lot more than had been agreed to. So I got my wish. I told Ron that I wanted to become his direct assistant. Ron was the territorial manager, and I wanted to become the assistant territorial manager. I now offered him another proposition. I said, 'In the next month I will get your people to double the best month they have ever had. If I don't, I am to be fired. If I do, I am your assistant.' Ron didn't want to agree to fire me, but eventually he agreed. We went around in his Cadillac convertible to all the cities in the Northwest where he had operations. I remember it vividly. I began to work for Parents in January 1962, and we started on our trip in February. We went through snowstorms. We had meetings with everyone, and everyone got so fired up that they did indeed double the best month that they ever had. Ron got a big bonus from Parents, and the president of the operation came out from New York to see what we were doing."

A few days after talking with Werner about Ron Baldwin, I flew to Portland to meet him. Ron has been successful with Parents since those early days with Werner. In the late sixties, he went to New York City to become the president of Parents. In 1972 he returned to the West Coast, and now operates the successor to Parents' Magazine Cultural Institute in the Pacific Northwest.

He and his wife Shirley met me in an office on the outskirts of Portland. Ron is a very large man. He was dressed informally, and sat behind his desk reflecting on the success of his friend Werner Erhard. He seemed calmly amused by his memories. "Most people had the same reaction to Werner," Ron said. "Here was a guy with such dynamism that you just had to know and be around him. I watched him very carefully for the whole seven years that he worked for me. My own success was very much dependent on Werner's doing his job. When I first met him, he wasn't, outwardly, all that different from the way he is today. He is just as intense now, but in a more quiet and relaxed way. He is serene now. And he wasn't then.

"From the start, he was interested in *everything*. He never stopped. We took Werner and Ellen with us and the kids to a summer resort cabin that we had on a lake in Idaho, near Spokane, for a little vacation. In a single day there, he learned how to water-ski and to ride a motorcycle. He even relaxed in an intense way!

"The main thing was, however, his interest in learning how to be successful and how to help other people to be successful. There were no stones that he would not turn to find out more about that. Every time I saw him he had a new book about being successful or using your mind. He began to take courses connected with these things too. Each time he did this, it became part of him, and he would put it into practice.

"He had read *Psycho-Cybernetics* a few months before I met him, and he was full of that when I first knew him. I remember one afternoon when we were sitting in my living room and Werner was talking about psycho-cybernetics. My little boy, who was about three at the time, was sitting on the floor with his mouth open, just listening, just like he understood every word that was being said."

Ron confirmed that Werner not only read and talked about psycho-cybernetics, but tried to apply it to the people with whom he was working. "He worked twenty hours a day," Ron said. "Most of his thoughts, his time, his energy, were devoted to finding ways to help people to be more successful at their jobs. He could take bored, egotistic, confused people, and work with them, and turn them into well-balanced and efficient workers.

"Meeting Werner was really *the* irreversible encounter in your life. Your life was just turned around afterward. You were a better and more effective, and more honest and compassionate person. Werner was just *wonderful* with people.

"This is why I was never too disturbed by those things in his past. He told me about them almost at once. He was very open with me. That was a painful subject, a big cloud hanging over him. When Werner was with my own children, tears would often come to his eyes. Whenever we discussed the matter, I would always urge him to go back and straighten it out. He and Ellen knew that that is what they had to do, that they could not avoid it forever.

"What Werner did to his family in Philadelphia is hard to understand because he was the gentlest and most compassionate man I had ever met. People would come and sit in his office until midnight and talk with him about their personal problems, about things that didn't appear to have anything to do with success on the job. When Werner was talking with somebody he was able to listen intently to what was being said and really look completely into that person.

"It is really very interesting. He was demanding—more demanding than anyone else I had worked with. On the other hand, he was a pussycat, a pushover. He was reluctant to fire people. He would take back people that I would consider hopeless, and they would become a challenge to him. It wasn't a question of productivity, but of whether he could show some improvement with them. From a business point of view, this was a fault. I would not have wasted my time on somebody who had so little potential.

"It didn't matter who it was," Ron said. "It could be somebody who worked for him, or just anybody at all. His vocation was helping people. He just happened to run the sales organization too."

CASTING OFF THE VICTIM'S POSITION: FIRST BREAKTHROUGH

"Self-image" psychology was a natural enough interest for someone with a false identity. Yet as Werner worked through Maltz, Hill, and other writers, applied their theories and techniques to his job and personal life, and taught them to Ellen and to his business associates, he reaped a number of benefits that he had not bargained for. He "got out of the mire." As he put it, "I dropped the inconsistent behavior and way of being. I stopped scheming.

"Although my desertion of Pat and the children was always there in the background, clouding and invalidating my progress, my new identity—Werner Erhard—was now really taking on flesh. I wasn't the victim of circumstances anymore. I moved from having justifications for what was wrong with my life to having some sway over it. I could alter the quality of my life. It could be good instead of just tolerable. It could be turned on instead of ground out.

"I began to think that I *had* won—that I *was* beating the game, that I could go beyond my past, that my gamble in leaving Philadelphia was paying off, and that eventually I might even be able to go back and correct that situation. I had begun to satisfy my basic need for food and shelter, for relationship and esteem. I even began to be proud of myself. The 'Werner Erhard' that I had created was a good and honorable person, able, inspiring to others, a success in the world. I had made it possible for others to succeed, and people respected me."

He also now had a lot to lose. At any moment someone from the past might have turned up; his family could have learned of his whereabouts and come after him. His new identity could have tumbled down like a house of cards. For the moment, this danger—and the fear connected with it—was set aside, as Werner filled his life with goals for the future.

"In that first breakthrough in Spokane," he told me, "I began to get sufficiently beyond the upset and horror of my departure from Philadelphia to have some sense of my own value and to want to do something with my life. The orientation of my life changed from past to future. I became a nut about goals. I was full of hope. I began to see as a task for myself the cleaning up and completing of my life."

Werner and Ellen had found a comfortable apartment in a complex on West Fifteenth Street, in Spokane. Most other tenants of the complex were young like themselves, and they began to make friends. "Werner was often away on business," Ellen told me, "but there were always people around, and that made it easier for me. We had some good times together too. We went to Lake Coeur d'Alene, in Idaho, several times. I remember one morning in particular. We got up very early and went out in the middle of the lake to fish for perch for breakfast. Werner caught them and I cooked them. I can remember the smell in the air and the fish frying in the pan. They were delicious. Somehow that scene sticks in my mind as representative of Spokane. It was a comparatively calm mellow time."

Werner's chief responsibilities in his job were to train the managers of the Parents offices in the Northwest, to hire new management personnel, to open new offices, and to conduct a sales motivation program. He traveled throughout the Inland Empire, and also to Salt Lake City and Seattle, to open and develop offices.

After a few months, in the late summer of 1962, the president of Parents suggested to Baldwin that Werner be promoted, and put in charge of Parents operations in California, Nevada, and Arizona, with the title of Territorial Director, and with headquarters in San Francisco. At the same time, Baldwin was made Zone Manager for the entire Western area of operations, thus remaining Werner's immediate superior. The offices in the territory that Werner was to direct eventually ranged from Seattle in the north to San Diego in the south, and as far west as Denver. He was now in charge of hundreds of employees.

SIX Conversion

Whoever has passed successfully through an education for truthfulness towards himself, will thereby be protected permanently against the danger of immorality, even if his standard of morality should somehow differ from social convention.
—Sigmund Freud

INTO CALIFORNIA

In San Francisco, Werner and Ellen took an apartment at the end of Anza Street, near the Cliff House, directly overlooking the pounding surf of the Pacific Ocean. Late one night, about a month after they moved in, Werner lay wide awake in bed. "That time of night has always been significant for me," he told me. "This feeling stretches back to my boyhood, to those late night conversations of my family; and to high school, when I would stay awake reading. It is so quiet; the world is asleep. You are alone. If you listen, you can hear things that cannot be heard at other times.

"During that night I finally confronted my sins against my family. 'Sin' is a word I never use. Yet it is the correct word here.

"Prior to that, I had been avoiding the whole issue of my family—even when I worried about it. I had never before got close to the true nature of my relationship with my children, with Pat, with

91

my sister and brothers, and Joe and Dorothy. Each member of my family, one at a time, appeared in my imagination. I was with each of them, savoring them. This went on for hours.

"Finally, I got up from bed. Ellen still lay there asleep. I went into the living room, on the south end of the apartment, and sat in a chair, looking out the large window overlooking the ocean. I was able to look directly south, far down the coast, at the line of surf beating against the rocks below. As I sat there I had a conversation with God. It was a holy experience; it had not the circumstances but the experience of holiness about it. I was literally forced to rise from my chair, and then forced to my knees. And I prayed for forgiveness.

"During that night a great weight lifted from me, and for the first time I knew that, eventually, I would return home."

At his new office, in the Flood Building on Market Street, Werner had already begun to recruit a new staff. One of those he hired was a man named Robert Hardgrove. Hardgrove had been a journalist, a politician, a newspaper editor. "He was a beautiful man," Werner told me, "I have an enormous debt to him. An intellectual in a business where there are few intellectuals, Bob Hardgrove, more than anyone else, turned my attention away from motivational work, things like Maltz and Hill, and excited my interest in psychology, encounter, and consciousness. Bob opened my eyes to disciplines that were not *obviously* applicable to business."

Bob Hardgrove was a student of the ideas and techniques of Abraham Maslow and Carl Rogers, the chief theoreticians of the developing "human potential movement."[1] "The things that Bob told me about Maslow and Rogers made sense to me," Werner said. "My orientation now shifted again: from motivation and success, to growth; from personnel development to human development.

"Due to my relationship with Bob, I was in on the beginnings of the human potential movement, before it really 'happened.' I went to Esalen, where I did a workshop with Julian Silverman, and one with Will Schutz. I met Fritz Perls there, although I never did a workshop with him. While Esalen *the place* did not really play an important role in my development, the space created by Esalen was crucial.

"I continued of course to use motivational technology. It had not lost its value. Now, however, I began to integrate it with growth techniques. We did a lot of work in encounter, in sensitivity groups—and in self-revelation sessions. We spent, literally, thousands of hours in individual and group sessions.

"So it was in San Francisco, in late 1962 and early 1963, that my emphasis began to shift from success for its own sake. Business became for me a vehicle for having people to work with. Being successful in business was the dues that I had to pay to do what I really wanted to do. What I wanted to do, and by now was doing, was working with people; I saw what I was doing then as a sort of counseling. For I saw, under the influence of Maslow, Rogers, and others in this field, that people who are healthy and developing as human beings are naturally successful in their jobs. Then *you* don't have to motivate *them;* they motivate themselves.

I ntersection
THREE: MASLOW AND ROGERS:
HUMAN POTENTIAL AND DETERMINISM

Hill and Maltz wrote for ordinary folks. Their message was, "You, too, can be successful, happy, fulfilled." Both were eager to show ordinary normal people that they had immense *potential* beyond normal expectation. Neither thought of his work as therapy: Hill did not talk of therapy at all, and Maltz implied that it was beyond the scope of his book. Both were, in any case, writing for people who had no hope of affording ordinary therapy. Had either Hill or Maltz wanted to start a movement, he could have called it a "human potential movement." But such an idea would hardly have occurred to them. Both saw themselves as reminding their readers of commonsense wisdom about individualism, self-reliance, and imagination; in the case of Maltz, the common sense happened to be bolstered by a popularized version of cybernetic theory.

With Abraham Maslow (1908–1970) and Carl R. Rogers (1902–) we leave the indigenous humanistic and pragmatic tendencies of the American business marketplace and move into the university. Here things become more complicated: one's conclusions must be framed, interpreted, tested, in the context of the intellectual problems, tendencies, and results of European theory over the past several hundred years. The ideas of Maslow and Rogers introduced Werner to this broader, and less distinctively American, context.

Maslow and Rogers were both graduates of the University of Wisconsin, and both were university professors of psychology. Maslow was professor at Brandeis University. Rogers held a succession of distinguished posts at Ohio State, Chicago, and Wisconsin, and finally became director of his own institute in La Jolla, California.

Although they led successful careers, both rebelled against basic ideas of the established psychological and psychiatric professions. In their intellectual lineage, they were far removed from the reigning empiricism of American academic life, as derived from the eighteenth-century British philosophers John Locke and David Hume. Their intellectual roots were, rather, in Germany. Both were influenced strongly by Gestalt psychology, as developed in Würzburg in the early decades of the twentieth century. Gestalt psychology—which was in its turn shaped by the ideas of the great German thinker Immanuel Kant—contains a radical critique of British empiricism.[2]

Here we encounter again the split in American intellectual life between the ideology of the universities and the ideology of the American marketplace. For the ideas of Maslow and Rogers often come quite close to the "commonsense" business philosophy of Hill and Maltz; yet the academic community first regarded what they had to say as more like common ignorance. Thus the rebellion: the human potential movement had to combat the reigning academic notion that "human potential," in the sense given to it by Maslow and Rogers (as well as by Hill and Maltz), was physically and psychologically impossible, and perhaps even a "meaningless notion." The strongest ally of the human potential movement in this struggle has been the American business community. It was the conflict again between the American skyscraper and the colonial mansion—to use Santayana's expressions—between American Will and American Intellect.

Although Maslow and Rogers are often treated together, their ideas and approaches differ in many ways. For example, the concept of self-image plays no formal role in Maslow's work; whereas Rogers, like Maltz, emphasizes something very similar to self-image—what he refers to as "self-concept" and "self-structure." Like Maltz, Rogers treats self-image in a cybernetic way (although he does not invoke cybernetic language), emphasizing its function in ordering, regulating, and controlling behavior. One of the main aims of Rogerian therapy is change in the client's perception of himself. As he puts it: "It is this concept of self which is reorganized during therapy."[3]

What unites Maslow and Rogers is their battle with entrenched psychological and psychiatric viewpoints and attitudes, both theoretical and practical. This battle moves on a number of fronts.

1. Optimism. Maslow and Rogers's work is permeated by an optimism that stands in sharp contrast to conclusions drawn from clinical psychology within the dominant Freudian and behavioristic traditions. It is not a sickly or giddy Pollyanna optimism; Maslow and Rogers do not contest the facts about human behavior that have led other psychologists to more pessimistic reflections: they do not deny or minimize psychosis, brutality, mass murder. Rather, they counsel a certain caution in drawing conclusions about essential human nature from the facts of human aberration. Conclusions about the nature of man, and the possibilities of human society, Maslow and Rogers insist, should take into account not only the abnormal, the deviant, the ill, but also the normal and the *positively* exceptional.

The "pebble or crystal" from which all his later thought stemmed, Rogers explained, was the "gradually formed and tested hypothesis that the individual has within himself vast resources."[4] Maslow's venture into "humanistic psychology" was inspired by his own attempt to account for the exceptional qualities of two of his own teachers: Ruth Benedict and Max Wertheimer. "I could not be content," he wrote, "simply to adore, but sought to understand why these two people were so different from the run-of-the-mill people in the world." Thus Maslow charted as his lifework the study of unusually healthy and creative people.

Two questions inform the investigations of both these men:

What accounts for gifted individuals, people of goodness and genius?

How can these qualities be cultivated and enhanced in society at large?

There is large agreement about the characteristics of individuals who are negatively abnormal: who are, say, psychotic or criminal. But what characterizes the positively abnormal? To answer this question, Maslow investigated the lives and behavior of historical figures and those among his contemporaries who seemed to have realized their potentialities.[5]

He found that such individuals had a more accurate perception of reality; a heightened acceptance of themselves, of others, and of nature; that they were spontaneous, detached, desired privacy; that they were autonomous, resistant to "enculturation," but not rebels against authority; that they were capable of fresh experience and of rich emotional reactions; that they did not need groups and institutions and political parties for personal identification, but tended to identify with the human species as a whole; that their interpersonal relations were of an unusually developed quality; that they tended not to discriminate on the basis of social status, age, sex, race: they were more democratic; they were creative. And they had a high incidence of peak—or "mystical"—experiences in the course of their lives.

An obvious objection to any such inventory of virtues is that it must be culturally biased. Maslow vigorously counters this suggestion. In the course of doing so he developed his theory of the "self-actualizing individual," according to which such *essential* qualities appear *naturally* and *spontaneously* in *all* persons when certain *basic human needs* are fulfilled. Thus, whereas genius, imagination, creativity, mysticism, have often been viewed as abnormal behavior manifesting deep-rooted neurosis or character disorder—as "freakish" in their way as deviant crime—Maslow, by contrast, viewed them as natural and truly normal virtues of the human species at its best.

Basic human needs, Maslow wrote, include food, air, clothing, shelter, social contact, sex, safety, love and belonging, and esteem. Once *all* these needs are satisfied, the individual will naturally turn to his *meta-needs*, having to do with self-actualization, and will develop into the sort of person characterized by healthy qualities. A natural *need* to self-actualize and a natural motivation toward growth come into play when basic needs are met.

"I think of the self-actualizing man," Maslow writes, "not as an ordinary man with something added, but rather as the ordinary man with nothing taken away. The average man is a full human being with dampened and inhibited powers and capabilities."[6] By the same token, neuroses are "deficiency diseases," stemming from the failure to satisfy some basic need.

2. Groups in Which to Grow. Rogers was, as a therapist, not satisfied to tinker with individuals out of context. Rather, he turned to the ecological aspects of therapy and growth, to search after and define "facilitative conditions" that would have to be present in various environments—in one-to-one therapy, in families, or in groups—to further personal growth and self-actualization.[7]

The experience of growth, of learning to be free, best takes place in a situation that approximately satisfies one's basic needs. It must be a "safe space," a "close warm, understanding relationship in which there is freedom *from* such things as threat, and freedom *to* choose and be." Such a safe psychological climate enables the individual to reduce his defensiveness and to express his feelings. After reducing their defensive rigidity, individuals begin to *hear* one another; communication takes place. Change comes to seem possible, even desirable, rather than threatening.

The therapist, for example, must present himself, in his relationship with his client, as a human being without professional front; he must *have*—not affect—a warm, positive, and accepting attitude toward the client; his care must be unconditional, unreserved, unevaluative—no matter how the client is behaving. In the course of creating the conditions under which the client's defensive façade may crumble, he must meanwhile be unconditionally willing for that façade to enter their relationship. The therapy must be *client-directed*, not an attempt to impose a viewpoint or an interpretation on the client. The therapy must, in short, be directed toward satisfying the client's basic needs.

Corollary to this, Rogers points out how many econiches work against such development and growth. A therapist, for instance, might be splendidly trained, to the highest professional standards; and his interpretations might be both brilliant and sound; yet if he fails to respond to the client in a "facilitative" way, if he fails to create the right kind of space around the individual, the individual's growth is hindered rather than fostered. Many families and friendships also provide econiches that hinder personal development. They are mutual protection rackets that work to defend façades rather than to satisfy basic needs.

Rogers became particularly interested in groups—training groups and encounter groups—in which growth would be furthered faster, and more efficiently and cheaply, than in conventional therapy. T-groups, or training groups in "sensitivity," were established after the Second World War, partly under the influence of the Gestalt psychologist Kurt Lewin. These began in Bethel, Maine, in 1947; they developed in the National Training Laboratories (NTL) in Washington, D.C.; and then spread throughout the country. The initial thrust of the NTL groups was to industry, aiming at managerial and executive education. By the mid-sixties, Esalen Institute, in California's Big Sur, became an important center for the development of such approaches, although by now "sensitivity training" tended to be deemphasized in favor of "encounter groups," as pioneered by Rogers in Chicago some years earlier. After the dynamic and charismatic group leader Fritz Perls chose Esalen as the headquarters for the application of his particular brand of "Gestalt therapy," the Esalen style of growth and self-actualization through groups won national attention.

By no means were all these groups conducted on Rogerian lines: those of Perls, for instance, were much more directive and intrusive. But the many different sorts of groups gave Rogers and his associates the opportunity to explore group dynamics intensively, and also to develop practical techniques and methods for encouraging human growth in group situations. As Rogers's assumptions influenced the new discipline of "humanistic psychology," other workers added a battery of complementary techniques—to reduce defensiveness, to enhance communication and openness, to identify and treat neurotic patterns. They found that people became more open and capable, in certain kinds of groups, than they had ever been with their own families; and, moreover, that people hungered for groups wherein they could

express themselves and communicate openly without defending
their façades—where they could relate closely to others and share
deep experiences without threat of being ridiculed or diminished.
Where one approaches a state "where all is known and all
accepted," Rogers writes, "further growth becomes possible."[8]

Although many universities still look upon encounter groups "with
scorn," as Rogers put it in 1970, the main issue between Rogers
and the professional establishment did not concern the use of
groups as such, so much as the question of group leadership.
Whereas the establishment would restrict the practice of therapy to
those certified by the medical professions, Rogers—like William
James before him[9]—battled to open up practice to professional
psychologists and even to laymen. This particular battle has
engaged Rogers for nearly his entire professional career, beginning
in the thirties, when he met his first attack and almost lost his
position in Rochester, New York, because of it.[10] From the thirties
to the middle fifties, Rogers was almost alone in his battle to keep
medicine from gaining a stranglehold on the "helping professions."
As one commentator on his work put it: "Somehow he knew then
what many have come to know now, that no single profession or
discipline has a corner on the market of knowledge about human
affairs. His lonely battles with medicine, psychiatry,
psychoanalysis, and psychoanalytically-dominated professions such
as psychiatric social work are largely forgotten. It is difficult,
sometimes, to remember the days when even highly trained
psychologists could not practice therapy. Armed with impressive
research findings and a bold vision, he forced the door open and
held it open for all who followed."[11]

3. Determinism. The philosophical assumptions distinguishing
Maslow and Rogers's approach from those of the dominant
academic schools cover a broad front. In particular, academic
psychology leans strongly to the sort of behaviorism associated with
the name of B. F. Skinner, of Harvard University.

Without reviewing Maslow and Rogers's critique of behaviorism in
detail, I want to call attention to one issue that has arisen in their
battle with Skinner: the matter of determinism, and its denial of the
reality of free choice. For determinism is an issue that is important
in this story. Werner had ruminated on this issue as a boy: "If God

already knows everything I'm going to do, it doesn't matter; I might as well do anything. But that doesn't seem to work either. Because I could only do what I'm going to do because God already knows I'm going to do it." Werner confronted the issue again in his essay: "All that I do and am to do was written in the books long before I was born, but still you couldn't say the devil with it and do as you really pleased. Well, I guess you couldn't say it because it was written that you wouldn't. Funny, you can do what you want but there is only one thing to do, so you do it."

Funny indeed. The issue of determinism provides a kind of watershed in philosophy. On one side are grouped those accounts that see man as an active, purposive, and free initiator of his own existence; on the other side are those that see him as essentially passive, shaped, molded, controlled—victimized—by God, the environment, socioeconomic circumstances, or some other forces. Those accounts that fall into the second group tend to be deterministic—and to sponsor that Werner calls the "victim's interpretation." The approaches of Hill and Maltz, and of Maslow and Rogers, fall into the first group. They depend on rejecting the victim's position—and determinism. Not that they minimize the extent of causality in human life. Maslow, for example, has written that the neurotic rarely engages in free choices. But both insist that *some* choice does exist, particularly for self-actualizing persons. Werner's own later position differed from all of these. While rejecting the victim's interpretation, he also, paradoxically, *accepted* determinism, and charted a place for choice *within* a determined universe.[12]

The controversy about determinism is an ancient one. It appeared in antiquity, and became an important—if controversial—element of traditional Christianity. Some great Christian theologians, such as Luther and Calvin, were determinists; others, such as St. Augustine, were indeterminists. Christian doctrines about the attributes of God led in both directions. Medieval theologians observed—as Werner did later—that an *omniscient* God, knowing everything, must know the future. And if the future is known to God in advance, then it is fixed, determined, in advance. On the other hand, God is also *omnipotent*, all-powerful, and thus can do anything. Therefore he can change the future, which is thus *not* determined. This "paradox" was not the only difficulty: as Werner also later noticed, it was hard to reconcile the doctrine that one is wholly dependent on God with the doctrine that one is morally responsible for one's actions. If one's behavior is wholly determined, if one could not have done otherwise than one did, how can one be held morally responsible?

The determinist theory held by Skinner and other contemporary psychologists and philosophers has nothing directly to do with Christianity. In its origins in the seventeenth century, determinism was often part of an attempt to *combat* the Christian doctrine that God could miraculously intervene in history. A universe governed by natural law left no room for miracle.

Yet the idea that the universe is governed solely by the laws of nature does not by itself amount to a determinist view: to accept that nothing happens in violation of natural law is not necessarily to accept that the future is implicit in the past, or that the future may be predicted from knowledge of the past.

Thus three separate doctrines can be distinguished:

Causal Governance. This is the idea that nothing happens in violation of natural law; i.e., that everything happens *in accordance with* natural law: there are no miracles. Maslow and Rogers do not dispute this.

Metaphysical Determinism. This is the doctrine that past and future are both fixed in the same sense. The metaphor of a motion picture film has been used here: the stills of the film that have already been run off are the past; the one showing at the moment is the present; the ones remaining to be run off on the reel constitute the future. The part of the reel not yet run off is just as fixed—and in the same way—as that part which has already been run off.[13]

Scientific Determinism. This doctrine adds to Metaphysical Determinism a claim about knowledge. It contends that the future not only is fixed but *may also be foreknown*—without limit—not by relevation or intuition, but by scientific calculation. This view was brought to its strongest formulation by the French physicist Laplace, who imagined a powerful calculator—he described him as a spirit or a demon—who could predict the future course of the

world to any specified degree of precision provided he possessed all
the laws of nature plus a sufficiently precise description of all past
events. "Assume," Laplace wrote, "an intelligence which could
know all the forces by which nature is animated, and the states at
an instant of all the objects that compose it; . . . for [this
intelligence] nothing would be uncertain; and the future, as the
past, would be present to its eyes."[14]

Virtually all arguments for determinism today are arguments on
behalf of Scientific Determinism. Although Metaphysical
Determinism is widely believed, no strong independent argument
has ever been posed on its behalf. If Scientific Determinism is true,
of course, Metaphysical Determinism must also be true, since it
follows logically from it. But what if Scientific Determinism is
false?

How is Scientific Determinism defended?

It is often presented as a criticism of common sense. On a
commonsense view, there are two sorts of things in the universe:
clocks and clouds—clocklike things, and cloudlike things.[15] Clouds
are physical systems that are, like gases, irregular, disorderly,
unpredictable. Clocks, on the other hand, represent systems that
are regular and orderly, and highly predictable in their action. Our
earthly clocks are regulated by astronomical clocks; so perhaps the
best examples of clocks come from astronomy. The phenomena
of ordinary life could thus be ranged between these two extremes.
Animals will, depending on their ages, be closer to the cloud
category. An old dog or cat, grown rigid in its behavior, will
be more clocklike than a young and quite unpredictable puppy or
kitten. And the weather, the very domain of clouds, will be
extremely unpredictable.

The Scientific Determinist opposes the commonsense account. He
says, in effect, that all clouds are *really* clocks, and that common
sense reflects not the real nature of things, but only our ignorance.
If we only *knew more* about clouds, we would, so it is promised, be
able to predict them as we do clocks. Each time science has
successfully extended its reach into some new area, this promise has
been redeemed. The argument for Scientific Determinism thus
relies on the fact of scientific success and on the supposition that

evidence of increasing scientific predictability in *some* areas argues
for the eventual extension of scientific predictability into *all* areas
without limit. It is this promise on which Skinner and other
contemporary determinists are trading.

Few writers on determinism ever notice its nightmarish and
preposterous implications. They fail to notice that if this doctrine,
championed in the name of science, is true, then science itself is an
illusion. It would not just be *some* things that are fixed from all
eternity: *everything* is so fixed, including the results of science: the
results of any particular scientific argument are determined. Even
the result of any argument about determinism is determined: that
one person shall become a determinist is fixed—*without any regard
to the weight of any argument;* and that another shall become an
indeterminist is similarly fixed. Scientific argument thus becomes
illusory. If one's opinions are *fully* determined by natural laws and
initial conditions, then they do not depend on the force of an
argument or on the weighing of evidence. If Scientific Determinism
is true, we may believe or reject it; but we do so not because we
judge the argument in its favor to be sound, but because facts and
laws determine that we shall so believe or fail to believe.

Maslow and Rogers noticed and confronted these implications.
Rogers, in particular, repeatedly challenged Skinner on this point.
On Skinner's view, as Rogers reports in his biographical statement:

> The environment, which is part of a causal sequence, is the sole
> determiner of the individual's behavior, which is thus again an
> unbreakable chain of cause and effect. All the things that I do, or
> that Skinner does, are simply inevitable results of our condition-
> ing. As he has pointed out, man acts as he is forced to act, but as
> if he were not forced. Carried to its logical conclusion, this
> means, as John Calvin concluded earlier, that the universe was
> at some point wound up like a great clock and has been ticking
> off its inexorable way ever since. Thus, what we think are our
> decisions, choices, and values are all illusions. Skinner did not
> write his books because he had chosen to present his views, or to
> point to the kind of society he values, but simply because he was
> conditioned to make certain marks on paper. Amazingly to me,
> he admitted as much in one session in which we both partici-
> pated.[16]

Rogers himself saw things differently. In the course of growth, of self-realization, an individual comes to greater freedom for himself, less compulsion by other persons and circumstances. Rogers wrote:

> In the relationship with an effective therapist . . . the client moves gradually toward a new type of realization, a dawning recognition that in some sense he chooses himself. This is not usually any sudden burst of insight—it is a groping, ambivalent, confused and uncertain movement into a new territory. The client begins to realize, "I am not compelled to be simply the creation of others, molded by their expectancies, shaped by their demands. I am not compelled to be a victim of unknown forces in myself. I am less and less a creature of influences in myself which operate beyond my ken in the realms of the unconscious. I am increasingly the architect of self. I am free to will and choose. I can, through accepting my individuality, my "isness," become more of my uniqueness, more of my potentiality."[17]

That determinism is a nightmare does not mean that it is false. Both Rogers's client and his "effective therapist" might be deluded about the scope of choice in their lives. The weakness in the discussions of Maslow and Rogers is that, although they notice the devastating consequences of the doctrine, and compellingly reject it, they do not argue effectively against it. Fortunately for their position, this sort of Scientific Determinism has during the past forty years been as thoroughly undermined, by both philosophical and scientific results, as one could ever expect any philosophical doctrine to be. Indeed, when examined on the micro level, in their molecular structure, clocks turn out to be clouds! Far from all clouds being clocks, all clocks are clouds: clouds of particles whose positions are neither determinable nor determined.

Further, as the philosopher of science Sir Karl Popper has argued, determinism is not even—as was widely supposed—necessitated by classical Newtonian physics.[18] D. M. MacKay, Popper, and other writers have given additional arguments, both formal and informal, drawn from systems analysis, logic, mathematics, computer theory, and elsewhere, to show that Scientific Determinism is untenable.[19]

Among these arguments, perhaps the most convincing, as well as most easily understandable, is the argument from the unpredictability of the growth of human knowledge. It can be shown logically that there is no way to predict a genuinely new idea or scientific theory. Yet the course of human history and the state of the world are strongly influenced by the growth of human knowledge. This means that we cannot predict the future course of human history and the future states of the world—at least to the extent to which they are influenced by the growth of human knowledge. Our ideas, created out of nothing and made into form, become part of the world and *enter* the causal sway. Thus the world is undetermined, the universe is open, to the extent that we can free ourselves from past pictures, patterns, theories, ideas, and bring into being something new. As Rogers puts it, man is the "architect of himself."[20]

CONVERSION IN BEVERLY HILLS

It was in an Esalen-oriented context, under the guidance of Bob Hard-grove, that Werner encountered Encounter—and the theories of Maslow and Rogers. To support his own intuition and his reading in the popular works of Hill and Maltz, he now had theoretical arguments and some evidence. He became convinced both by their arguments and by his own experience that philosophy and psychology had exciting and urgent practical applications, that ordinary people had within them untapped potential—which, if tapped, could release a nurturing satisfaction beyond their highest hopes.

As this happened, he became alarmed by the amount of pretense that he began to discover in his life. "As a result of the work that I had done in motivation, and later in human potential, the patterned behavior in my own life began to free up," Werner explained to me. "What I mean by 'patterned behavior' is one's habitual way of representing oneself, often thought of as 'just the way I am.' There is, for example, being funny to avoid an issue, or being outgoing to deflect real contact or intimacy, or always having to have a comment, or the inability to be quiet, the compulsion to fill up all the space with talk. There is also being stupid so as not to get the point, and meaningless social interaction, going through the motions.

"To say that I *became* aware of this kind of thing in my own life as patterned behavior is to imply that I hadn't previously been aware of it. That is so. What had seemed earlier to be just the way I was now clearly revealed itself as patterns or mechanisms which I happened to have.

"As you break up these patterns, you begin to get in touch with your natural integrity. And as you get in touch with your natural integrity, you break up the patterns more. Thus a beneficent cycle or spiral begins, a spiral which becomes the deadly enemy of pretense.

"I don't mean that there aren't any problems in your life anymore after you discover your own integrity. There were *plenty* of problems in *my* life—most conspicuously my relationship with my family in Philadelphia. That that was there, still unhandled, was the biggest pretense in my life: I was still living a lie. Yet, instead of having the *appearance* of integrity—pseudo-integrity—plastered over the dishonesty in my life, the real fundamental underlying integrity began to emerge, and to break up the old patterns which permitted the dishonesty.

"My business contributed some of the circumstances under which I began to watch my own pretense and my own patterns in operation. I realized that we were pretending to succeed, whereas in fact we were not. We were getting by—very well—but had no mastery of the situation. We were stringing ourselves and the management along with our good intentions, and our good ideas and plans, but we weren't really executing anything like our potential yet. We weren't creating.

"So I became fascinated by the whole issue. I began to impose on myself—overriding the various techniques and exercises of encounter and of Rogerian and Maltzian psychology—the discipline of telling the truth absolutely. Some time early in 1962 I began to tell the truth unflinchingly. If I said that something would happen, you could bet that it would—you could bet everything you owned. When you start to tell the truth, you begin to look at your offhand remarks, and to examine every single one of them. You begin to notice the lack of fit between the word and the object. You begin to realize that you almost never tell the truth exactly. And you realize that anything less than the truth is a lie: you cannot 'pretty much' tell the truth. To 'pretty much' tell the truth is to lie."

Werner now sees this truth telling as essential preparation for an immensely important experience that he underwent in Beverly Hills in the autumn of 1963. In the spring of that year, he had transferred his base of operations from San Francisco to Los Angeles, locating his office in Beverly Hills. From here he continued to manage the same territory, and flew regularly to San Francisco and the other cities where Parents had offices under his supervision. He and Ellen found an apartment on North Clark Street. Ellen was pregnant, and on August 2, their first daughter, Celeste, was born.

Late one evening in early October, he was sitting alone in his office after the staff had gone home. Looking toward the window, and yet not looking out it, he had a mystical experience—or what he now describes, using Maslow's term, as a "peak experience." It was one of those experiences that Maslow says are common among self-actualizing individuals—of profound concentration and intense feeling, of unity, wonder, acceptance, and comprehension.

One of the few things about which philosophers agree is that a mystical experience is ineffable: beyond language and unable to be described—and that it is intolerable that it should be so.[21] So I wanted to ask Werner to tell me about it, and to explain what is involved in a peak experience.

I found him in his library, on the ground floor of Franklin House. Around the walls, in built-in shelves ranging from floor to ceiling, there was testimony to his interest in the world of literature. Over five thousand books were there, carefully cataloged according to the Dewey decimal system. It is a general library, with entries in all categories, and is particularly strong in philosophy, psychology, consciousness research, religion, biography, and art. The works of Sri Aurobindo, sturdily bound in white, filled one shelf; books on motivation by such writers as Maxwell Maltz, Napoleon Hill, and Dale Carnegie filled another. Several sections were devoted to classics in psychology by Sigmund Freud, C. G. Jung, B. F. Skinner. Oversize books on Chinese and Japanese art filled a corner section.

In the light of the late afternoon sun the shadows of the tall Chinese talking jars, which stand on the floor and on top of the bookshelves, lengthened, playing against the pottery lions at Werner's feet.

Werner had been drinking cappuccino. When I asked him for an account of his peak experience, he put down his cup, and stroked his chin doubtfully.

"That is not so easy," he replied. "There is the experience, and then there is the report or explanation of it. In a sense it is absurd even to try to report or explain a peak experience, since such an experience essentially concerns the limitations of reports and explanations. All I can do is to talk around the subject.

"A peak experience is, first of all, an *experienced* experience. Now I know that phrase sounds funny, but I use it as a kind of shorthand for referring to the fact that most of what we think of as experience in our lives is highly schematic and conceptual, and so rigidly organized that true experience can rarely break through it. That is, most of what we call experience is in fact not experiential. So this was a moment in my life when experience broke through the wall of theory and concept that I kept between myself and true experience.

"You can in this sense have a peak experience of anyone or anything," Werner said. "I could for example have a peak experience of *you*. Ordinarily, my experience of you is filtered through my concepts and memories: I experience you through the concept that you are a professor, that you are such and such in age, that you dress a particular way, and so on. I see you as fitting into *my* life in some particular way. I attach a value or importance to you in terms of myself and my projects.

"In a peak experience, all that drops away. My experience of you is no longer mediated by my own position. Who you really are penetrates through the screen of my own conceptual structures and my hierarchy of values. I experience you as you are. And although I am more detached and more objective, I sense you more intensely.

"The peak experience that I had in 1963 was a peak experience of what I call Self. That is perhaps unusual. People are more apt to have peak experiences which are related to other people, or to their work; or related to nature or to art. Such peak experiences are splendid things that may profoundly affect life. Any peak experience carries you out of your ordinary state: you see in a larger context.

"But the peak experience that I had was not related to a person or to my work, not to the ocean or to the sunset or to art, not to any of that. It was a profound sense of Self. I truly experienced *the* Self—not *my* Self: the word 'my' belongs in the world of *concept* about Self, not *experience* of Self. I was carried out of my ordinary state, not merely to another state, but to the context for all states, the context of all contexts.

"Of course in 1963 I didn't have the means to express the matter in this way. Although I had experienced Self, I didn't yet know how to talk about it. It was only later, as I worked through Zen, and Scientology, and other disciplines, that I began to understand the matter better."

Werner looked away, then looked back at me and grinned. "As I say this," he said, "I distrust these words. It is so easy to misunderstand them. People so often get the impression that there is something anticonceptual and anti-intellectual about this. And that couldn't be further from the truth. A peak experience is not a warm bath of experience where you just feel good. It is not a time when your intellect and your concepts get fuzzy. It is a high noon of the spirit, when all shadows disappear. It is as if you see your concepts stretched to their furthest limits—and worn out. That discipline that I put myself under—of telling the truth unflinchingly—just wore out my concepts.

"So the concepts that you go beyond in a peak experience are concepts that are inadequate and are perceived to be so—not concepts that are so fuzzily perceived that you couldn't begin to say whether they are adequate or not. A peak experience doesn't come in a stupor; it comes in a blaze of clarity."

I asked Werner what were the consequences of this experience.

"Well, that is important," he said. "You know, I had mystical or peak experiences before: for example, just after I graduated from high school, lying on the beach at Atlantic City. But I never did anything with them. They had no real consequences—except perhaps to create within me the space to have a more significant experience of this sort.

"But this new experience had all sorts of effects. It put me in a quite new state of being. For one thing, it made my life magical for a while. My ordinary experience totally altered. It was as if it just never rained where I was. I was in incredible shape personally, and my organization became incredible too. The people who worked with me transcended themselves. Now I had people with whom I could share what was happening with me.

"Quite apart from giving a lyrical, magical cast to my life," Werner continued, "my experience had the effect of reorganizing my values. Until then, I had functioned from the values with which I had grown up, chief amongst which was the idea of success and security, of making it—of getting to the top of the pile of bodies.

"Afterward, I saw the folly of merely making it. I saw the stupidity and hypocrisy of my conventional values. I began to get the kind of skeptical head—skeptical of reality, skeptical of convention—that is attributed to people from the drug scene—to many of whom similar things obviously happened.

"Such a shift in values is also typical of religious conversion," Werner reflected. "It can also happen when people begin to meditate—or find a guru.

"Of course, I had been gradually giving up my old values anyway. My focus had already shifted from success to growth under the influence of Maslow and Rogers. But everything that I had been doing gradually, suddenly culminated in that experience. I was in the success business, and suddenly realized that life is not about success. Life had come to be about fulfillment and satisfaction.

"At the time, the only metaphors I had to explain what had happened to me were psychological, moral, and religious. The experience was truly a conversion experience. The word 'conversion' is often applied narrowly to religious experience—whereas in fact it belongs across the spectrum. Chiefly, it is a death of one's old values, and a re-birth with new values. Those things that previously were important are no longer so. I could still enjoy material things, but they no longer held any meaning for me for their own sakes.

"I made a mistake in interpreting and describing this first peak experience," Werner said. "I supposed that I had got what people refer to when they speak of enlightenment. So I called it enlighten-ment. Years later, I saw that it was not enlightenment; it was conver-sion. Yet this mistake was fortunate in its way. It kindled my interest in those disciplines and practices that cultivate the search for enlight-enment.

I asked Werner what impact all these experiences had on his un-derstanding of Hill and Maltz, and what, in particular, were his dis-agreements with them.

"It is not that I came to disagree with Maltz and Hill," he replied. "But in my encounter with Maslow and Rogers, and in my peak ex-perience, I began to grope my way into a context in which the insights of Maltz and Hill are contained and illuminated, but also transcended.

"Their approach to the individual is mechanistic; it involves tin-kering with the mechanisms and belief systems of the Mind. Yet a mechanism that produces failure and one that produces success pro-duce only different circumstances. Both are still mechanisms, and neither has the capacity to produce satisfaction.

"Satisfaction is intrinsic to the Self, as I was at this time just be-ginning to glimpse. Any mechanisms, such as those employed by Maltz and Hill, that fail to recognize and allow the Self block the ex-perience of satisfaction that is intrinsic to the Self.

"If the tools employed by Maltz and Hill are held in a wider con-text; that is, if they are recontextualized, they become invaluable. When contained in an inadequate context, they are of limited value. Even when they produce success, they can be destructive."

A contradiction, and a kind of mystery, enter the story at this point. Werner had attained a "profound sense of Self" in the course of what Freud calls an "education towards truthfulness in himself." He attained his peak experience as a result of "telling the truth *unflinch-ingly*." And yet . . . he was still living a lie. Everything he said was true, except for some of the most important things that he said about himself—about his name and his past, for instance. The truth-teller was a man who lied about himself. So, fervent and yet insecure in his own truth-telling, he reassumed, in the services of the truth, the righteousness that he had so recently laid down. He now became a crusader for the truth and an enemy of lies.

During his high state, on one of his trips back to the Bay Area, Werner met a young woman who worked with Bob Hardgrove in the San Francisco office. "I met her," he told me, "at that magical time. Everything I touched went right, and my relationship with her happened in a kind of natural high. She was the first woman that I had ever known who had no act going with me. There was no concealed motive in her relationship with me. She wasn't trying to get married; she wasn't trying to make me wrong or establish her supremacy; she wasn't trying to make sure that I didn't dominate her.

"Thus I had an opportunity, in my relationship with her, to experience a woman directly. It was as if I were thirteen years old again. All the worldliness that I had regarding women—having now been married twice, having been with a lot of women—was gone. I now found that I didn't know a thing about them.

"It may seem funny to say this, but a great deal of my ability to create space for my wife, Ellen, came out of my relationship with this woman. A lot of whatever value I have with women in general comes from that relationship. That relationship was hallucinogenic, psychedelic, mind expanding. I really learned to *see* during it. I remember going with her to see the photographic exhibition of Ansel Adams at the DeYoung Museum in November 1963. It was called "The Eloquent Light," or something like that. I could *see* in a totally new way as a result of my experience with her.

"I remember lying on her bed looking out the window through the telephone lines at the branches of the trees right after the visit to the Ansel Adams exhibit. That must be what being stoned is like. I was really stoned.

"She also taught me how to make love. That too was a whole new thing for me. I was like a kid. She taught me by her responsiveness, by her own total involvement. She just totally let go. This was closely related to my peak experience: in effect, I began to make love outside of my concepts about making love.

"She was beautiful too," Werner continued. "She was the kind of woman that people would turn around to look at when you were walking down the street together. She was a kind of horsey woman, that kind of beautiful. She wasn't brassy beautiful. So I had this warm beautiful woman, and an incredible sense of expansion, and a shift in perception—all at once."

Ellen was not to hear from Werner of this affair until several years later. Later she said of this time: "At the end of 1963, I began to be aware of a basic change in Werner. He had been working on himself to develop a quality of being absolutely trustworthy. Out of months of intensive practice he seemed to change dramatically. I saw that he stopped trying so hard, and at the same time, he became more effective. The ability of the people around him also expanded and he seemed to carry with him an all-pervading sense of well-being. For several months there was no stopping him. Although I spent a lot of time making him wrong in those days, I never doubted that he could stop the rain from falling and move mountains."

In January 1964, right in the middle of all this, Parents transferred Werner to the East Coast, to an office in Arlington, Virginia. He was now to be Zone Manager of Parents' Southeast Region.

ENLIGHTENMENT LOST

Werner might have achieved for the first time a profound state of being, the kind of state that is often called enlightenment, yet his relationship with his family remained a quagmire of unfinished business. His new office was in Arlington, Virginia, near Washington, D.C. Philadelphia was part of the zone of which he was now in charge, and he was to visit it many times during the next seven months. He and Ellen talked of contacting their families, and decided against it.

"At this time I began to tease myself with the idea of returning to my family," Werner told me. "Taking a job near Philadelphia was in itself a teasing of myself, and an inching toward an eventual reunion.

"One evening I drove out to Plymouth Meeting, past Joe and Dorothy's house. The lights were on. I drove away. And after a while I came back again—and then drove away again. I was reaching toward them, and then withdrawing. I *knew* I was not going to go in. And yet I went that close. I don't pretend that this was rational.

"I was thinking about *how* to go back, how the hell I would do it. But I wasn't strong enough to reenter that entanglement. I couldn't yet face it.

"There were, of course, things that I could have done. I could, for instance, have sent Pat and the children some money. I could now afford it. But that wasn't the real issue. I knew from my friend John Croft, who had been keeping an eye on the family for me, that they were getting along.

"The real issue still lay within myself. Despite the changes that had been going on within me, I was still untransformed. If I had gone back then, there would no doubt have been a reconciliation. And then it would have been the same entanglement as before.

"At some level within me, I knew this, and had the good sense not to return then. This was one instance in which my 'righteousness' did not interfere with the correct course of action. It would have been conventionally righteous to 'do my duty' and to return. Here is a case in which my integrity was battling with my morality. I could not go back until I had something *real*—not just money or my physical presence, and certainly not righteousness—to contribute to the redemption of that situation."

Werner began to reorganize the East Coast Parents organization along the lines that he had developed on the West Coast. He recruited college-trained women, who had made up the bulk of his staff on the West Coast. "I wanted people who could appreciate the materials they were selling," he told me. Some of the old pros in the office disliked Werner's style, and left the organization. But sales and production went up.

After less than eight months in his new position, a problem came up. "My manager in Philadelphia had rehired a person who had worked for Parents at an earlier time," Werner told me. "After the man had been back about three months, the story surfaced that at that earlier time he had used some funds that he had not earned. I think it was a matter of $500, a so-called 'imprest fund.'

"The president of Parents told the Philadelphia manager that the money would have to be recovered by deductions from the man's paycheck. The Philadephia manager protested, and I assured him that as long as I was Zone Manager, the man would not have to repay the money.

"My position was that we had already hired the man. It was too late *now* to tell him that we were going to recover the money from his earnings. Had we made that a condition of rehiring him, it would have been different. But we hadn't. I saw it as a question of integrity.

"The president of Parents didn't agree. He told me that he had to take back the money—and that was it. Now it became a question of who was going to be right. I declared that I would resign if they took back the money. And on my next visit to Philadelphia I assured the man there, again, that the money would not be taken back as long as I was Zone Manager.

"Sure enough, several weeks later they did deduct the money

from his pay. I was in Atlanta when it happened, and heard about it over the phone. I got on a plane immediately, flew to New York, walked into Parents' headquarters, and resigned. It was all very dramatic, very heavy."

Werner leaned back in the chair where he was sitting and laughed at the memory. "You need to remember," he continued, "that I thought I had arrived from California in an enlightened state. One hallmark of the enlightened state is that you *lighten* up. And here I was being heavy. During those months on the East Coast I lost my high state, my peak experience. All that was left was my concept of it.

"I resigned my job out of righteousness: a false concept of honor and truthfulness. I was being what I now call a 'dead hero.' I got to my high experience by telling the truth and delivering on what I said. But my interpretation of what I was doing was faulty. I turned my *experience* of honesty into a *concept*. I was telling the truth *in order to be right*. But you don't tell the truth in order to be right. You tell the truth in order to tell the truth. I hadn't yet got that.

"I destroyed my own high state by *believing* in it. I became a crusader for the truth. I thought truth telling had something to do with me—or with who I thought I was: the 'persona' Werner Erhard —of all things! Being a 'truth-teller' became part of my persona.

"Thus I lost what I thought was enlightenment because I didn't have the context in which to hold it. I was naïve—almost pedestrian—in the way I conceptualized peak experiences and enlightenment."

When Ron Baldwin heard of Werner's resignation, he telephoned to offer him back his old job on the West Coast. In late August, Werner and Ellen packed their bags, left their apartment in Arlington, and turned their backs on the steaming heat of the Eastern summer to return to the perpetual spring and autumn time of San Francisco.

SEVEN Quest

Since everything in life is but an experience perfect in being what it is; having nothing to do with good or bad, acceptance or rejection, one may well burst out in laughter.
—Long Chen Pa

TWICE BORN

In his great work, *The Varieties of Religious Experience*, the American philosopher and psychologist William James identified two very different kinds of person: the "once-born" and the "twice-born" man.[1]

The once-born man appears to fit effortlessly into a "rectilinear or one-storied" conception of the universe of our experience. For him everything is as it seems, and the values of this life are calculated in pluses and minuses. Happiness and satisfaction consist in living on the "plus side" of the account, rather than on the minus, or debit, side. Such a man will, in the course of growing up, experiment with, dabble at, religions and disciplines; he will decorate his life with them; but he will not become absorbed by them. Such things will not be central to him.

The twice-born man, the "homo religiosus" or "homo philosophicus," experiences reality differently. For him, as James writes, "the world is a double-storied mystery. Peace cannot be reached by the simple addition of pluses and elimination of minuses from life. Natural good is not simply insufficient in amount and transient, there lurks a falsity in its very being. . . . It gives no final balance, and can never be the thing intended for our lasting worship. It keeps us from our real good . . . and renunciation and despair of it are our first step in the direction of the truth." To achieve satisfaction and happiness, one must see the falsity of the one-storied world—one must "die to it"— and be born again with new values that transcend those of the first world.

The Werner Erhard who is known today is obviously a twice-born—or perhaps even a "thrice-born" man.

The identity Werner Erhard had been born in 1960, on his departure from home and family, when Jack Rosenberg and all that was associated with him became expendable. But Jack Rosenberg had not died at that time. Werner Erhard had Jack Rosenberg's values, and his unconscious patterns. Carried forward into the new identity were the values of the old.

His peak experience of 1963 was, as Werner himself now states, a classic conversion experience: a change of values. He was born again. Werner Erhard was finally more than a name. The values of Jack Rosenberg—particularly those connected with success—died, at least for a moment; and there was a glimpse of new value and of a new way of living, in which satisfaction—a state of being whole and complete—was more important than success. Now at last Werner Erhard had created some values of his own.

Then he slipped back into the old mode. But he became a backslider with a difference. The endarkenment in which he now found himself differed markedly from the endarkenment in which he had previously lived. He now had a "sense of sin," as it were—a keener sense of what he was missing, a sense of being less than one might be.

From this moment he seems not only hard-driving but also hard-driven: driven by the dialectic, the tension, the interface, among three identities: the identity with which he had begun: Jack Rosenberg—itself a composite of parental identifications; the identity which he had created for himself: Werner Erhard; and the new self—he later called it *the* Self—which he had glimpsed, and which was both his true self, his true identity, and something quite beyond all identification. For the next seven years he would move within the tension created by these three ways of being, by these double or treble identities at cross-purposes.

He drove himself and his associates into deeper and deeper inves-

tigations of why people and things are the way they are. Enlightenment was not a passing experience: it was the truth about himself,
about all men, and about the world. The search for enlightenment,
the search for identity, the search for truth: these were for him all the
same.

IN SEARCH OF ENLIGHTENMENT
Although neither Werner nor Ellen knew it then, in returning to
the Bay Area in August 1964, they had returned to what was to become their permanent home. They stayed with Ron and Shirley
Baldwin for two months, and then moved into an apartment canti-
levered out over the water in Sausalito. The village of Sausalito nestles
at the southeastern tip of the Marin County peninsula, which stretches down from the vineyards of Napa to the Golden Gate. Facing onto
Richardson Bay, and sheltered from the larger bay by Tiburon,
Belvedere, and Angel Island, it is a magical place, perhaps the only
village in America where one may walk down the main street and
think one is in a European—a Swiss—lakeside village. Until one
looks up to see, just four miles across the bay, glittering and beckon-
ing, the San Francisco skyline rising majestically and abruptly from
the water. Only on weekends is the traffic on the main street, Bridge-
way, heavy. The freeway traffic can be neither seen nor heard: skirt-
ing the town, it runs high in the hills above and behind Sausalito.
The traffic, rather, is in the water. Ferries churn back and forth across
the Golden Gate, from Sausalito and Tiburon to the city. Sailboats
and fishing boats dock at the Sausalito harbor. A colony of houseboats
line the north shore.

When Werner and Ellen moved into their new apartment, Ellen
was pregnant. On December 27, their second daughter, Adair, was
born.

Though Werner's attention was again focused across the harbor,
in the Parents office on Sutter Street, in downtown San Francisco, his
real concern after his return was his state of "endarkenment." The
central concern in his life became his quest to regain enlightenment.
He was absorbed in this quest, driven by it.

"Having lived in this new way," he told me, "it seemed pointless
to live in the old way. As I reflected on what had happened to me, I
realized that my peak experience had little to do with my studies in
motivation, and couldn't be explained by what I was learning in
humanistic psychology and the human potential movement either.
And even if they could explain it, such explanations produced no mas-

tery of the phenomena, no ability to cause it. I was casting about for a way not only to understand it but to re-create it. It was Alan Watts who first gave me a clue as to where I had been and where I was going."

Alan Watts (1915– 1973) was an English philosopher who, after a distinguished career in America as an Episcopal clergyman, renounced the priesthood and became known as a brilliant expositor and advocate of Oriental religions, of Zen in particular.[2]

"Watts did two main things for me," Werner said. "He opened up the connections between what I was doing and the traditional Oriental philosophies. And he pointed me toward the distinction between Self and Mind.

"When I studied yoga as a boy I didn't realize its spiritual import. Other Oriental disciplines that I studied I saw at first only as techniques. Alan Watts opened me to a wider sense of all these things, and particularly of Zen.

"Until my return to California, I knew him only from his books, a few of which I had read just before going back to the East Coast. After I got back to California, I got in touch with him personally. I remember sitting in my office, telling the secretary to find out where he was. It turned out that he lived in Sausalito. He was a neighbor!

"I started to go to the seminars that he held on his houseboat. I also listened to his tapes over the radio and vividly recall listening to one of them while driving home one night. It was extraordinary, and moved me deeply.

"I was at his houseboat once at a discussion of the Buddhist principle of nonaction. I had begun to grasp some of the fundamental precepts of Buddhism, yet I couldn't get them by myself alone. I remember asking Alan why he was teaching.

"He just smiled at me, and pointed out the window, to a bird flying. There was no reason why he was teaching, he replied. He taught, he said, just as the bird flies.

"I struggled with that. I had really been asking him about myself, not about himself. I remember initially being put off by what he said, as if he hadn't answered me—just as people are put off today when I don't 'answer' them. I wasn't yet ready for a Zen answer.

"Another time, Alan was giving a seminar with Charlotte Selver and Charles Brooks. Charles was talking about spontaneous movement, and called for a volunteer to help illustrate. Alan just got up and danced across the room with absolutely no reservations. It was an extraordinary performance from this powerfully intellectual guy. His intellect was overlaid by a quiet asceticism. Yet he could wholly let go, and dance at will. He didn't just talk about such things; he could do them. He practiced what he preached. His performance allowed me to get in touch with the capacity for living in that way. I had an enormous respect and admiration for him." Werner smiled. "I really loved him.

"He also had a Zen-like capacity for irreverence. I remember another meeting with him years later, after I started *est*. It was a meeting in San Francisco, called 'The Changing Way,' or something like that. I had been invited to talk. After my talk I was invited to dinner, and went into the dining room. It was full of yoga masters. Practically everybody was dressed in saffron robes. Just then Alan swept into the room. He was going to have to miss dinner in order to give his own talk, so he came in to say hello first. He knew everybody in the room, and was open and warm with them—but in a reverent and correct Buddhist way. He went around and greeted each of them formally. I was the last person at the table, and he hadn't yet noticed me. When he got to me the cloak of reverence fell away. He threw up his arms and cried 'You rogue, you,' and embraced me.

"I enjoy reminiscing about him so much I almost forgot the thing for which I am most indebted to him. He pointed me toward what I now call the distinction between Self and Mind.

"This evolved gradually for me," he said. "It went through a conceptual level before I got to experience it. I was able to understand the concept of the Self through the sense of frustration I had with motivational psychologies. Hill and Maltz, for instance, directed themselves to the Mind: to personality, position, life story.

"Although reprogramming the Mind, when accurately applied, does produce *success*, it is not a source of *satisfaction*—of being whole and complete, fulfilled. Of course, many who use these programs *do* experience fulfillment in their lives. But their fulfillment comes out of who they *are*, not out of those programs. Unfortunately, people sometimes attribute their own wholeness to these programs. Serious misunderstandings stem from that.

"In refining my understanding of the difference between success and satisfaction, and pondering the relationship between the two, it became clearer that Self—which is nonpersonal, nonpositional, nonnarrative—is the source of satisfaction.

"Reprogramming the Mind can of course produce something *called* satisfaction. A satisfaction that comes from succeeding through motivation or self-image can more accurately be called gratification. It may involve a sense of having gotten it, an approval of what you are doing. This can produce a temporary high. But one falls back from such a high. Worse, one may retain the belief that one now has it.

"From my first contact with Alan," Werner said, "every discipline I touched taught me more about the Self—though this is not always what it was called. Sometimes it was called Being, or Essence, or Buddha nature, or Ground of Being. Although this is what was happening with me, I was sleepwalking. In the labryrinth of my mind, the Self—the state beyond positions, beyond identifications—was the thread of Ariadne that kept me steering toward my final destination. I didn't grasp the full implications of the distinction between Self and Mind until I encountered Scientology. But after my encounter with Alan, the context in which I was working shifted."

The Zen that Werner assimilated he began to apply not only to his personal development but also to his sales force. He began to describe his office as a "laboratory" or "research machine." In it, he tried out, with his organization, one discipline after another. He tells the story that when he asked the Parents home office whether there was any objection to his using Zen, he was told that there was none—as long as he didn't get any on the walls.

Intersection
FOUR: ZEN

With this rebirth of consciousness everything becomes new, beautiful and true. This lively and fresh consciousness is the creator of a world called zen.
—Yamada Mumon Roshi

I was sitting with Werner and the *est* trainers and trainer candidates in the meeting room on the fifth floor of *est*'s central headquarters on California Street in San Francisco. The previous week a Zen monk had visited the trainers for "Trainers' Day." Now Werner was talking about Zen.

"Of all the disciplines that I studied, practiced, learned, Zen was the *essential* one. It was not so much an influence on me; rather, it created space. It allowed those things that were there to be there. It gave some form to my experience. And it built up in me the critical mass from which was kindled the experience that produced *est*. Although the *est* training is not Zen, nor even anything like it, some features of *est* resonate with Zen teaching and practice. It is entirely appropriate for persons interested in *est* to be interested also in Zen. While the *form* of Zen training is different from the form of the *est* training, we come from similar abstractions."

Werner began to speak of the historical origins of Zen. The name "Zen," he explained, is a Japanese rendering of the Chinese *ch'an*, which in turn comes from the original *dhyāna*, meaning meditation. Zen emerged in India within the framework of Buddhism, and was brought from India to China by Bodhidharma around A.D. 520. Bodhidharma is a figure of legend, which meant, as Werner put it, that "either he existed or he didn't." Historical points are not all that important in Zen. In any case, Zen developed in China during the seventh to the ninth centuries, assimilating elements of Taoism and an earthy and practical Chinese sensibility. Zen has been practiced continuously in China since this time, and some of the greatest Zen masters have been Chinese. In the West, Japanese forms of Zen are more familiar. Zen was imported from China into Japan in the twelfth and thirteenth centuries, and importantly influenced Japanese culture, affecting—literally— almost every aspect of life.

"You have heard," Werner elaborated, "of the importance of Zen in the fine arts, in Zen painting, in sumi, in rock gardening, in flower arrangement, in the tea ceremony. Zen also contributed, through the samurai movement, to chivalry, archery, swordsmanship. Zen transforms life.

"Zen was not built by clever men," Werner went on. "The men who built Zen were inspired. What I mean is this: some Buddhist philosophies are as reasonable, as palatable, as the rest of religion. Often the reasonableness and palatableness look like they were put there to make the product salable. In Zen, that has been transcended. Zen does not appeal to mere rationality or comfort or sense. It is highly intrusive, far more intrusive than Buddhism as a whole—just as *est* is more intrusive than, say, much of the human potential movement or Rogerian therapy.

"Zen is a particular approach in a broader Buddhist discipline that has enlightenment as its purpose. The distinctive element in Zen is instantaneousness leading to transformation, rather than process leading to change. The great teachings of the Buddha sometimes led to the search for a gradual change of state. There is nothing gradual about Zen. Although even this is not quite accurate. As Zen masters often say about enlightenment: 'Not gradual, not sudden.'"

Werner smiled. "It is of course absurd to try to 'sum up' Zen in a list of concepts and practices. Zen transcends conceptualizing. It even avoids words that people can turn easily into conceptual systems. All I would like to do is to mention some important aspects of Zen that convey something of its flavor. These aspects are only bricks; and it would be very un-Zen for a pile of bricks to make a wall: Zen is not systematic.

"First, Zen aims to harmonize body and mind with true nature. Along the way, however, it may blow the mind. There is a typical Zen story about Nan-in, a Japanese Zen master of the last century, which illustrates this. Nan-in one day received a university professor who came to inquire about Zen. After a while he served tea.[3]

"Nan-in poured his visitor's cup full, and kept on pouring and pouring.

"It is not polite in Japan to notice such things, but eventually the professor could not restrain himself any longer. 'It is overfull,' he said. 'No more will go in!'

" 'Like this cup,' Nan-in observed, 'you are full of your own opinions and speculations. How can I show you Zen unless you first empty your cup?'

"Another point of emptying your Mind is to realize your own perfection," Werner continued. "This was the Buddha's own realization on attaining enlightenment. As Yasutani-roshi, the Zen master, explains, all human beings, whether clever or stupid, male or female, ugly or beautiful, are whole and complete just as they are. When we work through the churning images of our minds back to our original perfection, we see that every being is intrinsically without flaw. That is, one is as one is.

"Third, there is the nonjudgmental, nonevaluative acceptance in Zen of everything that is, as it is. I call this love, and in the Orient it is sometimes called compassion. The Zen adept does not behave evaluatively toward persons or objects. In fact, he doesn't behave at all. It is as if the things he were perceiving were perceiving themselves and making use of his senses. He is able to take the viewpoint of the person or thing with whom he is in contact and to grant it beingness. He does not impose his own will on the other, and he also does not permit himself to be influenced by the will of the other. He lets be what is.

"Fourth, there is the emphasis in Zen on the here and the now. There is a wonderful Zen story about this that I cannot resist telling you.

"Two monks named Tanzan and Ekido," Werner began, "were once traveling together down a muddy road. A heavy rain was falling. As they came round a bend, they met a lovely girl in a silk kimono and sash, unable to cross the intersection because of the mud.

" 'Come on, girl,' said Tanzan at once. Lifting her in his arms, he carried her over the mud.

"Ekido did not speak again until late that night when they reached a lodging temple. Then he could no longer restrain himself. 'We monks,' he said, 'don't go near females, especially not young and lovely ones. It is dangerous. Why did you do that?'

" 'I left the girl there,' Tanzan replied. 'Are you still carrying her?'

"For the Zen adept it is all important not to go through life carrying around yesterday or tomorrow on one's back. When he is hungry, he eats; when he is tired, he sleeps. This seems so simple. Yet how many people do this? Most people when they are eating have no idea what they are doing. Their minds are far away—engaging in plans, memories, fantasies.

"As you can see from these stories and anecdotes," Werner went on, "Zen drops some of the righteousness of other approaches to Buddhist values and brings in irony and wit—and earthiness.

"Zen is known not only for these ideas and attitudes—which of course cannot adequately be described and must be experienced—but also for a number of practices that enable one to live without Mind, in realization of one's own perfection, nonjudgmentally in the here and now. The essential practices in Zen are Zazen, or sitting meditation, and the koan.

"Zazen is a practice that enables the practitioner to experience him or herself as what is—as Self, as the context for existence rather than something which exists. Many people erroneously think that Zen is somehow about doing meditation in order to attain some special experience. Of course it is not. Zen is about the suchness of sitting, not the technique of sitting in order to gain something, although novices might at first be taught merely the technique of sitting.

"Another important part of Zen is the koan. Koans are mind-breaking riddles or paradoxes. Some famous ones are: 'What is the sound of one hand clapping?' and 'What was my face before my parents were born?' The koan is intended to break down ordinary rationality—whose power lies in mere explanation, and which is therefore a defense against the truth. The koan is intended to boggle one's mind so that there is a shift in being from that state where one can explain and justify to that state wherein one can align and relate. The koan is also used as a testing device that allows the Zen master to tell where the disciple is in his or her progress toward the desired state.

"An important aim of these exercises is a kind of concentration or Mind control, which is known as *joriki* and which promotes experiential knowing. This is not ordinary 'concentration.' Stemming out of a practiced being-here-nowness and control over the checkerboard of our thoughts, it is a dynamic power. Once mobilized, it permits us to act instantly yet entirely appropriately even in the most abrupt and unexpected situations. One who has developed *joriki* is no longer a slave of his random and uncontrolled thoughts, his passions or his environment.

"Thus, the goal of Zen does not lie somewhere in time. It is neither in the future nor *not* in the future. In Zen, one is working toward enlightenment from and in a context of already being enlightened.

"This brings up the question whether one needs to or ought to practice all the Buddhist rituals in order to know Zen," Werner said. "I don't see that many of the rituals and the spirit of Zen are inextricably connected—except historically. It is interesting that some contemporary Zen scholars and masters see matters similarly." Werner called our attention to Koji Sato, one of the most influential contemporary interpreters of Zen.[4] In one of his essays, Sato introduced Zen as "one of the highest ways of personality training and adjustment that may be used by any person without regard to his religious beliefs or political ideologies."

"The kind of Zen that Sato was talking about," Werner explained, "has the name 'bompu Zen' in Japan today. There is a good account of this in the lectures of the Zen master Yasutani-roshi, who says that this kind of Zen is for everybody and anybody. It is a Zen practiced to attain physical and mental health."

Werner reached for another book, Philip Kapleau's *Three Pillars of Zen*, containing Yasutani-roshi's introductory lectures.[5] He began to read aloud. "Through the practice of bompu Zen," Yasutani had said, "you learn to concentrate and control your mind. It never occurs to most people to try to control their minds, and unfortunately this basic training is left out of contemporary education, not being part of what is called the acquisition of knowledge. Yet without it what we learn is difficult to retain because we learn it improperly, wasting much energy in the process. Indeed, we are virtually crippled unless we know how to restrain our thoughts and concentrate our minds. Furthermore, by practicing this very excellent mode of mind training you will find yourself increasingly able to resist temptations to which you had previously succumbed, and to sever attachments which had long held you in bondage."

Werner looked up and said: "There is another thing about this kind of Zen that I would like to share with you. That is its attitude to science. Everybody knows that Zen is thoroughly unreasonable. Of course it is: it takes an unreasonable approach to the chattering of the human Mind, and aims to transcend it. But Zen is also compatible with Western science. Of course, Western science is also often unreasonable."

Werner reminded us that Koji Sato had stressed Zen's applicability to physical and mental health, and also its compatibility with science. Erich Fromm, Werner said, had also written of Zen in this vein, saying that just as the Orient must go to the West for natural science, so must the West go to the Orient for a scientific religion: Zen. Fromm wrote: "Paradoxically, Eastern religious thought turns out to be more congenial to Western thought than does Western religious thought itself."

Werner paused. "But people won't understand this. They won't get it. It needs to be seen that Zen is not a religion in the Western sense. Neither for the most part is Buddhism. A Zen person practicing any religion would practice it with a Zen quality. So there are undoubtedly Zen Christians and Zen Jews and Zen Muhammadans as well as Zen Buddhists.

"I learned this some years ago, when I began to apply Zen to business. In business I had to meet a criterion: anything I used had to produce results. This forced me to separate out those things that were effective from those that were not—which were perhaps simply traditional or had gotten attached to the discipline in the course of history. There is a lot of that in almost any discipline. Within the discipline it may well be charming. I loved the things that I saw in Japan in the Buddhist temples. I was moved and charmed by them. They were totally appropriate there. But many are not essential when what you are looking for is effectiveness rather than to become a devotee. You can let Zen permeate your life without being a member of a particular religion."

What Werner had said about the late Koji Sato interested me. I had heard of him before, and decided to look up a journal that he had founded, and that I had never seen. A few days later I drove down the peninsula to Stanford University, went into the stacks of the library, and hauled down from the shelves the worn volumes of *Psychologia*, the journal that Sato had founded when a professor at the University of Kyoto. It is a curious journal, written chiefly in English; occasionally there are articles in German and French as well. The range of the contributors is striking. Sato's aim had been to build a bridge of communication between Zen practitioners in Japan and Western psychological thinking. Thus there appear in its pages articles not only by Japanese philosophical and psychological writers, but also by some great Western psychologists, including C. G. Jung, Erich Fromm, Karen Horney, Karl Jaspers, Aldous Huxley, and others.

It was fascinating to read in *Psychologia* that the Japanese began to investigate the physiological and scientific aspects of Zen long before many people in the West became interested in altered states of consciousness and consciousness expansion. Zen appeared in Europe in a specifically psychological context as early as 1905, when a professor of psychology at Tokyo Imperial University attended the Fifth International Congress of Psychology in Rome, and read there a paper on the "Idea of Ego in Eastern Philosophy," in which he reported on states of mind developed in Zen practice at Engakuji Zen monastery. His ideas were immediately compared with the new ideas in Gestalt psychology that were being developed at that time in Germany.

In the years that followed, Japanese scholars began to take interest in such questions. By 1920, a survey had been made of the experience and effects of what is now called *Zen training*. By the 1930s, experimental research on Zen training was being attempted; and it was proposed that electroencephalographic studies of the effects of Zen training be made. This was finally carried out some years later. By the late thirties, D. T. Suzuki, well known in the West as an interpreter of Zen, published a book on its psychological basis, and a professor of chemistry at Kyoto University gave a physiological explanation of Zen training's effects.

By the late forties and early fifties, this approach to Zen had become widely known. Koji Sato began to publish a series of works on Zen, psychology, and physiology; and in 1956, he founded *Psychologia*. Sato was particularly fascinated by the possibilities of *short courses in satori*. Commenting on the long periods of time involved in traditional Zen training, Sato remarks, "Generally speaking, Western people cannot have such a time-consuming training. Therefore, it is quite natural for Westerners to wonder if there could be found any way to attain Zen enlightenment [*Kensho* or *satori*] if possible in a shorter period of time than they are often told is necessary."

Precedent is important in religion; and fortunately there is Buddhist precedent for a crash course. In one of the most important sutras of the Pure Land sect of Buddhism, "Kon-muryoju-kyo," it is written that "one can realize Buddha in one to seven days' practice." A discipline of the famous Zen master Hakuin (1685–1768) attained a Zen enlightenment experience in two days and two nights of intensive practice. Hakuin himself, in his book *Orategama*, advises that one may be able to "solve the great matter of rebirth in the Pure Land" (which is seeing into one's own nature) within three to five days.

Building on such precedents, a number of such "crash courses in satori" were developed in Japan, and Sato wrote extensively about their results. Two things that he said struck me. One was the unqualified and enthusiastic way in which he reports the medical benefits of the Zen trainings. Among the ailments said to be cured or radically alleviated by Zen practice are the following: neurasthenia, gynecological diseases, consumption, asthma, uterine myoma, hysteria, obsessive neuroses, emphysema, gastric and duodenal ulcer, insomnia, indigestion, high blood pressure.[6]

I was also struck by the rapturous way in which Sato speaks of the experience of satori itself. Sato himself prefers to speak in the words of Master Hakuin, and I shall close this Intersection on Zen by quoting Hakuin's own words on the moment of enlightenment:

> Those who wish to witness the Profundity, one hundred out of one hundred, one thousand out of one thousand, can have their eyes opened if the Great Doubt can present itself. When the Great Doubt presents itself, it is empty and boundless on all sides, it is beyond life and death, it is like lying in thousands of layers of ice, sitting in a crystal vase, it is to feel extremely clear and cool, extremely neat and clean. All is forgotten: when sitting, standing is forgotten; when standing, sitting is forgotten.
>
> . . . It is as if standing in the boundless heaven. In such a situation, if one rushes forth at a stretch, without fear or reflection, one will suddenly feel the crushing of the wall of ice, the breaking down of the palace of crystal, and will have the greatest joy which has never before been experienced in his forty years, nor even been heard of. At this time one realizes that life and death or nirvana are all like a dream of the previous night, even the immense number of the worlds are like foam in the ocean, all the sages and saints seem nothing but flashes of lightning. This is called the period of "reaching the bottom of ourselves, attaining the glorious enlightenment, throwing off all encumbrances of the ego." One cannot tell it to others, nor explain it to others. One can only grasp it by experiencing, as one feels for oneself cold and hot by drinking water. It is to melt all space in a wink and to look through all time, from past to future, in one thought. Is there any joy comparable to this in the worlds of human and heavenly beings?

THE ZEN ART OF BOOKSELLING

Although Werner still saw himself as an endarkened being, those in his "laboratory" began to perceive him otherwise. He taught them, through what they came to call the "Zen art of bookselling," that they must attain *satisfaction* from selling books. That was the least of it. He began to say things that seemed quite odd: that he aimed to do no less than to transform merchandising, and thereby to transform business civilization itself. What they were doing together, he said, was not really selling. That was only the *form* of what they were doing. What they were really doing was *communicating*.

Elaine Cronin, a native of Boston and a graduate of Georgetown University, began to work at the Parents' office in San Francisco in late 1964. She would later work closely with Werner in founding *est*, and she would manage the Chicago, Seattle, and Hawaii centers of *est*.

She described to me their first meeting. "The first week I worked for Parents, he came in to speak at a morning meeting. To attend that was like nothing I had known before. He told us that people were really great, that most of us are asleep or half-awake, that we had immense potential, that people really did want to be alive. I wanted to be part of that right away.

"He was going over to Sausalito to see Alan Watts at this time," Elaine said. "He would tell us about Zen, and would throw into the morning meetings things that Watts said, or quote what Erich Fromm had said, or anything else that he was reading or experiencing. Eric Berne's *Games People Play* had just been published and Werner and Bob Hardgrove used that with us too.

"Werner read all the time," Elaine said to me. "We could be driving down a street, and he would say, 'Stop the car,' and we would get out and walk for blocks looking in store windows. Just because it was fascinating and interesting to him. It was the same with books: he would pore over them and get all sorts of things out of them."

I asked Elaine to tell me about selling books: in particular, whether the things that Werner taught the salespeople in their morning meetings were only intended to increase their personal potential, or whether they were also to be applied in sales.

"You're missing the whole point!" Elaine replied. "I saw working for him as a way to have the things that he was talking about come out of me—*and* out of the people with whom I worked and had relationships. It was as if these potentialities were in me, and only rarely emerged. About forty of us worked out of the San Francisco office. In our selling we worked with mothers on an individual basis, counseling

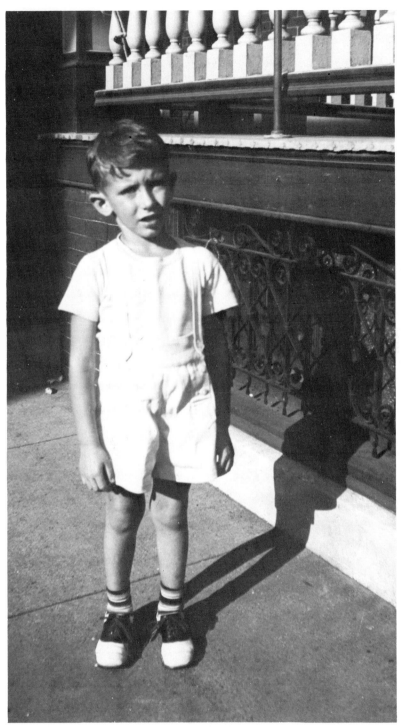

Werner in Philadelphia, 1939.

opposite:

With his parents, 1942.

With his parents, Joan, and baby Harry, 1951.

Werner and his bride Pat
on their honeymoon in 1953.

opposite:
Werner at A Be-in, San Francisco, 1974.

With Swami Muktananda.

With Ellen, 1974.

With his children.

© Michael Dobo

(Foreground:) Erhards: Adair, Celeste, Lynn, Debbie, Werner, Clare, St. John. (Standing:) Jack Erhard, Pat Campbell, Andrea Kleibisch, Nathan Rosenberg, Joan Rosenberg, Gail Rosenberger, Harry Rosenberg, Ellen Erhard, (Seated at right:) Dorothy Rosenberg, Joe Rosenberg.

Hunger project,
New York.

Transformation event,
Boston

Masonic Auditorium,
San Francisco.

about preschool children. Our relationships with them were definitely altered by our experience with Werner.

"Let me give you an example," Elaine offered. "The Parents mothers' program was directed to the potential that could be developed in preschool children. Mothers didn't always realize that their children's education could begin at an early age. A lot of them thought that education only happened in school, and that the role of the home was incidental. We told them about the initiative they could take in working with their children before they got to school. Werner was always interested in moving people in the direction of developing their potential. This was putting them at what Werner later called 'cause.'

"People came in from all over the country to attend those morning meetings," Elaine went on. "Word got around about how valuable they were. Once in a while someone would ask whether he had ever thought about being a teacher. He would say, 'Not really. It might be fun.' Werner is a very moment-to-moment person, and never thought about it. He didn't say that he would do such and such a discipline for a specified length of time. Things just opened up, and he came into contact with more and more people and learned more and more approaches. At this early time he was really far out, but he hadn't yet assumed responsibility for being far out. That came later."

Elaine's account was amplified for me by another woman who joined Werner's staff during this period. Gonneke Spits joined the Parents office in San Francisco over a year after Elaine did, in early 1966, and has worked constantly with him ever since. She sold books for both Parents and Grolier. (She would later help to start *est* and manage both the Los Angeles and Hawaii centers of *est*, and finally become the manager of Werner's own office.) Gonneke is a beautiful, well-educated, and well-connected Dutch woman. She is blonde, and resembles Jane Fonda. She comes from a prominent Amsterdam family and is a graduate of the University of Amsterdam. Her English is flawless.

In early 1966 Gonneke had reached San Francisco in the middle of a round-the-world odyssey that had already lasted two years. Her cash reserves were running low, and she decided to take a job for a few months before going on to the Orient, and then back to Europe. She answered a Parents ad in the *San Francisco Chronicle*, and then came to work.

After working for Parents for about a week, she went, with the rest of the staff, on a camping weekend at the Russian River, north of San Francisco.

"I felt like an outsider at first," she told me. "I thought that these people were weird. I sat there talking with an English girl, with whom I thought I had something in common. Later I walked over to the Russian River. It was there that I saw Werner for the first time. He was standing up to his knees in water. I wondered what he was doing. I couldn't figure it out. He was just looking into the water, and just standing there watching the water go. Here was this man serenely standing up to his knees in the Russian River watching the water. I thought he was ridiculous, and yet I also had a strange feeling of wonder."

Gonneke was successful in working for Parents, and soon became a manager in the San Francisco office. I asked her to tell me about the staff meetings and the "laboratory sessions" with Werner. "Every Sunday afternoon Werner would come up with something new to do in the managers' meeting," she said. We would listen to tapes and read books. Frequently he would just take a subject—like 'commitment' for example—and work on it with us.

"He would explain how mothers have a commitment to their children—whether they are succeeding with them or not. So when we encountered the mothers in the field we had to recognize their commitment.

Then we could talk about their children's education in a way that made sense to them. Werner pointed out how we too were committed to producing results in life.

"That is only one example," Gonneke said. "He was always working on some idea, and would pass on to us what he was thinking. We were a laboratory in which he was doing his research. The field was our test ground.

"That is why I stayed with him despite the opposition of my parents," Gonneke said, smiling wistfully. "My parents were distressed at the idea of my selling door to door or having anything to do with a sales operation. Had I taken a job like that in Holland, I would have become a social outcast. My parents flew over to California to find out what I was up to and tried to talk me out of it. They wanted me to do something 'important' with my life, and saw what I was doing as a tragic waste of talent. I had position, money, brains, an education, good looks—and I was selling books from door to door. They could not understand that. What particularly bewildered them was my commitment to it.

"Of course, what I was doing was important, and I was continuing my education. The opportunity to be associated with Werner was more than worth all the obvious disadvantages of the job. Selling books was only an excuse to do the other things."

Gonneke frowned. "It was really hard. We did have to earn our paychecks too. After learning those things, we couldn't just con our ways into homes to sell somebody something. We had to do it straight.

"Werner was unwilling for us to work without integrity. He kept cutting us off from our ability to manipulate. The mind wants to sell, to convince, *to manipulate*. So he was doing the opposite of what a sales organization usually does. He was literally destroying our ability to sell. You sell when you are in trouble. Then you convince. And we were not to do that. Yet it is much easier to sell than to do the other thing.

"Selling is completely a mind thing," Gonneke repeated. "In selling you often dominate or play a right/wrong game. We had to learn that it doesn't matter who wins the argument; that had nothing to do with our being there.

"Werner was unyielding about this. If the mother didn't want us there, he wanted us out fast. Can you imagine how hard that is? My paycheck depended on selling the lady some books. You finally work your way in, you're sitting there, and you experience the feeling that she doesn't want you in her home. She would even buy a book to get rid of you: she could manipulate too. Werner hammered into us that we were to leave in such a situation."

I asked Gonneke what happened in the field when they were successfully avoiding selling. "We got those people in touch with their experience of being mothers and wanting to take care of their children and experiencing that they could do that," she replied. "The point was that they should get value out of the time that they spent with us whether they bought anything or not.

"As it turned out, they *wanted* to talk about their children. Many of them rarely had anybody to share with about their kids. They had frightening teachers to talk to. Often they had a horribly inadequate feeling that they were supposed to know something about raising children and didn't. They read books about raising children, which they didn't understand. We said, 'Listen, if you want to read to your kids, do that. It doesn't make any difference what you read. *Just read to them*. You don't have to do it right.'

"It was wonderful when the mothers got that," Gonneke said, beaming enthusiastically. "When they became aware that what they wanted was not the program, but to work with their children—and that they could do that. I would get letters from them about the things that had been happening with them and their children. They would thank me for selling them the program, but that is not really what they were talking about. They were talking about my recognition of what they wanted to do.

"This is how we were taught to go to somebody's door." Gonneke got up to demonstrate to me. "We'd knock on the door, and then when it was answered we would *step back*. When you stand too close to the door it frightens people. It gives no space. So we stepped back. We went through our routine in a really respectful way, recognizing that they had pictures in their minds about what somebody is going to do with them when they come into their house.

"Werner trained us for hours just to handle that door and entrance business. We would work on that every night.

"Werner taught us that if we had integrity in the situation, then the space would be safe for the mother to make a choice. We wanted them to have a *choice*, not to force a decision on them. Sometimes a mother would ask me what she ought to do. I might say, 'Well, I don't know. Let's talk a little more,' and ask her what she thought. I didn't do this to manipulate her, but because I knew I couldn't go into what we called a 'close' unless I was certain that that was the right thing to do. If things did go well, I might eventually say, 'You know what? I think you ought to get this.' And then she might agree. If in my experience I found that she didn't want to buy after all, I would say, 'You know, I don't think you ought to do this.'

"It took courage to work this way. But for us it was unethical to sell to someone who didn't want you there. It provided a short-term gain but no satisfaction.

"The field is a hard master. Sometimes, in those days—I was in the field constantly for five years—I would be so upset about something. But nobody who opens the door gives a damn about what is going on with you. If you can't get off it and just *be* with that person, you'll have a horrible time of it. Nobody knew or cared how much education you had or how well you behaved socially or who your friends were or how much money you had or anything like that. Your 'act' was irrelevant. You were just somebody at the door. You had to 'get off it,' as Werner now puts it.

"People don't understand the field," Gonneke concluded. "Everything that I have learned comes out of my experience in the field. And from having Werner there: as unreasonable as he was. He couldn't care less how happy I was. Like a Zen master, he just kept me out there banging my head against the wall. He never got drawn into the drama of it. He just kept us at it. He taught us the Zen art of bookselling. So I learned to produce something out of nothing. I learned that you did this by means of intention—and by getting off it. That is the hardest school."

Ron Baldwin had told me about the one-to-one counseling that Werner did in his office with his staff, and I asked Gonneke if she had any experience of that.[7]

"Did I?", Gonneke looked surprised. "I certainly did. I spent hours with him myself. Werner really cared for the people who worked for him. Let me tell you about one of those episodes. There was a girl who worked for me in the field who always seemed to me to be a little strange. She wasn't bad at the business, but I didn't know what was going on with her. At one point she came to me, in the office, and started to tell me something about drugs. She was being so odd that I didn't know what to do with her. She started to tremble.

"I called Werner and asked him to look at her. I didn't yet know what was happening. What she had been trying to tell me was that she was going through withdrawal. She'd been on heroin for seven years, and had finally become secure enough, with us, to get off it. On her own.

"Werner immediately saw what was going on. He moved all the furniture out of his office onto the balcony and into the hallway. There was nothing in the room but one lamp. She went through withdrawal right there. There wasn't much talking for him to do with her. All he did was hold her and then she'd start getting so much pain that she would start fighting again. But he would just hold her. I was sitting over in the corner, and he would call me over, and we'd hold her, until the pain had passed. He just held her for hours, while she was screaming and fighting and kicking and biting.

"She was so strong physically. At one point we had her pinned against the wall, and he was sitting on top of her, and I had my feet against her back, holding her because she was so violent, and in so much pain. We fought to hold her down to prevent her from hurting herself. She wanted a fix, but had entrusted herself to us. Finally, at about three o'clock in the morning, she collapsed. Werner took her to Ellen and put her to bed, where she remained for about two weeks.

"After she left Ellen, we took her to a drug rehabilitation center. But that didn't work out. She got some drugs from a pusher right in the rehabilitation center itself, and fled back to us. She was petrified, knowing that she wasn't safe even there.

"Werner decided to take responsibility for her, and worked out a regimen for her. He was ruthless in his compassion for her. He knew that she wanted to get off of it. With her agreement, we agreed to work her until she dropped. We moved her into an apartment right across from our office. I managed her money for her, and gave her only a dollar a day. Anything additional, she had to justify to me. She came to the office first thing in the morning—before eight o'clock. And she was the last one to leave at night—usually not before 1:00 A.M. She had no free time. All her time was spent with us. She even cleaned the office.

"What we were doing was supporting her in her intention to beat her addiction. We had no time for sympathy. We were doing our own jobs. Our approach was that she either had to get off the drugs or to leave us. We didn't play games with her.

"What was remarkable was that there was never any doubt that Werner would support her in getting off her habit—as long as she did want off it.

"As she became stronger," Gonneke said, "we eased up, and gave her more independence. She never returned to drugs. That episode was for me the beginning of our doing what people say cannot be done."

With Elaine and Gonneke, Werner had developed the beginnings of a loyal cadre with whom he could work, people who had—as Werner put it—"high intention." "People who have no intention," Werner told me, "just go through the motions. They make mistakes, they can't handle things, nothing around them works, they don't do things completely, they complain all the time. What gives people superiority at a task is true intention. That makes you attuned to everything. You handle everything, and your mind doesn't give you reasons for not noticing and not handling things. I don't enjoy people who have low intention. I don't enjoy playing for low stakes. I like to play for stakes. I want the person with whom I am interacting to have something at stake. If I have a conversation with you, I want you to have something at stake. I want you to have an intention for me to understand you, for me to get what you have to say."

Yet another woman of exceptional power and high intention was to be added to Werner's staff the following year. Laurel Scheaf, a native of Ohio, a graduate of the University of Wisconsin, came to work for Parents in September 1967. She became a sales manager, and then the manager of Werner's office. (In 1972 she would become the first president of *est*, later resigning in order to become a trainer candidate.)

I spoke with her, in her office on the seventh floor of the *est* headquarters in San Francisco, about what Elaine and Gonneke had told me concerning the Parents program for mothers.

"What you need to understand about what Elaine and Gonneke told you is that Werner wasn't just implementing Parents' sales policy." Laurel looked up as she spoke, her eyes penetrating and bright. "Werner devised a new approach to selling Parents material. He trained us to communicate, not to sell. As a result, we sold better, *and* everyone involved felt much more satisfied about it. We felt that what we were doing was worthwhile, and so did the mothers who bought programs from us. This approach to selling has now been carried over to some other organizations that use direct sales techniques.

"It was this, more than anything else," Laurel said, "that enabled Werner to recruit and keep the people who worked for him. Most of us were 'overqualified' for door-to-door selling. But we had our own school, and our own community."

EIGHT Experiments

After his conversion in 1963, Werner made an obvious and dramatic change. His pattern of failure *appeared* to have been broken. When success was no longer his highest goal—when he had been converted from it—he began to succeed in all his business activities. He made large amounts of money, as much as $10,000 a month at times; and in 1967, in testimony to his success, Parents appointed him Vice-President.

In fact, however, the pattern had not been transcended. He was still, after all that he had been through, operating in Dorothy's identity—which required him to fail. He failed precisely where the remaining identification with Dorothy touched him most immediately —in his relationship to Ellen.

No longer a harbinger of development for Werner, Ellen—like Pat before her—now became his victim. He had a series of affairs. By 1968, when Ellen was pregnant with their son St. John, the marriage reached its nadir.

I was talking about this with Werner and Ellen in the kitchen of their home high in the hills of Marin County, across the Golden Gate north of San Francisco. On one side of the house rose the slopes of Mount Tamalpais. Below there spread out a watery vista of the Bay Area. In the foreground lay Richardson Bay; in the distance, the San

138

Francisco Bay, stretching south between Oakland and San Francisco to San Jose. Light banks of fog had drifted into the bay in the late morning. Buffeted by the wind, the fog contested the strong sunlight, creating outside the distance, the silence, the dramatic tranquillity of a Chinese scroll.

Ellen had just served a fragrant camomile herb tea. As she sat down again at the table she began to answer some of my questions about their relationship.

"Our marriage survived that period perhaps only because I could not go back to cry on my mother's shoulder," Ellen said. "I always knew about Werner's affairs. Not because anyone told me. He wasn't hiding what he was doing. I could tell by the way he behaved when he came home that he had a 'withhold,' a 'perpetration.' " Ellen paused to smile at the *est* terminology that she was using. (In *est* terminology, a *perpetration* is something that reduces the aliveness of another person—whether a specific act or a break in some agreement that had been made to further aliveness. A *withhold* is a failure to acknowledge a wrongdoing, or to correct or follow up on a perpetration.) "I didn't have the words for it then, but I knew what was going on. Finally, he moved out. I could have cared less if he never came back. As far as I was concerned, the marriage was over."

Ellen looked up. "But you know," she said. "It wasn't just the affairs that upset me. I felt like such a dud, such a failure, next to him. I always knew he was extraordinary, but I hadn't at first realized *how* extraordinary he was. I should have begun to see it when he left Philadelphia with me to go to Saint Louis. The initial remarkable thing is that he set out on that quest at all. We all know what can happen to people in difficult situations. They can give up, take to drink or pills, or something like that. After all, Werner could have stayed with Pat in Philadephia; he could have played around with other women, and sold cars and made a lot of money, and gradually degenerated into a sad and ordinary old age. Or he might have married someone else and done the same.

"But nothing like that ever happened. He never got stuck. Not even with success. He took a much more dramatic path, taking on a new identity and trying to work out a new life for himself. He was always growing, always pushing in a new direction. There was always something new.

"On one level I just didn't want to keep up with that pace. In fact, there was a level on which I just *couldn't* keep up. I felt neither willing nor able to be that powerful. I resisted his success. And I knew that he knew this. I knew that he was disappointed in me because I wasn't keeping up with him in his investigations and disciplines. And if I fell behind here, I certainly couldn't inspire him. In order to support him in what he was doing, *I* would have to grow too. That frightened me. Then when he started to have affairs, I saw that as a token of my *utter* inadequacy. That hurt! I was terribly afraid that he would leave me, and at the same time I had fantasies about leaving him. And then he *did* leave me!"

Ellen looked over and smiled at Werner. "Then St. John was born. And Werner came into the delivery room on June 3, 1968, to watch his birth. That altered a lot of things."

Werner nodded and broke into the story. "The doctor had called to ask whether I wanted to be present when the baby was born. When I said that I did, he mentioned that he would need Ellen's permission. He was obviously doing marriage counseling. Ellen's allowing me into the delivery room was clearly a statement on her part of her willingness for things to work again."

Ellen returned to her story. "We came home from the hospital, gave St. John to the nurse, and went out together. We went to The Dock, a restaurant in Tiburon, and just sat and talked for a couple of hours. I told him that I didn't want to make up, and he asked me to give it a chance.

"I did, and for several weeks things were marvelous. Then they began to deteriorate again. We still weren't communicating. I didn't even tell him that I didn't like him to play around, that I didn't want to have a relationship like that."

Werner began to comment on what Ellen had said. "What Ellen has just said is accurate," he reflected, "except for what she said about my never getting stuck. I did get stuck. I got stuck with our marriage. I literally *could not* end it. It is a law of nature that you cannot be satisfied with something that you are stuck with.

"Why was I stuck? I was stuck by my image of who I was. I thought I was Werner Erhard, the truth-teller. If I were to break my vows again, if I were to destroy another marriage, I wouldn't be Werner Erhard anymore; I would be the liar Jack Rosenberg again. Jack Rosenberg could botch a marriage; but Werner Erhard had to do it right.

"This was my old familiar righteousness—the same righteousness that led to my resigning my post in Washington in 1964. In my mind, the righteousness of my position relieved me of responsibility for the quality of the marriage. I *had* to put up with it no matter how bad it might be, because there was no way for me to get out of it without losing my self-righteous image of myself.

"As a result, I put a lot of energy into pretending the marriage worked, and *trying* to make it work, and *working* at making it work, ad nauseam. Underneath the soap opera was a nonsensical heroic epic in which the worse the marriage got, the more of an internal hero Werner Erhard—that unflinching crusader for the truth and man of his word—became."

Werner paused in his account and smiled wryly at us. "These unconscious patterns really do make puppets out of us. I was repeating the same pattern that I had used on Pat. My marriage with Ellen was functioning, at this point, in a way almost directly parallel to the marriage to Pat. I had even been in the same situation *exactly* with Pat: I wasn't living at home, she was having a baby, I came into the hospital, then things got a little better for a while. And so on. This shows how little I had really moved from my old entanglement, despite my desperate search for satisfaction and for enlightenment."

And so, in a state lacking in satisfaction, all he could do was to keep on searching, to keep on trying.

THE DALE CARNEGIE COURSE

In late 1967, at the height of the crisis with Ellen, and after his study of Zen, Werner took the oldest and most successful of all personality development courses: the Dale Carnegie course. Carnegie himself had modestly launched his course in 1912, in lectures at his local YMCA. Designed to teach people to conquer fear—and using public speaking as a vehicle for this—the course rapidly became successful, and was franchised by Carnegie for presentation throughout the United States and abroad.

Werner was impressed by the course, and arranged for his employees to take it. For Valentine's Day 1968, he gave Ellen a gift-certificate enrollment.

Initially, Ellen was furious. "I was pregnant at the time, with St. John. And what do I get for a present? A course on how to win friends and influence people! Why not a 95-pound box of candy?

"Well, I did take it. It was an intensive course held over a series of weekends. I went into it still very annoyed, but when you get into a roomful of people who are interested in learning 'how to win friends and influence people,' you cooperate. One of the first things you do is to get up in front of the room and relate a story about yourself. From the day I went in until the day I finished the course, I won prizes every time I did something.

"That surprised me," Ellen said. "I was sure I was going to hate it. I don't like to speak in front of people. I certainly didn't like being looked at when I was pregnant. Yet I enjoyed the course from beginning to end."

When I mentioned to Werner what Ellen had told me, he burst out laughing at the memory.

"People think of the Dale Carnegie course as some sort of business scheme—as a bag of tricks to change your presentation of yourself—your same old self—so that people will like you instead of hate you.

"In fact, it is not like that at all. The Dale Carnegie course is essentially about the development of human potential, and is put together with sophisticated principles. Dale Carnegie's genius is not usually appreciated, because he expressed it in his course, more than in his writing. The material he developed is more subtle than the explanations of it given in his books. Even his own instructors sometimes don't appreciate the brilliance of the course. It is put together so well that the result is produced every time, regardless of the instructor. It transcends personality."

"It's put together in a simple way. As Ellen told you, every student gives two two-minute talks every night. The idea is that you aren't to talk about what you think you know—since you don't know anything—but you *are* to talk about your experience. That is what you *really* know. The first talk is about your current circumstances— who you are, where you live, what you do for a living. You sit up on a table with three or four other students for confidence. The second talk is about an incident from your childhood. The instructor gives you immediate feedback. He might interrupt you in the middle of your talk.

"The Carnegie instructors are really able at this. They are real humanists; and humanity is at the basis of what Carnegie does. He draws out human qualities. As you talk, you stop pretending and truly share yourself.

"They give a pencil as a prize for the best talk," Werner said. Two of the awards are given by the students, and the third comes from the instructor. The instructor uses his award to encourage people or to acknowledge something that he wants emulated, or perhaps to acknowledge a person whom the group is not recognizing.

"I had a terrible time in winning a pencil. I earned my living talking, yet I didn't win a pencil. At the beginning I could explain it away. I could say to myself that the pencils were awarded on a sympathy basis to the people who broke down the most. But by the eighth week that argument didn't even convince me anymore—and I still wasn't winning pencils.

"My mistake, as it turned out, was in giving a great talk every week. The Carnegie course is not about giving a great talk. It is not about proving yourself, but about being yourself. I wasn't sharing myself; I was presenting 'Werner Erhard.' My presentation of myself got in the way of my sharing of myself. I found out that I would have to share myself to win the award."

I asked Werner what had attracted him to the Dale Carnegie course and how it compared in importance with Zen.

"There is no comparison," he replied. "My experience with Zen and other disciplines enabled me to get things out of the Carnegie course that are not usually found there.

"What particularly interested me in the Carnegie course were the techniques and format. I was beginning to think about starting a course of my own, and of consulting for other firms. I knew that my real talent was in working with people, not in running a business. Having developed methods in the laboratory of my own firm, I thought that I could apply and market them elsewhere. I even thought about becoming a Dale Carnegie instructor. I signed up and paid for the instructor's course, but I never began it.

"I did once assist as a volunteer at a course for Carnegie instructors. There were two sessions. One was on excitement; the other was on enthusiasm. I learned the difference between excitement and enthusiasm by watching the head psychologist of the Carnegie course mis-explain them.

"Most people have never experienced enthusiasm," Werner said. "It is an inspired state. Whereas excitement, which is a common experience, is only a high-energy state. The Carnegie instructor tried to get across this difference, but it remained unclear to me. I went away confused about it. Over the next several months I got clear about it in terms of what I call Self—something that I had begun to understand in Zen. Excitement is related to personality and Mind; enthusiasm is related to Self. When you reach the Self, you get enthusiasm. The enthusiasm may be quiet or humorous or exuberant or buoyant. It is there naturally, whereas excitement is something added on or put out.

Excitement is noise or outer form. You can fake or pretend excitement. Enthusiasm is what you are essentially. You can't pretend it. Everybody is already enthusiastic. One reveals or discovers one's enthusiasm.

"This is an example of something valuable from the Carnegie course, which I couldn't have gotten without my experience of Zen.

"I was later able to translate other Carnegie principles into the material that I use. I haven't used it in the *est* training, but I do use some Carnegie principles in the training of *est* trainers, and also in the training of *est* seminar leaders. I also developed some related techniques of my own. There is the mirror technique, for example. Sometimes I have people do two-minute talks into a mirror. That is an attempt to get immediate results without much instructor feedback. I first used the mirror in Los Angeles, when I was training personnel for Parents. One woman just couldn't get something. On the spur of the moment, I went into the bathroom, took the mirror off the wall, brought it out into the training room, and stood her in front of it. She was a tough hard woman—and she just melted in front of the mirror. Her beauty and softness and tenderness emerged. She was able to observe her own act in the mirror; the moment she saw it, it dissolved. She got to be more herself.

"I was moved by that," Werner added. "The whole world shifted for me as she went through that. I saw that mere honest direct feedback—without explanation or evaluation, without what I now call 'make-wrong'—can remove layer after layer of pretense. That became a principle of mine."

SUBUD AND THE MARTIAL ARTS
As the years went by, Werner investigated one discipline after another. From his relationship with Hardgrove, and his readings in Maslow and Rogers, flowed further contact with Gestalt, with Encounter, and with Transactional Analysis. Pursuing the themes he was learning with Alan Watts, he also turned more and more to the Orient. He took an "Enlightenment Intensive" with H. Charles Berner, the founder of "Abilitism." And after studying Zen, he took instruction in the martial arts.

The chief lesson that he learned from the latter, and particularly from judo, concerned the dangers of positionality. "I used to show my associates a film on judo from the Japanese consulate," Werner told me. "Part of it was done in slow motion, and you could see that the master never moved in to attack until the instant when his opponent stopped to think. The phrase 'stop to think' is perfect. That is exactly what happens, as you can see clearly in slow motion. The instant your opponent takes a position—that is to say, stops—he is vulnerable."

Werner also nonchalantly probed areas that would have been forbidden ground to most academic investigators and even off limits to Alan Watts—whose practice of Zen never strayed far from the respectable. Werner probed the bizarre, eccentric, exotic, and utterly disreputable new movements and religions that were growing in California, and ransacked them for notions and practices of value to him in his own quest. He had everything to gain and nothing to lose. As Santayana said of William James, Werner "gave a sincerely respectful hearing to sentimentalists, mystics, spiritualists, wizards, cranks, quacks, and impostors—for it is hard to draw the line."[1]

For nearly a year, Werner participated in Subud. Subud is a religious community founded in Asia in the thirties by the Indonesian Pakh Subuh, who is known as Bapak to his followers. Subud became famous in the fifties, when the film star Eva Bartók became Subud's disciple, and when J. G. Bennett, one of the most prominent disciples of Gurdjieff, embraced Subud, proclaiming Subuh to be the "Avatar," or "Awakener of Conscience," described in Gurdjieff's book *All and Everything*. Werner sat in attendance outside the latihan hall—the room in which the Subud meetings are held—waiting for his mind to be "opened." Later he participated in latihan itself, which is a form of meditation aiming at "inner stillness" and opening of the mind to meaning and "divine energies." Even more exotic groups were to follow.

CHANGE: STOPPING AND STARTING
In late 1968, Werner's business began to intrude into, rather than to complement, his quest. After selling their magazine sales business to Time-Life, Inc., Parents began to reduce the size of their management in New York. Then they began to cut back in the subscription book and materials division. As they did so, Werner's own territory and responsibilities rapidly contracted. The Los Angeles office was closed. The San Francisco staff shrunk from forty to twenty-five. There were rumors that the whole division would be shut down, as indeed happened a year later. Reading the signs, Werner resigned amicably from Parents in April 1969, to become a division manager for the Grolier Society, a subsidiary of the Grolier Corporation,

marketing their program for preschool children. He moved his entire organization of office and sales managers, instructors, and sales force from Parents to Grolier.

Grolier sales were good, but, unlike Parents, they were in other kinds of difficulties. Hiring Werner was one of a series of urgent measures taken by Grolier to fend off public attack and bolster their corporate image. By 1970, the Grolier Society had become the target of suits brought by the state alleging fraudulent sales techniques and practices. California eventually won permanent injunctions against such practices, and the Grolier Society is no longer active.

Werner had nothing to do with either the complaints or the suits. As John Wirtz, then vice-president of the Grolier Society, has testified: "The complaints against Grolier Society already existed at the time Werner was hired, and the executives of Grolier were looking for ways to correct the regrettable practices that resulted in these legal actions. Werner's demonstrated ability to develop programs of integrity, honesty, and straightforwardness and his ability to develop high-caliber people who could manage and carry out their own programs made him especially interesting to us.

"Nothing that Werner or anyone in his division did was in any way associated with the legal action against Grolier Society in the state of California," Wirtz stated. "Quite to the contrary, he demonstrated that one could develop an organization that combined success and integrity."

Yet his new job was not the change that Werner wanted to make. It differed little from what he had been doing for seven years, and gave him too little scope to counsel and to train. As soon as the new business at Grolier was going smoothly, he turned his attention back to his own personal quest—but now with much closer regard to the idea of offering to the public the program that he had been developing.

It would take two more years, and two more major steps— Scientology and Mind Dynamics—before he was to create the independent training program toward which he was still sleepwalking. His crucial entry point for both these steps was his old acquaintance Mike Maurer. Mike and he had met in Spokane. Mike had worked for him briefly in San Francisco at Parents, and in early 1968 he began to work for him again.

While shopping in a jewelry store in Sausalito one afternoon, Mike was introduced to Peter Monk, an Englishman, an engineer from Los Gatos, California, who turned out to be a member of the

Church of Scientology, a maverick and highly successful new religion started in the fifties by the American science-fiction writer and originator of Dianetics, L. Ron Hubbard. Mike introduced Peter to Werner. "I had no idea what Scientology was," Werner told me. "But I did what came along and agreed to have the Scientology communication course that Peter was doing presented to our organization. The course was arduous. There was no brain work in it, just exercises that at first appeared to have no relationship to life. There also was a two-person, two-hour, eyeball-to-eyeball confrontation. I did the exercises. I saw their point, and I saw how to apply them. The course was brilliant."

Werner bought from Peter some of L. Ron Hubbard's books on Scientology. He read part of Hubbard's *Problems of Work*, as well as parts of *A New Slant on Life*, and a book of aphorisms called *When in Doubt Communicate*. He read all of Hubbard's *Original Thesis*, as well as part of *The Phoenix Lectures*.[2] As he did so, he became deeply interested in Scientology.

So did Mike Maurer (who later joined L. Ron Hubbard's "Sea Org" headquarters). Ellen came home one afternoon to the house, "and there," she said, "were Werner and Mike in the living room doing Scientology on one another. They were talking all in jargon and I got very irritated about it."

Werner encouraged his whole staff to take the Scientology communication course, and hired Peter Monk to help train them. Meanwhile, Mike and Peter started to do what Scientologists call "auditing," which is the application of Scientology processes. Working first with Peter and Mike, and then at the Scientology organization, Werner went through five Scientology levels, and received a total of about seventy hours of auditing. At the organization he also took a short course introducing what are called "locks" and "secondaries" (various levels of traumatic experience).

"I got a lot of benefit from auditing," Werner told me. "It was the fastest and deepest way to handle situations that I had yet encountered. I immediately wanted to learn to do it.

"The most important theoretical insight that I got from Scientology concerned the Mind. I had been working to understand the Mind since the shift in my values following the peak experience in 1963. I had begun to understand it through my study of Zen, where I began to distinguish between Mind and what I later called Self. But not until I encountered Scientology did I see clearly that Mind is at the root of all the trouble; and that the trouble lies in its positionality. Previously

I had still thought of Mind as a useful tool. With Scientology, I was able to characterize the Mind more accurately, and to cease justifying it. This greatly clarified what I was doing."

Werner paused, and reflected. He turned to me again and said, "At this point I began to be able to go beyond Mind as it is ordinarily conceived. For example, I was able to get back to my 'memories' of past lives.

"I know that sounds shocking. Yet within our mental systems there are—so I have learned from personal experience—symbols or archetypes that represent the past of humanity. 'Memories' is perhaps not a good word, since it implies that you were there, and I don't mean that. These are patterns that you *know* and that yet have nothing to do with your individual history.

"One thing that I went looking for, when I got in touch with past lives, is the source of the feeling of being under pressure. Since getting back to the source of that feeling—in a state of 'active imagination,' or trance, or altered state of consciousness, whatever you want to call it—I have never again been troubled by feeling under pressure.

"After my experience with Scientology, I saw what it means to see the Mind as a machine. I can now operate my Mind accordingly, with exactitude. I can do the familiar mind over matter experiments—the control of pain and bleeding, telepathy, those things. Many people can do such things, and they are well known in the yogic tradition. These yogic practices amount to a systematic reduction of mechanicalness in one's life. At some point, after reducing your mechanicalness—and going beyond Mind—you regain abilities that are transcendent to form and position, abilities that you had been prevented from using by your mechanicalness. One can also attain these abilities working within the Mind. Yet, however successful this may be, it remains an extension of mechanicalness rather than a transcendence of it."

Werner smiled again. "As the yogis well know, there is knowing, and there is the demonstration of knowing. The world keeps grinding you into the demonstration of knowing, and into proving it. This reduces knowingness."

Intersection
FIVE: SCIENTOLOGY

As I worked through the tall pile of works of and about Scientology by L. Ron Hubbard, I became more and more puzzled. The books were in their very appearance off-putting: uniformly and cheaply bound in green board covers, poorly printed on cheap paper, outlandishly expensive. The style was ghastly: poorly organized, pretentious, humorless.

And yet, these books were brilliant. On many issues, Hubbard went to the heart of the matter with a penetration lacking in more "respectable" material. His techniques were to the point and often more effective than the usual stuff of psychiatry and psychology. And they were presented with a care for exactness in application that manifested the author's seriousness.

Scholars such as myself, when attempting to become oriented in a new area, go about their business in a fairly direct way: they search out the original texts of the discipline or subject matter that they are attempting to understand; and they read the secondary material—the critical material that has been published *about* the original texts—in order to see how the material has been appraised and judged, what the current state of discussion may be.

With Scientology, neither primary nor secondary material is easy to
come by. The primary material—the official Scientology
publications and works by L. Ron Hubbard himself—is not
usually for sale in commercial bookstores; nor is it usually available
in public and university libraries. I eventually obtained the basic
works of Hubbard by buying them at the local Scientology
mission. Even there, I was told, additional books could be made
available only if I were to register for some Scientology courses.

With secondary material the situation was worse. Here is a
movement with many thousands of adherents in English-speaking
countries, which has been wholly created in the past twenty-five
years. All evidence suggests that adherents tend to be of
intelligence above average; the movement is basically oriented to
intelligence, to reading, study, training. Yet the movement has
virtually escaped critical attention. I was unable to find a single
serious journal article about the subject by a professional scholar in
philosophy, religion, or sociology. Nor has any study of it appeared
in such journals as *Commentary* or *The New York Review* or
Encounter. There were several dozen short magazine reports of
Scientology, all on a superficial descriptive level, mostly concerned
with gossip about the personality of L. Ron Hubbard, or with
crises in the Scientology organization. Of course hundreds of short,
superficial newspaper articles on the subject had appeared in British
newspapers during several crises of the past ten years. About five
books have been published, most of them by British writers. Most
of these attempt an exposé of the Scientology organization. Only
one of them, *Cults of Unreason*, by Christopher Evans,[3] makes even
a stab at treating the whole phenomenon of Scientology seriously,
and it is chiefly a historical account rather than an assessment of the
basic ideas and techniques of Scientology. The only American
writer of distinction to discuss Hubbard has been Martin Gardner,
the mathematician, in a brief account of Dianetics in his book *Fad
and Fallacies*.[4]

This neglect of Scientology—this lack of genuine curiosity about
its basic tenets and techniques (as opposed to its more sensational
features) and lack of appreciation for its merits—is the more
peculiar when one considers the impact of Scientology on the
consciousness movement. The consciousness movement has
benefited from and been enormously influenced by ideas and

techniques taken from Scientology; yet its leaders generally are reluctant to acknowledge influence from Scientology, perhaps fearful of being tarred with its brush.

There is a phrase from Scientology jargon that nicely sums up the relationship between Scientology and the society in which it is growing: the Scientology organization is "out of ARC on the third dynamic." Hubbard's "third dynamic" has to do with the survival of the individual through the group with which he is affiliated and through symbiotes of that group. "ARC" refers to Hubbard's triangle of "Affinity/Reality/Communication," which he uses to demonstrate the close connection of these three phenomena: if one is out of communication with another person or group, one's sense of reality about the other will be diminished, as will one's feelings of affinity. An increase or decrease in any one of affinity, reality, or communication leads to a comparable increase or decrease in the other two. This explains Scientology's stress on enhanced communication as the route to sanity: to a realistic appraisal of the way things are and of one's relationship with persons and things.

Yet Hubbard as a writer, and Scientology as an organization, are out of touch with the normal means of communication in the Western world. This results in an unrealistic and needlessly adversary attitude of the Scientology organization toward the society in which it lives. And a huffy—"Well, if that's the way you're going to be, we'll just ignore you"—attitude on the part of society.

Werner Erhard is virtually the only consciousness leader, and the only person of distinction in American society, to have stepped outside this childish quarrel between Scientology and society, and to have acknowledged both his indebtedness to Hubbard and his emphatic differences with him.

It is not hard to give a general description of Scientology. Scientology is a form of what philosophers call "philosophical idealism." "Idealism" here refers not to *ideals*, but to the supremacy of Idea or Spirit over Matter. Several great Western philosophers, notably Bishop Berkeley (1685–1753) and G.W.F. Hegel (1770–1831), have been idealists; the type of idealism espoused by Hubbard, however, is a variant more usually associated with

Eastern philosophy, particularly with Buddhism. Although Hubbard rejects several tenets ordinarily connected with Buddhism—such as the idea of nirvana and of a oneness with the universe that transcends individuality—he acknowledges the influence of Eastern thought, particularly of the Vedas, on his own development, and in one place describes Scientology as the "Western world's first workable organization of Eastern philosophy."

For Hubbard, the most important thing in the universe is a godlike creative force called the "thetan," which is itself the creator and definer of universes. The thetan does not exist in space and time, and has no mass or energy. It is the true Self of the individual, his soul, or "essence," and is immortal.

The world of matter, energy, space, and time—the MEST universe, as Hubbard calls it (from the first letters of the words "matter," "energy," "space," and "time")—is, in something like a Buddhist sense, *illusion*. It is created by the thetans, and has no independent existence. The thetan is a "MEST production unit." Reality —the MEST universe—consists in the overlapping or shared agreements of the thetans. The MEST universe result from con- siderations—postulates—made by thetans; the MEST universe is perceived solely because thetans consider that they can perceive it.

Man as we know him exists in a fallen state. He has forgotten his essential, immortal Self. He has entrapped himself in the MEST universe. He even believes himself to be wholly MEST. No worse fate could have befallen him. For the MEST universe is a universe of force and slavery, where honesty, justice, reason, and integrity are impossible, a universe wholly at war with the thetan essence, which is naturally good, honest, just, full of integrity. The way to happiness is to win freedom from this entrapment by the world of mass, energy, space, and time, to regain thetan freedom and creativity.

So far, little in Scientology differs from Buddhism and other Oriental philosophies that search for escape from the "wheel" of birth and death. There are also similarities with gnostic and Christian attempts to free the spirit from the flesh.

Scientology begins to differ in the account that Hubbard gives of the manner by which theta is enmeshed in MEST, and of the way by which it may free itself from it. In a detailed account of the way in which free spirits are stuck, entrapped, "solidified" in matter, Hubbard states general principles governing life and underlying human knowledge. By applying these principles he proceeds to construct a technology to free the thetan from his material prison.

We are imprisoned by the MEST universe to the extent to which we *agree* with it, consciously or unconsciously. Hubbard quotes the Buddha's Dharmapada, "All that we are is the result of what we have thought. It is founded upon our thoughts. It is made up of our thoughts."

The chief mechanism whereby a thetan goes into agreement with the MEST universe, and becomes MEST, is for Hubbard the "reactive mind," an extremely stupid stimulus-response mechanism that is not under the volitional control of the thetan. This mind is run by its memory bank: by mental "pictures" from the past, including "engrams," which are records of experiences containing pain, unconsciousness, and real or imagined threats to survival—"traumas" in more conventional psychological language.

Every time the individual encounters a new experience reminding him in any way of an earlier trauma, the reactive mind goes into operation and the person goes unconscious, automatically acting as he did earlier. Since the reactive mind operates according to a logic that "everything is like everything else," *any* new experience turns out to "restimulate" the reactive mind, and thus the person is continually jerked unconscious, simply reacting in a stimulus-response fashion. Thus he is overwhelmed by the MEST environment; the object of almost continual inflow from MEST, he no longer has space in which to create; he "goes solid." He is hemmed in by traumatic memories, and by all the agreements that he made with other persons and with the MEST universe. He comes to think that he *is* his MEST body, and forgets his non-MEST origins.

As he reflected on these matters, Werner came for a time to accept, with minor alterations, Scientology's characterization of mind. He rejected, however, the idea of the thetan, and later characterized the Self in a way that differs markedly from Hubbard's description of the thetan.

The goal of Scientology is to retrieve the individual from his agreement with the MEST universe: to reduce the apparently infinite power of the MEST universe over him to zero; and to increase the apparent zero of his own personal universe to infinity.

One way to escape the power of past traumatic incident was featured in Dianetics (the discipline first introduced by Hubbard), and lies in the individual's *duplicating consciously,* in his own subjective universe, the painful experience that rendered him unconscious. The conscious re-creation of the painful incident has the effect of dimming or liquidating the power of the incident to control his reactions, thereby freeing him from the incident.

This much of course parallels psychiatric treatment. What Hubbard adds is, first of all, an account in literally cosmic terms of why the technique works. In terms of this account, he specifies which techniques will rehabilitate an individual, and which are bound to fail. Those that work conform to the cosmic principle.

What is this principle? It is the principle of "duplication," a principle that violates the principle of conservation of energy. The way—the only way—to destroy anything is to create a perfect duplicate of it. Duplicated, it would not change or alter; it would *disappear*, vanish from the universe. Hubbard means exactly what he says here. This is where the punch behind his philosophical idealism comes into play: if MEST is originally created out of thought, thought can make MEST disappear. If I were to make a perfect duplicate in my mind of my headache—in the same place and the same time—that headache would disappear. To the extent that I can duplicate consciously in thought a painful traumatic episode or incident that has me in its grasp, to that extent the incident loses its power over me. Hubbard calls these conscious duplications "mock-ups."

On the other hand, to the extent to which a particular therapeutic technique does *not* aim at disappearance, but rather simply attempts to force a change, or to alter or cover up a situation, it is trying to use MEST on MEST; and the troubling situation will persist, although perhaps in a different form.

Scientology, as opposed to Dianetics, is less concerned with mocking-up traumatic incidents from the past. According to Hubbard, one may virtually *ignore* an individual's reactive mind and instead concentrate on rehabilitating his ability to construct a personal subjective universe. One's personal subjective universe, one's universe of imagination, is one of the first casualties of MEST. In childhood the imagination is condemned; as the MEST universe presses in, one gradually ceases to garnish it with one's dreams, and thus becomes its slave.

But, when one rehabilitates creative ability, and reexercises the imagination, one automatically brings the reactive mind under better control, reducing its command value. As Hubbard writes, "When one has compromised too long and too often, when he has been betrayed and ridiculed and is no longer able to create what he believes to be desirable, he descends down to lower levels and in those levels, he is still more compelled to face the MEST universe, and as such, loses much more of his ability to handle the MEST universe. When an individual's ability to create his own universe is rehabilitated it will be found, strangely enough, that his ability to handle the MEST universe has been rehabilitated."[5]

Hubbard takes it as something like a proof of the illusory character of the MEST universe that the rehabilitation of the imagination and the creation of illusion in the act of imagination serve to rehabilitate one's ability to view, and to handle and control, the MEST universe. One might take Werner's own case to illustrate the point here: by consciously creating, in his imagination, a fictitious identity for himself, he became more able to handle the "realities" of his life than he was from the fixed, agreed, identity of Jack Rosenberg.

However this may be, and whatever one may think of the cosmic theses in which Hubbard couches his remarks on imagination, much of the contemporary consciousness movement agrees with him, on the technical level, about the importance of rehabilitating the imagination in the attempt to bring people to fulfill their potential. Psychosynthesis, psychodrama, "mind games," and other approaches depend on this notion.

In addition to a general account of how man fell from his creative state, and how he may regain it, Hubbard provides a wealth—a psychologist's gold mine—of detailed analyses of what might be called the "machinery of unconsciousness," the different devices that keep people stuck in automatically patterned behavior. He also presents a variety of charts and scales that give a phenomenological description of human experience, and perhaps the most elaborate typology available in contemporary psychology. Finally, he develops a battery of techniques and "processes" for rehabilitating the imagination and defusing the power of the reactive mind. In these techniques the greatest value in Scientology is to be found. They do not of course lend themselves to summary treatment.

In this brief account, I omitted some sensationalized features that have served to discredit Scientology in the eyes of many. For example, various writers have presented evidence to suggest that Hubbard has at times made exaggerated claims about his past and his scientific qualifications. Others have ridiculed some marginal elements in Hubbard's thought: his speculations, for instance, on genetics and the history of the universe. It is true that Hubbard sometimes presents Scientology in a wildly eccentric garb. Rather than dwelling on marginal matters, in which I too see little value, I have tried to indicate the core of the system. That too is peculiar enough, but no more peculiar than the views of most Buddhist and Christian sects. An overscrupulous preoccupation with the peculiarities of the viewpoint may prevent an appreciation of the considerable merits of its techniques.

After working through the books on Scientology, and studying it as well as I could without becoming a member, I had an opportunity to talk with Werner again, and to ask him to evaluate it and to state the differences between *est* and Scientology.

I wanted to know, first, how Werner regarded L. Ron Hubbard, the founder of Scientology. "I have a lot of feeling for Ron Hubbard," Werner told me. "His genius has not been sufficiently acknowledged. That is partly a matter of timing.

"Ron was telling people things that were foreign to them. They couldn't get what he was saying. When he tried to make it believable, he was trapped by the need to build a bridge from where people were to his own insight. To the degree that he *needed* to be understood he undermined what he had to say. In that respect, I have had an easier time than he. Partly because of his contribution, I had less of a gap to cross."

When I asked Werner to sum up the differences between *est* and Scientology, he reflected for a moment. "Although the *est* training is quite different from Scientology practices and processes," he replied, "I am not surprised that people find traces of Scientology in *est*. In *est* we use variations on some of the Scientology charts, and as a result the terminology overlaps a bit. In essential respects, however, the two are different.

"The essential difference between *est* and Scientology is twofold.

"The first has to do with Scientology's emphasis on survival and its idea that the purpose of life is survival. *est* sees the purpose of life as wholeness or completion—truth—not survival.

"Completion is the state in which that which is, is and that which is not, is not. So the purpose of life as I see it is to be complete, in one's relationship to oneself, to others, and to the universe.

"Being in a state of completion is tantamount to being satisfied," Werner continued. "And to be satisfied is to be in a state where the moment is sufficient unto itself. To say it more conversationally, by 'completion' I mean 'aliveness,' by which I refer to the state of love, vitality, happiness, and full self-expression.

"This does not mean that *est* is opposed to survival. Of course one has a responsibility for survival, not only for oneself, but for others and societies and organizations too. But that is not the *point* to life. Nor is it a sufficiently accurate fundamental context to empower you in life.

"The other main difference between *est* and Scientology lies in the treatment of knowing. Ron Hubbard seems to have no difficulty in codifying the truth and in urging people to believe it. But I suspect all codifications, particularly my own. In presenting my own ideas, I emphasize their epistemological context. I hold them as pointers to the truth, not as the truth itself.

"I don't think that anyone ought to believe the ideas that we use in *est*. The *est* philosophy is not a belief system and most certainly ought not to be believed. In any case, even the truth, when believed, is a lie. You must *experience* the truth, not *believe* it.

"So in *est*, by contrast to Scientology, the epistemology is altered from a well-conceived belief system to something other than belief, to a context in which one is sensitive to the dangers and pitfalls of any and all beliefs and belief systems.

"As a result of these differences," Werner concluded, "my relationship to Scientology differs from my relationship to Zen. Of all the disciplines that I practiced, studied, learned, Zen was the *essential* one.

Although the forms of the *est* training and Zen training are different, Zen and *est* come from similar abstractions. By contrast—despite any apparent similarities of form—Scientology and *est* come from different abstractions. Scientology sees the world through a well-developed belief system, and its context is survival. Neither belief systems nor survival are important in *est* and in Zen."

MIND DYNAMICS

During his encounter with Scientology, Werner continued to prepare his own communications and training course. In order to discover how existing training courses were organized and advertised, he sent Peter Monk and Mike Maurer from one course to another to check attendance, promotion, effectiveness. In October 1970, Mike and Peter attended an introductory lecture for a two-weekend course called "Mind Dynamics."[6]

As Elaine Cronin told me, "Mike and Peter came back from Mind Dynamics very excited. The things that they had gone looking for—attendance figures, promotion, and things like that—hadn't impressed them. What impressed them were the people who were presenting it. They seemed to be in good shape. They knew how to relate to their audience, and didn't get into arguments with the people in it, as amateurs and people who are not in good shape often do. Most important, Mike and Peter seemed to think that the course itself was valid and original. They kept repeating to Werner, 'This thing is just fantastic.'"

What is Mind Dynamics—this "fantastic" course? It was indeed probably the most spectacular mind-expansion program ever staged. It featured extraordinary demonstrations and intensive training in memory feats, in enhancement of psychic powers, ESP, precognition, and psychic diagnosis and healing. There was comparatively little philosophical theory in it, but a wide range of techniques drawing on hypnosis and autohypnosis, and on autogenic therapy, in addition to rather more exotic techniques cultivated by the famous Texas "natural psychic" Edgar Cayce, and by José Silva, founder of Silva Mind Control, as well as a number of colorful effects drawing from Rosicrucianism, Theosophy, and other disciplines.[7]

Clairvoyance, extrasensory perception, and healing have always been reported in connection with the hypnotic trance. Yet because of their controversial nature, many students of hypnosis and trance states have kept firmly away from them. Mind Dynamics went to the other extreme, giving impressive demonstrations that were purported to be examples of these phenomena, and contending, moreover, that *anyone* could—through Mind Dynamics—learn to cultivate such powers in himself.

Alexander Everett, the Englishman who founded Mind Dynamics, now lives in San Francisco, and early one morning I drove to meet him in his house in the Sunset District, a few minutes' walk from the Pacific Ocean and from Golden Gate Park, where he jogs four miles each day. He is a tall, elegant and youthful man, who recited a blessing as I entered and when I left. After seating me comfortably on a couch in his living room—from which I had a view into the adjoining study and workroom—he began to talk about himself and about the programs that he had developed.

He told me how he had, as a young man in England, founded several schools for boys, including Shiplake College, in Henley-on-Thames, inspired by Kurt Hahn, the German educator and founder of the Outward Bound program and of the famous Gordonstoun School in Scotland. "I wanted to reach the spiritual level that Aldous Huxley wrote about in *The Perennial Philosophy*," Alexander told me, "and I wasn't able to do that in my school. So I gave it away. I packed my bags, and set off to travel the world. I went to Greece, to Egypt, to India, searching for methods to reach the inner spiritual state. I studied Christian Science, the Unity School of Christianity, Rosicrucianism, Theosophy. I came to America because of the Unity School, in Kansas, where I worked for a year intending to become a minister. I made some progress there, but I still didn't find a way to reach the spiritual level effectively. By coincidence, the British consul in Kansas put me in touch with someone who wanted my help in setting up a private school in Texas.

"In Texas, I got involved with the Edgar Cayce group. Cayce spoke of himself—I think correctly—as a natural psychic. I recognized that he was indeed able to go to the subjective level that I had been searching for, to contact the divine level of being. But I met the same old problem. Although Cayce himself reached these realms, the members of his group couldn't say *how* to do it. It was the same thing that I had encountered with Madame Blavatsky, with Rosicrucianism and Theosophy, everywhere. Some of these people could themselves get to the subjective level; but they didn't know how to teach you to get there too.

"José Silva, whom I met and worked with in Texas, was the first who could show people the way. He is a friendly Mexican, a beautiful guy. I learned from him techniques to get people into subjective states. But we also had some disagreements, and eventually we parted.

"I decided to set up my own trip," Alexander continued. "To the things that I had learned from Silva, I added what I knew from other disciplines. For example, I had learned in Theosophy the power of imagination and visualization. I added a color system to take you from one subjective level to another. The basic objective of Mind Dynamics, as I set it up, was to get people to a higher dimension of mind, from which level their entire lives would be more effective."

Everett won the backing of a California entrepreneur, the late William Penn Patrick, and with his financial support set up Mind Dynamics.

Spurred on by the enthusiasm of Mike Maurer and Peter Monk for Mind Dynamics, Werner took the course in November 1970. Werner was so impressed by it that, immediately after completing it, he arranged to train to be a Mind Dynamics instructor himself, as did Peter.

To do this, he would need his staff's support. During the Christmas holiday of 1970, Werner called Gonneke, Laurel, Elaine, and a few other members of his staff together. After demonstrating some Mind Dynamics techniques to them, he announced his decision to lead the course, and asked for their support and cooperation. Each of them agreed to take the course and to assist at Mind Dynamics events. Then Werner outlined plans whereby Laurel—who had in the previous three months completed the Dale Carnegie course and also taken a course in Dianetic auditing for Scientology—would not only continue to run the Grolier office, but would also train to be a Mind Dynamics instructor.

The first obstacle, the instructors' course, proved to be elementary. Alexander Everett, the founder of Mind Dynamics, just brought ten candidates together for ten days and, as he put it, "I taught them all I knew. Only one in ten had the character and the strength to succeed in the course." Werner made it, and was at once put in charge of the San Francisco area, where he was to lead his first Mind Dynamics training in February 1971.

Just at this moment, Werner's old career put in a final appearance. Ron Baldwin, now president of Parents, flew in from New York City to offer Werner a new job. Parents' Home Service Institute, another organization in the Parents family, had just been established. "I was prepared to offer Werner the regional directorship for the New

York area," Ron told me. "It would have brought him a salary of $100,000 a year. Although there was as yet no way to be certain that he would make anything of Mind Dynamics, Werner turned me down. Oddly, I had the feeling that he made the right decision. When I watched him do the Mind Dynamics course—I took it during my trip to California to see Werner—I knew immediately that he had found the right medium for his talents."

Mind Dynamics—like *est* later—used guest lectures as its chief means of recruiting trainees. Werner had given two of these in January. "We just printed up tickets and invited everyone we knew," Laurel Scheaf told me. By the second lecture 150 people were in attendance; and by the first weekend of the course itself, in February 1971, thirty-two people had signed up for it. That course, held at the Holiday Inn at Fisherman's Wharf, was the smallest one Werner ever gave. It became an instant success, with enrollment more than doubling each month. By June, Werner began to give courses in Los Angeles too.

Werner's Grolier staff supported him wholeheartedly—working long additional hours on weekends and during the week in order to arrange and produce the course. But they were also initially puzzled and bewildered by it. "I was not at first interested in consciousness," Laurel told me. "I slept through most of the first session." Elaine Cronin, who was sharing an apartment with Laurel at the time, reacted differently. "What happened to me," she told me, "was frightening. I woke up the night before the final day of the training, from a sound sleep, as if lightning had struck me. Everything just opened up, and I could see everything from the beginning to the end of time. I called Werner—it must have been four in the morning—and told him that I couldn't make the session in the morning because I was sure I was going to die. And he just said, 'Oh, what's it like?' He kept asking, 'What did you see? What happened?'

"During this night I began to see people as light, and to see auras," Elaine said. "That lasted for about a week."

Ellen also changed her tune. She had initially been exasperated with the whole business. "I came home and found Mike Maurer and Werner at it again," she said. "This time they were working a 'case' in the living room, as if 'diagnosing' a physical condition. This was one of the techniques taught in the course. I wondered whether it was genuine, or whether they were throwing each other clues." After taking Mind Dynamics herself, she changed her mind. "I saw something exciting in Werner, something that hadn't been there in Subud or Scientology, or anything else. When he began doing that course he really opened up.

"You know," she reflected, "when girls are growing up they hear that their young men will have to go out to work, and that once in a while—only once in a while—they will find a niche where they just fit in. This was finally happening to Werner."

PART III Transformation

Both speech and silence transgress.
   —Zen saying

*Now he understood it and realized that the inward voice had been
right, that no teacher could have brought him salvation. That was
why he had to go into the world, to lose himself in power, women and
money; that was why he had to be a merchant, a dice player, a
drinker and a man of property, until the priest and Samana in him
were dead. That was why he had to undergo those horrible years,
suffer nausea, learn the lesson of the madness of an empty, futile life
till the end, till he reached bitter despair, so that Siddhartha the
pleasure-monger and Siddhartha the man of property could die. He
had died and a new Siddhartha had awakened from his sleep. He also
would grow old and die. Siddhartha was transitory, all forms were
transitory, but today he was young, he was a child—the new
Siddhartha—and he was very happy.*
   —Hermann Hesse, Siddhartha

NINE True Identity

If one does not expect the unexpected one will not find it, for it is not reached by search or trail.
—Heraclitus.

Once you reach your True-nature, all evil bent of mind arising from karma extending over innumerable years past is instantly annihilated, like snow put into a roaring furnace.
—Bassui Tokusho Roshi

ONCE UPON A FREEWAY

On a midweek morning in March 1971, Werner Erhard walked casually to the car outside his home in Corte Madera, north of San Francisco. He was whistling a popular tune and thinking of the day before him. He planned to drive to his office, across the bay in San Francisco, where he was to lead a meeting of Grolier sales managers.

He was thirty-five years old now, and was growing a bit full at the waistline, but this was neatly concealed by his vest and tie. He took off his jacket, folded it, and laid it carefully on the seat. Then he walked to the front of the car. He was driving Ellen's black Mustang, and the fender had been crushed the day before, when someone backed into the car when she was shopping at the supermarket. He inspected the damage, kicked the fender lightly, and got into the car. He lit a cigarette, started the engine, and drove away toward the freeway.

Like many other commuters on that Marin County highway that morning, he was a pillar of the community, a successful businessman with a substantial income. Indeed, he now had two businesses— Grolier and Mind Dynamics. Unlike most other commuters, he had been pushed and pulled, buffed and polished, by several dozen disciplines, Eastern and Western, and was learned in both their theories and their practices. Although he did not yet know who he really was—and was meanwhile a sort of impostor—had he been asked about the Zen or Scientology accounts of Mind, he would have given a detailed and witty discourse about them.

There was not a trace about him of neurotic or destructive behavior. He emanated healthy confidence and good feeling. People brightened up in his presence. He was aggressive, charming, warm, supportive, and generous almost to a fault. A man of intense calm, he showed not a sign of resentment or guilt. He was a good organizer, an effective and rapid thinker. He was also a man of his word, respected and trusted by all his associates, with a devoted staff, several of whose members had been with him for years.

He was also a man of surprises. He lived, in a good-humored way, in a state of chronic potentiality. Never satisfied with what he had been or was, ever hopeful of the future, ever changing, ever growing, ever becoming more conscious, ever filling his human potential, he lived in a state of constant alteration. Not a saint in India would have been impressed.

Somewhere between Corte Madera and the Golden Gate Bridge, the man in the car on the freeway was transformed: the individual who emerged from the Mustang in San Francisco a half hour later was a different kind of being. Werner had had an extraordinary experience, and found what he had been searching for, in one discipline after another, for nearly eight years.

I met with him to ask him who, what, when, where, why, how.

"What happened? How did it happen?" Werner asked. "To relate the experience to time and place is to falsify it. It did not happen in time and space. Either I am inadequate to explain what happened or it simply cannot be explained in words. Or both. All my efforts to put it into words damage it.

"What happened had no form. It was timeless, unbounded, ineffable, beyond language. There were no words attached to it, no emotions or feelings, no attitudes, no bodily sensations. What came from it, of course, formed itself into feelings and emotions and words, and finally into an altered process of life itself. But that is like saying that the hole in the sand looks like the stick that you made the hole with. Holes in the sand and sticks are worlds apart. To put what happened into language would be like trying to describe a stick by telling you about the hole in the sand.

"Part of it was the realization that I knew nothing. I was aghast at that. For I had spent most of my life trying to learn things. I was sure that there was some one thing that I didn't know, and that if I could find it out, I would be all right. I was sure that there was a secret, and I was determined to find it.

"Then this happened—and I realized that I knew nothing. I realized that everything I knew was skewed toward some end. I saw that the fundamental skew to all knowledge, and to unenlightened mind, is survival, or, as I put it then, success. All my knowledge up to then had been skewed toward success, toward making it, toward self-realization, toward all the goals, from material to mystical.

"In the next instant—after I realized that I knew nothing—I realized that I knew everything. All the things that I had ever heard, and read, and all those hours of practice, suddenly fell into place. It was so stupidly, blindingly simple that I could not believe it. I saw that there were no hidden meanings, that everything was just the way that it is, and that I was already all right. All that knowledge that I had amassed just obscured the simplicity, the truth, the suchness, the thusness of it all.

"I saw that everything was going to be all right. It *was* all right; it always had been all right; it always would be all right—no matter what happened. I didn't just think this: suddenly I *knew* it. Not only was I no longer concerned about success; I was no longer even concerned about *achieving* satisfaction. *I was satisfied.* I was no longer concerned with my reputation; I was concerned only with the truth.

"I realized that I was not my emotions or thoughts. I was not my ideas, my intellect, my perceptions, my beliefs. I was not what I did or accomplished or achieved. Or hadn't achieved. I was not what I had done right—or what I had done wrong. I was not what I had been labeled—by myself or others. All these identifications cut me off from experience, from living. I was none of these.

"I was simply the space, the creator, the source of all that stuff. I experienced Self *as* Self in a direct and unmediated way. I didn't just experience Self; *I became Self.* Suddenly I held all the information, the content, in my life in a new way, from a new mode, a new context. I knew it from my experience and not from having learned it. It was an unmistakable recognition that I was, am, and always will be the source of my experience.

"Experience," Werner said, "is simply evidence that I am here. It is not who I am. I am *I am*. It is as if the Self is the projector, and everything else is the movie. Before the transformation, I could only recognize myself by seeing the movie. Now I saw that I am prior to or transcendent to all that.

"I no longer thought of myself as the person named Werner Erhard, the person who did all that stuff. I was no longer the one who had all the experiences I had as a child. I was not identified by my 'false identity' any more than by my 'true identity.' All identities were false.

"I suddenly saw myself on a level that had nothing to do with either Jack Rosenberg or Werner Erhard. I saw that everything is just the way it is—and the way it isn't. There was no longer any need to try to be Werner Erhard and try not to be Jack Rosenberg. Werner Erhard was a concept—just like Jack Rosenberg.

"Nor was I my Mind, patterned unconsciously, as it was, on identities taken over from my mother and father. I was whole and complete as I was, and I now could accept the whole truth about myself. For I was its source. I found enlightenment, truth, and true self all at once.

"I had reached the end. It was all over for Werner Erhard."

Was this enlightenment?

Werner sometimes calls it so, yet has expressed two reservations. First, the connotations of the word "enlightenment" suggest a kind of Eastern mysticism, whereas, as he puts it, "I don't require that context." Second, the transformation that he underwent was not in itself so much an *experience*, as a shift of the context in which he held all content and all process, including experience. Hence he sees what happened in 1963 as a "peak experience," and what happened in 1971 as a "transformation," and prefers not to use the word "enlightenment" at all.

THREE TASKS

Werner never reached the Grolier meeting that morning. He drove to Twin Peaks, overlooking San Francisco, and walked there for several hours, reflecting on what had happened and revising the training that he was doing in its light.

"That afternoon I saw that I had to do three things," he told me. "First, I had to share what had happened to me with others. I know that the idea of sharing such an experience puzzles some people, but that is because experiences of this sort are misunderstood. Having come to believe what is sometimes said about the ineffability of such experiences, people reach the conclusion that what cannot be described cannot be shared or communicated either. But it *can* be! You can't do this in the ordinary sense of communication: I can't have it and give it to you. But I can communicate in a way so that you get an opportunity to realize that you have it yourself already. Essentially, this is what the *est* training was developed to do. It provides a setting in which this kind of sharing takes place.

"Second, I saw that I had to take responsibility for my own ego, so that my transformation would not turn into just another ego trip. I had destroyed my previous experience by holding it incorrectly—by believing it and being righteous about it. I was concerned that I might do that again.

"What resolved this worry was realizing that it is ultimate ego to suppose that you can function without ego. I saw that I could let my ego be, and that when I did so, it would let me be. It would no longer impede me. Instead of my ego's running the show, I could run the show. It was a matter of my being willing to be at cause with my own ego, to hold it as something that belonged to me—not to resist or try to get rid of it, not to try to prove that I didn't have one, not fall into it, submit to it, or let it run me. Now this was a matter, in part, of taking responsibility for Jack Rosenberg and for Werner Erhard. It was all over for Werner Erhard. And yet now, for the first time, I could use that particular personality, Werner Erhard, as a means of expression, as a way to express the Self.

"That brings me to the third task that I saw for myself. To share what had happened to me, and to take responsibility for my ego, I had to confront and to take responsibility for those things that Jack Rosenberg and Werner Erhard had done from an untransformed space. I had to acknowledge those aspects of my life that came from lack of transformation. I had to 'clean up' my life. I had to acknowledge and correct the lies in my life. I saw that the lies that I told about others—my wanting my family, or Ellen, or anyone else, to be different from the way that they are—came from lies that I told about myself—my wanting to be different from the way that I was. All attachments come from lying about who you really are. When you don't have any real identity of your own—when you don't know who you really are—you will fault the identity of others. You won't grant beingness to others as they are."

ELLEN

Ellen was the first to notice the difference in Werner. "He suddenly gave up smoking," she told me. "At first I thought it was the 'get better' part of the usual 'get better, get worse, get better, get worse' syndrome. He was smoking three to five packs of cigarettes a day. A few years earlier he had stopped smoking for a month. It had been the worst month of my life. I actually encouraged him to start smoking again.

"This time, however, not only did the dreaded 'nerves' not materialize, but along with smoking he gave up coffee and sugar. He had been drinking twenty to thirty cups of coffee a day—with double cream and double sugar. He just lost the desire for dairy products. He also stopped using alcohol and there was a radical shift in his diet. He lost twenty pounds in two weeks, and his posture changed. Within a few months, years fell from his face.

"His insistence on being right and on using his wit and intellect to prove a point also mellowed," Ellen said. "He no longer dominated with his intelligence. He reached an amazing high state and seemed to have strange abilities.

"He was never mystical about this, although from time to time he seemed a little wistful, you know, as if he wanted to say, 'Here I could have been having a great time, and instead I had to find God!' Every now and then I saw him as wishing for a moment that he could go back.

"Then one evening he began to communicate with me again— perhaps for the first time. He sat down with me and told me about the affairs that he had had during the years of our marriage, and also about some other things that he had been keeping from me, including keeping a separate apartment and spending a lot of money I hadn't known about."

Werner confirmed what Ellen said. "I used to think I was stuck in my marriage," he said. "The lie that I had to remain with Ellen was held in place by my position that Werner Erhard could not break his word, and therefore had to stay with her—whatever the cost. After the transformation, it was obvious that *I* wasn't stuck with Ellen.

Only the position "Werner Erhard-the-man-of-his-word" was stuck with her. Once I saw that I was not that position, all the reasons and justifications for the marriage dissolved: they lost their solidity and their ability to dictate my feelings, points of view, and behavior. A choice appeared.

"The question became: Did I *choose* to be married to her? When I looked at that question, I found that I really *did* want to be married to this woman that I had been pretending to be stuck with for so long. It was appropriate for us to be married. I wanted to work out with her the form of a satisfying relationship of marriage and family. My God! How I loved being married and having my family!

"Having experienced the appropriateness of my marriage, all that was left was to clean up the mess that had been made from my un-transformed position. The first step was to communicate fully with Ellen, and to see how things were with her.

"I began by saying that there was no external justification for our being married—that the marriage had to stand on its own, to be complete within itself. I told her that I loved her and wanted to be married to her, and that I was willing to do what was needed to make the marriage work."

As they talked about their relationship, Werner and Ellen took note of the games—Werner calls them "rackets"—that they played with each other. Werner was the bad guy, and Ellen the victim. The worse Werner was, the righter Ellen became. "Ever since we left the East Coast together," Werner said, "she was dependent on me. She resisted her dependency by being righteous about my bad behavior—as if that made her less dependent.

"Our interlocking rackets produced great drama, as we justified our respective positions. They produced righteousness on both sides. The cost was the impoverishment of the marriage in terms of satisfaction and aliveness."

Several steps were necessary to transform the relationship. Ellen would have to give up playing victim and making Werner wrong. And she would have to be independent of him, so that she too could have a choice about the marriage. Werner undertook to support her financially and personally, whether the relationship continued or not. He took immediate steps to guarantee her financial independence. In September 1971, he started a new business—a cosmetic, vitamin, and food supplement distribution company—and turned it over to her. "Just as Werner intended," Ellen told me, "the success of that enterprise enabled me to experience my independence and ability. I saw that I could support myself financially, and could do things besides raising children and cleaning house." She managed the company successfully for the next three and a half years.

Werner had to get off his position too. "Hitherto I had been unwilling for Ellen to succeed as my wife. I set it up so that, in order to make it, she had to be what she wasn't. She had to look this way and do this, and not do that—all the things that she was not.

"If you look at the relationships around you, you see that few are nurturing. People are unwilling for others to make it with them as they are. For most of us, people don't seem to be complete as they are. They are not quite 'perfect'; they 'need' something. At best, people go along with one another. When we are unwilling to experience another person as perfect—as complete exactly the way he or she is—we are unable to experience satisfaction, love, or happiness in our relationship with that person. We have only the pale *concept* of love—instead of the nurturing, joyful, expansive *experience* of love.

"It took months for us to get through these barriers, and get straight about our marriage.

"As I confronted it, accepted it, allowed it, took responsibility for it, and created it, more of the barriers disappeared. As I expanded my experience of Ellen's all-rightness and became willing for her to make it as my wife, it became effortless to support her. She was all right. That meant that I could give her all kinds of power. And she gave it back. Now that Ellen did not perceive me as being bad to her, she could support me. From her support I had more power to give to her, and from my support she had more power to give to me. It spiraled up in a joyful, effortless spontaneity.

"Thus," Werner concluded, "we stopped righteously trying to figure out what was wrong with each other—what was whose fault, who was to blame for what, or even what was wrong with the marriage. We each took responsibility for the marriage by taking responsibility for ourselves in it."

As Werner worked through his relationship with Ellen, he shared the matter with his staff, and later with the graduates of the training. Now that he could accept the entire truth about himself, he could be known as he was, in his wholeness, to everyone. A mask— an "identity"—was no longer necessary.

Randy McNamara, who later became an *est* trainer, told me about this. "Werner would go into the seminars and would pour out the whole story of his past, and whatever was going on in his own life right then too. No matter how heavy or light—even when his relationship with Ellen was in a state of disaster. That opened people's eyes about their own relationships. You would sit there and be amazed. It wasn't really a seminar; Werner was doing his life with you. There were points in there where I thought he should just leave Ellen. But he was completing his relationship with her. He was transforming it in a way that served everyone who knew them."

Cleaning up his life, beginning with his relationship with Ellen, was only one of the "three tasks" that Werner saw for himself. Another was to share his transformation as widely as possible. The means to begin to do so seemed to be immediately at hand, in the format and platform provided by Mind Dynamics.

Yet Werner was uneasy about using Mind Dynamics classes to share the experience of transformation. "The discrepancy between what I was teaching and the Mind Dynamics syllabus grew enormous," he said. "Mind Dynamics was not the sharing of the opportunity to experience transformation for oneself. It was not a course *about* transformation. It was a well-presented package of useful techniques. So I became uneasy about continuing to work under its auspices. My experience, what I wanted to share with people, was not consistent with the structure, intention, and philosophy of the Mind Dynamics course."

From Werner's point of view, there were two main problems with Mind Dynamics: its attention to the Mind, and to mind programming; and its approach to physical ailments.

Charlene Afremow, who was Werner's own Mind Dynamics instructor, and who later became an *est* trainer-candidate, explained the first problem to me.

Charlene told me that the Mind Dynamics format was similar to that of *est:* the room was set up theatre style, around a podium and blackboard. Some superficial things were different. There was, for instance, more emphasis on transmission of information and on processes. Moreover, the information given was more technical, relating to brain waves, sleep processes, and different levels of consciousness.

"The important difference, however, was fundamental," Charlene said. "Mind Dynamics was chiefly directed to Mind programming and conditioning. It wired up the Mind, changed the Mind. It was Mind running Mind. Whereas the purpose of similar processes in *est* is to *unwire* the Mind, to decondition it, to dehypnotize the person. Techniques that address the Mind alone are for Werner only interimly valuable. If continued too long, they tend to strengthen the Mind—to validate mechanism and automaticity—and to kill off experience of the Self.

"Thus in Mind Dynamics you created more patterns and programs that you just had to handle later on. Whereas the *est* training aims to take things out of the Mind, to reduce its power, to avoid adding things to it. Werner is coming from a place beyond Mind, from Self, and from a conviction that the Self is able to act appropriately without benefit of patterns and programs."

A second important difference between Mind Dynamics and *est* had to do with the approach to physical ailments. Mind Dynamics course members, like those in Silva Mind Control, were taught to work "cases," along lines made famous by the psychic Edgar Cayce. The participants would go into a subjective or trance state—an Alpha state Alexander called it, referring to the brain wave that he claimed to be associated with this particular sort of trance state—and give a medical diagnosis of some named person who was not in the room and whom the participants had never met. "Cases" were the centerpiece of the Mind Dynamics training, and are a stunning combination of extrasensory perception, clairvoyance, and mind over matter at long distance! They are perhaps also, at least sometimes, an example of self-deception.

In not having cases in the *est* training, Werner expressed no disagreement in theory, but in practical policy. He concedes that Mind Dynamics "visualization" approaches to the diagnosis and treatment of physical ailments—whatever their explanation—may be effective. Nor does he object to qualified persons learning such techniques, and applying them to medical situations on their own responsibility.

What he was unwilling to do—and what he almost had to do while working within the Mind Dynamics format—was to engage in practical medicine or therapy. He was, as he put it, interested in something more important than "parlor games and medical tricks." He was concerned with an experience of transformation that would, by itself, benefit those who experienced it. He was unwilling to set himself up in tacit rivalry with medicine—as Mind Dynamics has been accused of doing; or to attack the medical and psychiatric professions—as Scientology had done in its early Dianetics days.

As a result of his approach, which physicians tended to understand and think responsible, a number of physicians began to enroll in the Mind Dynamics training under Werner, and many more have enrolled since the beginning of the *est* training.

One of the first doctors to take the Mind Dynamics training

under Werner was Robert Larzelere, a Berkeley internist affiliated with Alta Bates Hospital, formerly a member of the medical faculty of the University of California, San Francisco. He took the course in May 1971. By talking with Bob I was able to get some idea both of the excitement of the Mind Dynamics emphasis on medical "cases," and also some of the potential hazards.

"Before taking the training," Bob told me, "I was a conventional doctor. I had not been into disciplines of any sort. Even before signing up for the Mind Dynamics training, however, just on the basis of what I had heard, I realized how valuable it would be for my medical practice *if* it worked.

"I first saw a 'case' worked at the introductory lecture, which was held at the house in the Marina where Laurel and Elaine were living. There was a large beautiful living room there, and we sat around on cushions on the floor for the 'case' that Laurel and Gonneke announced that they would do. I decided to take for my turn a patient of mine, a young man who had had a thyroid cancer removed just three weeks earlier. He was of course not present. Laurel told Gonneke the first name of the man, and then Gonneke—with her eyes closed and waving her arms around as if she were feeling his body—came to what presumably would be the man's throat. Her fingers were extended and she stuck them into the little notch at the top of the breastbone and said, 'There's something missing here, that gland, what is it called? Oh, the thyroid. The thyroid is not there.'

"But that wasn't all," Bob said. "It got worse . . . or better. Gonneke continued to do the 'case,' and she said, 'It's not there, but I see it over here, outside the body. I see that it is green.' I said, 'Well, of course it's green. It's in a bottle of formaldehyde.' Gonneke got everything exactly right, and the only information that she had, which she got about a minute before she started, was the first name of the patient. I was the only person in the room who knew anything about him.

"After the training, I started to use this in my practice. I would close my eyes and make diagnoses before the patients came into my office. The funny thing is that I had been doing something like that all along. I just hadn't realized it. I'd always end up with just one diagnosis for any particular patient. I used to think that this was because of the history and the physical, and when I look back I see that that wasn't it at all. After taking the training, I could have dispensed with the history and the physical entirely, although of course I didn't, since that corroborated my diagnosis, and acted as a check.

"There are so many things that people don't know the cause of and why certain medications work and others don't," Bob reflected. "During the next year and a half my practice just got better and better. My patients noticed a dramatic change in the way that I practiced, and loved it, since for the first time they felt that they had a doctor who was paying attention to them."

I mentioned to Bob that he was of course telling me about Mind Dynamics, and remarked that 'cases' and medicine do not appear in the *est* training. I asked him why.

"Werner cut the medical stuff out of *est*," Bob said. "The use of cases stopped soon after he started *est*. It is all right for *me* to do these things. I am a qualified medical doctor. But it is unwise to give lay people the idea that they can treat their own illnesses. I don't doubt for a moment the value of the techniques. I have had too much direct experience with them. But anyone who is going to use them on himself ought to do so under the supervision of a medical doctor. One of the things that I responded to in Werner immediately is that he was clear about this. And then when he dropped Mind Dynamics and started *est*, the training got clear too."

STARTING THE est TRAINING

In mid-July of 1971, Werner announced to his staff that he was thinking of leaving Mind Dynamics and setting up a program of his own, and asked for advice. He pointed out the advantages, at least in the short run, of staying with Mind Dynamics. Alexander Everett had just offered him the vice-presidency of the organization, with a much larger income and a large measure of control over development of the course. The staff that he consulted—Laurel, Gonneke, Elaine, Jack Rafferty, and a few others—would have none of it. They strongly urged him to develop his own training.

The next step was to explore the legal and financial problems connected with that. Jack Rafferty, a former nightclub operator and television producer who had joined Werner's staff as a writer, put him in touch with the eminent and controversial tax attorney Harry Margolis, of Los Gatos, California. Margolis had become famous—and had earned the undying hatred of the Internal Revenue Service—by applying, in order to shelter the income of middle-class people, tax laws and international trust arrangements that had been passed by Congress in order to aid the very rich. The complicated—and ingenious—organizational set up for *est* that Margolis devised has been described in a detailed "Legal and Financial Statement" published by *est*.[1]

During the next two months a variety of alternative plans were canvased—whether to be profit or nonprofit, whether to organize as a church (which would have had substantial tax advantages and also skirted potential legal objections about medicine and therapy). Eventually *est* was incorporated as a profit-making educational corporation. Another key decision had to do with the market to which the training was to be directed. Three basic plans were reviewed. One was to direct it to executives who would pay a large fee for it, perhaps as much as $10,000. Another was to set up a franchise arrangement, similar to those being used by Mind Dynamics, Silva Mind Control, and other training groups. Another alternative, the one adopted, was to charge a small fee—initially $150—and aim the training to the maximum number of people.

Although Margolis and his firm handled legal and tax arrangements, Werner initially paid close attention to financial details. Ron Adolphson, one of Margolis's associates, who was responsible for the initial accounting system, described Werner as "one of the quickest minds for grasping financial information that I have come across." Werner found ordinary bookkeeping methods inadequate to report and reflect the state of the business in terms of cash flow, and devised graphs and charts to represent the kind of information that he needed to develop the organization. "By the time we left his office," Ron Adolphson said, "we were convinced that we had wasted our time in our professional education in accounting. We finally agreed that Werner's way of accounting was much simpler."

During the summer of 1971, Werner brought his arrangements with the Grolier Society to a close, timing his resignation in October 1971 with the first *est* training session.

In September he informed Alexander Everett that he would not continue as a Mind Dynamics instructor, and arranged to return all records and files to him. Everett's financial backer, William Penn Patrick, also backer of Holiday Magic, Leadership Dynamics Institute, and various other enterprises, made a last-minute attempt to persuade Werner to change his mind. The two men met privately for the first time, and Werner spent a day with Patrick. Despite considerable financial inducements, Werner declined to continue with Mind Dynamics. This was a fortunate decision. During the next six months massive legal actions were brought against Patrick. Holiday Magic was accused of illegal pyramiding schemes; Leadership Dynamics Institute was sued for sadistic practices. Legal actions and damage suits hit almost every organization with which Patrick had been associated, including Mind Dynamics. Patrick himself died in a plane crash in 1972, and Mind Dynamics, deprived of his financial support, collapsed in 1973.

In late September 1971, at the Mark Hopkins Hotel, Werner gave a final introductory lecture on behalf of Mind Dynamics. Two weeks later, at the Jack Tar Hotel, the first *est* guest seminar was held—with a thousand people in attendance. In October, the first *est* training was held.

Philosophy

TEN Philosophy

Culture places before each of us only one task: to promote the creation of the philosopher, of the artist, and of the saint within and without us and thus to contribute to the perfection of nature.
—Friedrich Nietzsche

A LADDER TO THE SELF

And so the *est* training was born. But how does it work? And what vision underlies it?

When he presents his own philosophical perspective, Werner loves to use an image from the writings of the philosopher Ludwig Wittgenstein. Wittgenstein spoke of philosophy as a ladder that one uses to climb.[1] The image is an ancient one in Western philosophy, going back to the Hellenistic Greek skeptic Sextus Empiricus. It has also been used in the yogic tradition.[2]

Werner's point is that you don't agree with or believe in a ladder. You climb it. And if it breaks you get a new one. Thus to treat his philosophical perspective as a system to be believed, or to be committed or attached to, is to miss its point. As he puts it: "The truth, believed, is a lie."[3]

The key to Werner's thought is the recognition of *Self*. As we have followed Werner's life, the notion of Self as true identity has emerged again and again, almost as a motif. Thus we already know a little bit about it. We know, for instance, that there is nothing personal about Self: that it is misleading to speak of *my* Self. The Self is beyond any individual, identification, form, process, or position—and gives rise to them. Nor is the Self "conscience" or (as in Scientology) some immortal spirit that resides within individuals. No position, the Self is the space or context in which all positionality in life occurs. No thing, the Self is the space of things. It contains the "screen of life" but never appears upon it. The Self, as Werner prefers to put it, is *the context of all contexts.*

It is after transformation that one recognizes the Self as that which one really is. One then "comes from" the Self. One's "ground of being" has been shifted from Mind to Self. No longer identifying oneself as this or that, one no longer comes into life as a personality, ego, or mind. Rather than having an identity, one is the space of identities. One is now complete—and from that state, natural creativity, vitality, happiness, true self-expression, all arise spontaneously.

PROTEUS/CHAMELEON/GOD/MOTHER

To recognize the Self as "who one is" is to take a distinctly non-Western approach to the problem of individual identity. This problem has been a major theme of Western sociology and psychology during the past several decades, particularly under the influence of the brilliant work of Erik H. Erikson and his followers.[4]

The most common Western approach to identity is to prize clear and defined identification, and to treat indefiniteness or diffuseness in identification as a serious problem that may lead to character disorder.[5] From this, it is but a short step to bemoan the "identity crises"—the vagueness, indefiniteness, confusion—that reign in the chief Western sources of identity and commitment, in particular, in the Western religions. What is "generally lacking," as Kierkegaard insisted more than a hundred years ago, is a "decisive categorical definition" for a situation in which "one does not know and cannot make out whether one is situated in paganism, whether the parson is a missionary in that sense, or whereabouts one is."[6] "Who can tell what vagary or what compromise may not be calling itself Christianity?", George Santayana asked more than sixty years ago. "A bishop may be a modernist, a chemist may be a mystical theologian, a psychologist may be a believer in ghosts." Santayana was observing, not complaining. After, all, he described himself as both an atheist and a Roman Catholic. What Santayana believes, someone jibed, is that "there is no God, and Mary is His Mother."

The most important traditional sources of identity thus themselves partake of the general confusion. Traditions not only have been evolving but have been going through agonizing self-analysis and have emerged lacking an inner core. Thus the man who now tries to acquire a character or a cause by identifying himself, through commitment, with a particular tradition often exchanges his "I am confused" for an "I am a member of a confused tradition." Doubtless he may gain thereby, at least temporarily, in personal happiness: now he has a name; he can at least say what he is. But he cannot so easily explain what it is to be what he is, not so much because he does not know as because no one knows, or because everyone has a different answer.[7]

In identifying the Self—the context of all contexts—as the source of individual identity, Werner steps outside this entire discussion. Commitments, belief systems, ideologies, traditions, identifications, and so-called "ultimate values" provide contexts—often valuable contexts—for individual existence; but these are not who one is; and it makes no sense to be attached or committed to such things. The Self, being the context of all contexts, is the context in which such things as commitments, identifications, and ideologies emerge, flourish for a time, and then decline, as do those things that are misnamed "ultimate" values. Thus one is the context in which content is crystallized and process occurs, and is not any individual content or process, not any individual form. Here there is a profound sense of the limitation inherent in all form. Here identity as fixed identification is seen as a liability: the more fixed one's identity, the less experience of which one is capable. The point is not to *lack* a position, but not to be positional: not to be attached or committed to whatever position one does have at any particular moment. One *is*—one experiences "aliveness"—to the extent to which one can transcend particular positions and can assume other viewpoints; to the extent to which one can create and be the space for other viewpoints to exist.

Part of this is, of course, in the spirit of traditional Western critical philosophy. One contemporary philosopher, Friedrich Waismann, of Oxford, put it this way: "A philosophy is an attempt to unfreeze habits of thinking, to replace them by less stiff and restricting ones. . . . Philosophy is criticizing, dissolving and stepping over *all* prejudices, loosening all rigid and constricting moulds of thought." Professor John Wisdom, of Cambridge, writes of the way in which the philosopher brings certain models that we use into the light. "He does this," Wisdom states, "so that he may control them instead of their controlling us. . . . Anyone who reflects upon people and tries to come at the truth does in some degree the same thing."[8]

Nonetheless, despite such intentions, Western terminologies provide little assistance in characterizing this state. It is not *skepticism* — which rejects all attempts at knowing, all formulations, all definitions, all crystallizations, all identifications, including any definition of its own position. Nor is it what seems at first blush to be the opposite of skepticism, and what is in fact its closest relation, *credulity*, which accepts all things, however contradictory, as vessels of the truth; which, regarding everything as holy, yet takes nothing seriously. It is closer to the *fallibilism* of Xenophanes or, in a modern dress, of C. S. Peirce and Karl Popper. This allows for the fallibility, the distortion of all forms, of all existing crystallizations in language, and yet maintains that one may, through form, through language, attain closer to the truth, measuring one's progress through . . . fallible criteria.

Nor does Werner's perspective *quite* embrace—although it again approaches—the protean sensibility that both Hermann Hesse and Hermann Keyserling found in Hindu thought, writing of the "supple individual" of infinitely polymorphous plasticity, who "gains profundity from every metamorphosis." As Keyserling's protean figure—in the course of trying out different forms and experiences—discovers how limited every form and experience are, and how one is linked to another, "the centre of his consciousness gradually sinks to the bottom where Being truly dwells." Once one has cast anchor there, there is little danger of placing an exaggerated value on any single form or phenomenon. Personality and character, being forms, also imply limitation. "No developed individual," Keyserling says, "can reverence 'personality' as an ideal; he is beyond prejudices, principles and dogmas." Such a supple individual, though perceived to be without character, may be as securely and firmly positive as any rigid individual. This is not the confused and disordered state of someone in the throes of an "identity crisis." The yogi says "neti, neti: I am not that," to all nature, until he becomes one with Parabrahma. "After that," as Keyserling says, "he denies nothing, he affirms everything . . . because no manifestation limits him any more, because now each one is an obedient means of expression to him. . . . A God lives thus from the beginning, by virtue of his nature. Man slowly approaches the same condition by passing through the whole range of experience."[9]

Although Werner's perspective approaches this particular formulation of Keyserling, it yet escapes the negative connotations of "protean." For Proteus, the Greek sea god, "the old man of the sea," not only had the power to assume any form he wished; he was also as "capricious as the sea itself."[10] And capriciousness—the capriciousness that one also finds in some Hindu accounts—is no part of Werner's perspective. Nor, to consider and then discard yet another metaphor, is Werner's perspective that of the *chameleon*. For such lightning-change artistry is a superficial sort of suppleness, skin-deep, for which the chameleon's characteristic very slow power of locomotion is itself a metaphor.

What Werner does do, in pointing to the Self, is to invite people to become philosophers. He has said: "Our culture does not encourage people to be philosophers, and this is perhaps the most devastating denial of freedom in our lives. My own aim is to open to people, through 'philosophical reflection,' a mastery of the philosophical contexts, the ground of being, the presuppositions and models, from which their lives spring. This in turn opens mastery of life. A master is for me someone who has realized his or her own philosophical context, and who transcends his or her attachments in any particular area." In speaking of "attachment," Werner uses an Eastern terminology for what many Western writers call "commitment." "When I speak of 'attachment,'" he says, "I designate the sine wave 'submission/resistance.' When you submit to something, or resist something, or hate something, or identify with something, you are attached to it."

The Self, for Werner, being the context of all contexts, is then the unsubmitting, unresisting, unformed matrix in which all forms, all processes, all metaphors occur. Who is one really? One is the context of all contexts, the *matrix*, the *mater*, . . . the *mother*. Dorothy, the mother, is still here, but in a transfigured form.

THE MIND STATE

Most people exist not in a state of Self but in a "fallen" or untransformed state: a state of Mind. This is a tragic state in which, as Werner sees it, people consider themselves *not* as the matrix, but as one of the things created in that matrix.

"Mind" is Werner's way of designating the entire cybernetic system of any individual, including conscious as well as unconscious processes, operating without reference to Self. Werner's account of Self resonates with a number of traditions in philosophy and religion, coming closest, perhaps, to the Buddhist account of Atman. Similarly, his account of Mind overlaps with various psychologies. Like all psychologies—as in Freud's account of the superego, the ego, and the id, and in Jung's account of archetypes—Werner's psychology is a hypothesis couched in metaphor. In Werner's case, the chief sources of metaphor for Mind are to be found in machinery.

What is the Mind for him?

The Mind is an automated warehouse of burdened, encumbered memories. It is a linear arrangement of complete multisensory records of successive moments (memory records), and operates according to a simple and undiscriminating system of logic that associates—even identifies—things that are in fact quite different. The Mind is a device whose purpose or, more accurately, design function is to ensure the survival of oneself or of anything that one identifies with oneself. "Survival," in the sense intended, goes beyond physical survival. It includes the survival of one's ideas, opinions, and self-conceptions, and thus results in being right and making others wrong, dominating and avoiding domination, justifying oneself and invalidating others.

To accomplish its purpose, the Mind scrupulously records those experiences that are necessary for survival. Experiences containing a real or imagined threat to survival successfully met are those deemed necessary for survival. Among the latter are those records containing pain and unconsciousness; loss or shock associated with emotional stress; and unwitting reminders of earlier records containing pain, shock, or loss. The most powerful of these records usually relate to one's parents, and originate in the first few years of life.

Whenever the present environment resembles *in any way* some such painful or stressful memory, whenever one encounters a situation that one *perceives* as threatening to survival—one in which one might lose, be made wrong, be dominated, be invalidated—the past memories are reactivated, called into play in an undiscriminating way, as "guides" to the avoidance of pain and threat. They exert a total command over behavior in the present, controlling body sensations, facial expression, posture, thinking, emotions, appearance, fantasies, attitudes, states of mind, everything. Since the Mind operates according to a logic of identification wherein everything resembles everything else, resemblances are everywhere: painful and stressful images from the past are reactivated continuously. Thus they permeate the present, whether the "resemblance" in question is relevant or not. Hardly any circumstance does not resemble in *some* way some previous painful circumstance. Everyone is hence in a state of upset all the time.

Illustrations of such mechanisms in practice are readily available.

One example concerns a youth who began to suffer during high school from a debilitating reaction. Whenever he was in small classes or seminars, he found himself overcome by what appeared to be a strange shyness. A question would be asked; he would know the answer; but just when he was about to raise his hand to answer it, his mind would go blank. Ordinary attempts to treat this as a case of shyness, however, did not work. For he was not shy in most situations. He had no difficulty in talking with one or two persons; and he did not suffer from stage fright when addressing a large group. Only the small seminar or class situation triggered his "neurosis."

Then, one day, he remembered an incident from his childhood. When he was five years old, he had attended the birthday party of his favorite cousin, a three-year-old girl. The children were seated in a circle in the middle of the living room, with the adults standing behind them. In the center of the circle was a pile of presents. Seated there was the little cousin, opening them one by one. In one package she found a complicated toy, which she could not figure out. The boy, however, knew how to make it work; and he darted into the center of the circle, saying "I can do it!" At this, his mother grabbed him and pulled him back—and everyone laughed.

Some fourteen years later, when he remembered this incident, and connected it with his disability, the shyness disappeared completely. *Immediately*, he was able to participate in seminars with ease. The mind-mechanism here is easy to understand: whenever he met a life situation—such as a small seminar or class—that resembled, however superficially, the painful image from the past, he was prevented from initiating the kind of behavior that had previously caused him pain: he was prevented from "entering the circle" and answering the question. The fact that the later situations were usually non-threatening was irrelevant as far as the mind-mechanism was concerned. What determined his behavior was the *spurious* resemblance between the size of the earlier group and the size of the later groups. Such is undiscriminating thought by identification—in which "everything is like everything else."

Another example illustrates how complicated this type of mechanism can get. It concerns a small boy named Christopher, and is divided into two parts, or episodes.[11]

The first occurs when Christopher is eight years old, early in the first morning following the end of his Christmas holiday. We find him lying slumbering in bed, sleeping late, as he had done on many mornings during the holiday. Suddenly he is abruptly and painfully awakened: his mother yanks him out of bed, and spanks him. She had been calling him repeatedly to rise, to wash and dress, and prepare for school. But he had not heard; he had slept on; he was still on holiday. Less than an hour later, on the way to school, trudging through the snow with his little sister, Mary, five years old, whom he had to guide to and from school each day, he begins to cross-examine her about their mother. "Do you like Mommy?" Christopher asks repeatedly. "Don't you hate her?" Sister protests her love of her mother; but Christopher is stubborn and persuasive—and he promises not to tell. Eventually, as they near school, Mary submits, and agrees that she does hate their mother. That evening, after returning home from school, Christopher takes aside his mother to tell her: "Mommy, Mary told me that she hates you." And then mother spanks Mary.

The second episode takes place about eighteen months later, in the summer, when Christopher is nine years old. His mother being devoutly religious, he is sent regularly to church. But he is a precocious lad and has begun to doubt the stories of God and Jesus. We find him sitting on the porch of his family's house, in the warm summer evening, talking with his father. "Daddy," he asks, "was there really a Jesus? Did all those miracles really happen?" His father replies in a reasonable way: "Well, we don't really know; they may have—but perhaps not." Christopher turns away almost immediately, goes inside to his mother, and reports accusingly: "Mommy, Daddy says there wasn't any Jesus." There follows a heated quarrel between Christopher's parents, one which his father, as usual, lost.

We can hardly begin to explore the nuances in the report of these two episodes. But it is obvious what pattern is present in both these stories about a clever wicked little good boy who had not the slightest idea what he was doing, and yet at the same time in a sense may have known very well what he was doing.

In the first episode Christopher had felt himself wrongfully punished. Certainly he was: mother could have gently roused him and sent him off to school while commiserating over the end of the school holiday. But we do not know how things were with her. Perhaps she was under extreme pressure of her own. Christopher was, at any rate, furious. His fury expressed itself as hate for his mother—and perhaps for all things feminine: his sister, school, his teachers, his having to care for his sister on the way to school. But Christopher also loved his mother; and he knew from his religious and moral training that one ought only to love one's mother. He could not openly express hostility toward his mother, and yet he could not bear *not* to have it expressed. So he virtually forced his little sister—only five years old and hardly aware of what was happening—to express, to *voice*, the evil sentiment. And then Christopher promptly saw to it that the crime was punished: he tattled on his sister, and saw her suffer the same punishment, spanking, that he had earlier endured.

The pattern is the same in the second episode. Christopher was unable or unwilling to express his forbidden doubts about religious teachings; he probably suspected that his father also harbored such doubts; and so, in a man-to-man talk, he tricked his father into voicing the forbidden doubts. Once again, Christopher saw to it that the crime was punished: his father was spanked verbally by his mother and stalked off in despair to the neighborhood saloon, perhaps thereby corroborating his wickedness in his son's eyes. In this extraordinary way Christopher's religious doubts were laid quietly, but devilishly, to sleep, not to be wakened again for nearly a decade, at which time he was thrust into a neurosis.

If one disapproves of Christopher's behavior, at the same time one need not hide a certain admiration for the skillful way in which he was able to manipulate his social environment. One of the chief reasons for this, of course, was the predictability of the mother. When we take a closer look at that, we find it to consist largely in a certain rigidity—doubtless partly due to and reinforced by the dogmatic moral maxims that she used as magic charms, as it were, to deal with her own environment. Christopher seems to have been able to predict, almost to the detail, the sorts of actions she would take in response to the information that he fed her. She did not question his reports; she did not inquire how these issues—Mary's suddenly voiced hate for her or her husband's religious skepticism—had been raised. When her code appeared to have been violated, she did not pause to make inquiries; she sought revenge. The life of his family appears to have revolved around Christopher in a curious way. He used the members of his family to commit the crimes he himself would like to have committed, and then called on his mother to bring down God's wrath on the criminals. He could do this only because he could trust that she would not examine the situation but would blindly defend her moral magic. He was a puppet using a puppet.

These two examples differ; yet each illustrates how preserving a position or identification can cut one off from experience and growth. For example, as long as the shyness mechanism worked, the young man was cut off from normal participation in his school classes. Christopher's patterned behavior cut him off from the healthy experience of expressing his hostility toward his mother, and ultimately soured his expressions of love for her; and it prevented him from experiencing the doubt inherent in sincere religious commitment, causing him to carry into adulthood a barely developed, quite childish form of faith.

No one is immune to such Mind mechanisms. But they can be "caught in the act" when one becomes sensitive to them. A story that Werner tells about his younger son, St. John, illustrates how this can be done.

"I took my son St. John to Hawaii with me for a couple of days last year," Werner told me. "That was a treat for me, because I don't get to spend as much time with him as I'd like. One of the things we did was to go sailing in a little boat with a lot of sail on it. It was a sixteen-foot catamaran with an oversize sail area. When you sail in such a boat, it doesn't ride flat in the water. It rides way up on its side. So you don't get to sit on the deck. You get to sit on the edge.

"Of course Hawaii is out in the middle of the ocean. When you get a little way offshore there, you are literally out in the middle of the ocean. The little boat goes up and down, the waves are very high, you get down in the troughs, and it looks like there is nothing but blue water anywhere. On that day there were twenty-five-knot winds and swells of six or seven feet.

"St. John was very frightened.

"St. John already, of course, knew the facts of the situation. I had already explained to him that the boat is not likely to tip over, and that, in case it does, the boat floats anyhow and we are wearing life jackets. But reassurances and explanations are not always enough to quieten fear.

"When we got way offshore he started to talk incessantly. He kept going on: 'Why don't we turn around and go back?' And 'I think we're out far enough. And besides that, I think that the mast is going to break, and the rope is falling down.' Or, 'I looked and there's a cloud up there and it's getting bigger and I'm shaking a lot, don't you think?' And 'I think we ought to turn around now and go the other way.'

"You know, he had it on automatic.

"So I said, 'Son, if you're frightened, you don't need to hide that. If you're afraid, it's all right to let me know that you're afraid. You don't need to go through that whole racket in order to hide the fact that you're afraid.' And he said: 'Yeah, I'm scared!'

"Now he sat there and was able to experience the fear. He was in fact frightened. But he did stop talking. He no longer had to hide the fear with his talk. So he could be quiet, and he was.

"When we got back in the hotel room and I was in the shower, he stood on the countertop looking over the shower door talking to me. And I asked him what he thought he ought to do about being frightened. How do you handle fear in life? How was he going to handle his being afraid in a sailboat?

"He had a very good idea about that. He said that what he was going to do was just not go sailing anymore. The logic of this was overpowering. I remarked that what you can do is to avoid all the things that are uncomfortable in life as a way of getting around being uncomfortable. You can set a high value on being comfortable. That is a solution, there's no question about it. I told him that that was the solution that most people took. For the most part, people get down in one little corner of the boat of life and play down in that corner, where it is nice and safe and where they are protected from all discomfort and all fear and all harm. And they are truly survivors.

"They even look good, because they are always dealing with something as totally familiar to them, as something that they can handle.

"I told St. John that it was possible to do that. The only problem with that is that you never get to the true joy in life. Life gets more and more stuck. Eventually, you make up really horrendous problems in order to have some variety in life. You know, you might get deathly ill or have some tragic accident.

"So my son thought that over for a while. I asked him whether he could think of any other way to overcome his fear of sailing.

"Then he came up with the idea that he could overcome his fear of sailing by being afraid of sailing. At that point he literally got excited about going sailing and being frightened the next day. He actually looked forward to being frightened, because he knew he had discovered for himself that the way you overcome being afraid of sailing—so that you can have the fun that he knew was out there—is by experiencing the fear. My son chose to expand rather than to contract.

"That is the whole story about self-discipline. If you are, say, afraid, the point is *not* to rub your nose in it, to inure yourself to it, to get used to it, or even to overcome it. The point is *not* to jam it down or suppress it. Rather, the point is *to choose to be uncomfortable* in order to allow being uncomfortable to be. When you let something be, it lets you be. That way, you attain mastery.

"What stands in the way of this is only your point of view. Your point of view is the point from which you view—which you therefore do not see. Your point of view is positional, and to get off it, to leave it behind, is always uncomfortable and frequently terrifying."

TO EGO

In these three examples, it seems that the uncorrected cybernetic machinery—the Mind—does not in fact serve one's own interests.

Unless, . . . *unless one is one's Mind!*

Which brings to the fore Werner's next remark about Mind.

People tend to succumb to their Minds. Or they simply *become* their Minds in the sense that they identify themselves with the cybernetic machinery. From this error "ego" arises and Self disappears, ushering in conditions and disorders that impoverish even a successful life. "Ego" Werner defines as the functioning of one's point of view in the attempt to cause that point of view to survive. For Werner, the verb "to ego" means "to perpetuate one's own point of view."

The purpose or design function of the Mind, as stated earlier, is the survival of oneself *or of anything that one considers oneself to be*. When one considers oneself to be one's Mind, then Mind perpetuates all the identifications that happen to pertain to that particular Mind.

What are some examples of things with which people readily identify?

I am my job résumé.

I am the soap opera behind that job résumé.

I am what I have.

I am what I have done.

I am as I appear to others.

I am what I eat.

I am my physical appearance.

I am my body.

I am my social and economic circumstances.

I am my sex life.

I am my hopes.

I am my aspirations.

I am my commitments.

I am my affiliations and memberships.

I am my education.

I am my resentments.

I am what I might have.

I am what I might do.
I am my original ideas.
I am what I can do.
I am my future.
I am my house, my territory, and my teddy bear.
I am what I have thought.
I am my philosophy.
I am what I have felt.
I am the enemy of my enemies.
I am my good deeds.
I am my sins.

Acting by reference to such identifications, such specific contents, the Mind proceeds to make itself right and others wrong, dominate and avoid being dominated, justify itself and invalidate others. It must behave this way because two opposing viewpoints cannot both be right: even the possibility of the rightness of another viewpoint is a threat to the survival of one's own. Once the individual identifies with his Mind, he becomes—to the extent of the identification—no more than a machine for fending off threats.

Here is a story that illustrates the absurd extremes to which such identifications may be taken. It concerns a misunderstood genius. Its hero had an old-fashioned upbringing during which he was deeply imbued with, and passionately believed in, the doctrines of God, the devil, and everlasting life. On reaching college, he was exposed to the glare of contemporary skepticism, and, after abandoning these doctrines, became a thinker. By luck or fate he was an original thinker: in a short space of time he solved several problems widely regarded as insoluble. But he suffered a fate common to great thinkers: those who encountered his thinking first thought his views absurd, then deemed them obvious and trivial, and finally said that not only were his views correct and important, but that they had discovered them themselves, *first*.[12]

Our hero was relatively indifferent to those who viewed his ideas as absurd, but twisted in agony both when people acclaimed his ideas *and* got them wrong, and when people stole them. (Occasionally the two categories overlapped.) Feeling misunderstood and misused and unappreciated, in retaliation as it were, he stopped publishing his ideas and, insofar as that was within his power, he stopped thinking. Just to show his enemies (those who failed to understand him or who stole his ideas) that he was still around, he published books on dead thinkers from time to time, as well as beautifully composed essays on topics in which he had no interest. These were widely and accurately perceived as tours de force.

But most of his time and his energies and his fantasies were devoted to his *filing cabinets*. For this man kept all his notes, and early manuscripts, and his voluminous correspondence, and bits and pieces of all sorts of things in rows of filing cabinets. For, he reasoned, it was important that the whole story of his life be *there:* the misunderstandings, the thievery, everything. Why? Obviously so that some researcher a hundred years hence would understand the importance of his work and how sadly he had been misused by his contemporaries. The future would justify him! His role in the present was to prepare for posthumous understanding. And so he led the provisional life.[13]

The unremitting, unredeemed folly of this case is obvious. Its hero is spellbound by a picture that has tremendous command value over his life, a picture of which he is, as Werner would put it, the effect. It is a crude and pathetic picture, a cardboard illusion, as if he would one day attain a surrogate recognition and immortality in the mind of some future Ph.D. candidate and would be more lively there and then than here and now. His present existence is enslaved to his *identification* with the records in his filing cabinets.

What a pity that this talented fool did not confront, did not fully experience, his own mortality. Had he looked death in the face, he would perhaps for the first time have experienced life.

Such identifications create what may be called "life programs." A life program, like a research program in the sciences, identifies priorities: it indicates where attention is to be focused, where energy is to be channeled, which kinds of behavior are to be endorsed, which are to be excluded. This is what a position fundamentally is. This particular life program commands that present existence be subordinated, even sacrificed, to a specific fantasy picture. Our hero has truly *identified* with his fantasy image; all his behavior blindly serves it. That image must be perpetuated at *any* cost: *it* must survive. And the entire setting is soaked in resentment, regret, and righteousness. Easily vanquished by the real or imagined rebuffs of his contemporaries, resentful of their lack of applause, salvaging in the present only his feelings of righteous disdain for them, he visualizes a future in which he shall be revenged by his triumph, and they shall be plunged into oblivion. Abandoning communication with his contemporaries, he stakes all on the applause of posterity. His life program sticks him in the past and in the future: he lives always and everywhere except here and now.

In examples like these, there emerges a contrast that is at the heart of Werner's perspective: survival or perpetuation of positionality *versus* wholeness, completion, and experience. Perpetuating one's position, however it may manifest itself—as self-image, ideology, fantasy, whatever—is the essence of the Mind state and the source of all dissatisfaction in life. The danger of the Mind state lies in its furthering precisely that which denies the state of Self. Whereas the Self detaches from and transcends any particular position, it is in the nature of the Mind state to be attached. The Mind fastens on to particular positions and attempts to perpetuate them. Whereas, in the state of Self, one knows naturally and acts appropriately; knowing and acting originating in the Mind—while always "reasonable"—are nonetheless irrational. For such knowing and acting must be consistent with those conceptual systems—embedded in explanations, rationalizations, and justifications—into which the Mind is arranged, to which it is thus committed, and which thus bar the way to true knowing and appropriate action.

By the same token, one cannot be free in the Mind state. One is at the mercy of the attachments that control and define Mind. In particular, one is the prisoner of one's past. The past has no power save through the Mind: there *is* no past—i.e., there are no accumulated attachments, convictions, commitments, beliefs, images of self, unconscious pictures of what has, will, or is supposed to happen—save through the Mind.

Unaware of Mind's effect in patterning and enslaving their lives, people live in a state of waking sleep, in a state of enchantment, of mesmerism, most of the time. Every day, in every way, they become more and more the way they have always been. The normal Mind state of consciousness is thus of an exceedingly low level. Far from acting freely, people in this state "just go off." They *ego*.

THE ECOLOGY OF TRANSFORMATION

In the course of articulating Werner's basic theory of Self and Mind, the fundamental existential and practical problem has become apparent. The state of Mind, which is the state in which most people live, is intrinsically unsatisfying; whereas the state of Self, an intrinsically satisfying state, is inhabited by few individuals, yet is a possibility for everyone. The problem is to propel one from Mind to Self. How is the transition from one state to the other—what Werner calls *transformation*—to be achieved?

Most approaches to the problem, most disciplines—including

psycho-cybernetics and Mind Dynamics—as well as most programs of social reform, fall prey to a fundamental error. They attempt to achieve satisfaction merely through *change in conditions and circumstances*, i.e., rearrangement of the stuff of the Mind state. They attempt to alter self-image, or to implant new psychological programs and patterns, or—in the case of social reform—to institute new governmental arrangements. Such approaches, admirable as they may be in rearranging the Mind state in worthy ways, cannot solve the problem and even miss the point. Falling short, absolutely, of transformation, they fail to produce satisfaction. *For the Mind state as such, not individual programs, conditions, and circumstances within it, lies at the root of dissatisfaction.* Only by transcending the Mind, in all its manifestations, and by acknowledging the Self as the source of who one is, can dissatisfaction be vanquished and wholeness be attained.

Yet if transformation is not to be attained through change, how can it be reached? Another way that will *not* work is, obviously, through reading about it—as in this chapter. In fact, *no* discipline or route leads without fail to the Self.

The problem here is akin, in more ways than one, to the biological problem of *emergence*, where the new state or life form is not merely a rearrangement of the components of the old, not merely a sum of its parts, but a state in which something genuinely new appears, a state in which *something comes from nothing.* [14]

Although one cannot produce, by recipe, conditions *sufficient* to produce a biological mutant, a transformed individual, one can perhaps identify and create *necessary* conditions that create space for such a mutant. *Here we reach a fundamentally ecological question: a question of the ecology of transformation.* What conditions foster and inspire transformation? What kind of econiche does one need, i.e., what are the personal, relational, and institutional conditions for transcending positionality and ego in all their forms? How are our lives and institutions to be arranged so as to expose beliefs, policies, positions, traditions to maximum examination? What are the social, economic, environmental, cultural, psychological, and philosophical conditions that best inspire the growth and development of consciousness and the creation of transformation, which deter man from becoming stuck in his belief systems, attachments and commitments, and from thus stunting his powers of exploration and discovery? [15]

It is as a contribution to such problems in the ecology of transformation that the *est* training and program, both on the individual and the social level, are conceived. The *est* training seeks to create the conditions under which individual transformation can occur; and the *est* graduate program and social programs seek to create the conditions under which individual transformation can manifest and express itself and in which transformed relationships and social institutions can be created. Something akin to the *est* experience would have to be part of any ecological niche in which transformation were possible and consciousness could thrive.

Training

ELEVEN Training

I tame every bear. I make even buffoons behave.
   —Friedrich Nietzsche

THE TRAINING
The *est* Standard Training, which Werner began to present in October 1971, creates an econiche for transformation on an individual level.

What is the Standard Training?

Many accounts of its details and circumstances have been published. The best of these is the novelist Luke Rhinehart's dramatic recreation of it in *The Book of est.*[1] My aim here is not to duplicate what has been done, but to give an account of the structure of the training, and to relate it to the philosophical ideas supporting it.

The *est* Standard Training is a new form of participatory theatre that incorporates Socratic method: the artful interrogation that is midwife at the birth of consciousness.

Like most drama, it has catharsis as one of its aims. Unlike most drama, it also aims to bring the participant to an experience of him or herself which is tantamount to transformation.

It is *not* the purpose of the training—although it is often misunderstood to be its purpose—to bring the trainee to a single "high" experience. Although people frequently do have peak experiences in the course of the training, the aim is not to produce some such experience for its own sake, but to *transform the trainee's ability to experience* so that he encounters all of living in an expanded way. Such a transformation is a contextual shift, from a deficiency orientation to a sufficiency orientation, "from a state in which the content in your life is organized around the attempt to get satisfied or to survive . . . to an experience of *being* satisfied, right now, and organizing the content of your life as an expression, manifestation and sharing of the experience of being satisfied, of being whole and complete, now."[2] Such a transformation may be crystallized in an instant, but it is not necessary for this to happen.

What the training does promise is that after such an experience—after the encounter with the Self—life is transformed in the sense that it becomes the process of freeing oneself from the past, rather than enmeshing oneself more deeply in it. Patterns and problems continue to appear; but instead of acting them out, dramatizing them, one begins to experience them—and eventually to "experience them out." As will become apparent in the next chapter, Werner's own life story provides an example of this process. And his story about sailing with his son also illustrates what happens. Prior to experiencing, and thereby transcending, his fear, St. John was imprisoned *within* it: he had no alternative but to express it mechanically. By noticing, and thereby stepping outside it, he could begin to watch it come up, and play itself out, from a vantage point beyond it. This is what is involved in what Werner calls "experiencing" a pattern. It is one thing to be the prisoner or captive of an ordinary automatic fear-reaction pattern; it is quite another thing to watch fear arise from a context in which the fear pattern itself has been transcended.

How is this transformation of the ability to experience accomplished?

The training provides a format in which siege is mounted on the Mind. It is intended to identify and bring under examination presuppositions and entrenched positionality. It aims to press one beyond one's point of view, at least momentarily, into a perspective from which one observes one's own positionality. Teaching no new belief, it aims to break up the existing "wiring of the Mind," and thereby to trap the Mind, to allow one to take hold of one's own Mind, to blow the Mind. Such tactics create the conditions into which Self can be revealed, into which transformation can occur, into which a mutant of higher consciousness can be born.

The setting for the training is arduous and its style is irreverent and intrusive.[3] There is *a* way to do things, a way that is not bent to the personalities or acts—the Minds—of the participants. As Werner puts it, "Your Mind can't get sympathy from this environment." In the training, ordinary ways to escape confronting one's experience are—with the agreement of the participants—sealed off in advance. On the concrete level this means limited access to food, water, toilets, bed. Alcohol and drugs are forbidden. There is limited movement; there are no clocks or watches by which to tell the time; one may not talk with others; nor may one sit beside friends. Internal crutches and barriers to experience—such as one's own belief systems—are also challenged by means of philosophical lectures and exercises in imagination.

No matter which trainer is leading it, the external form of the training remains the same. The trainer is a performer, leading trainees through it in a firmly set and artfully designed order. The dramatic integrity of the training is in part dependent on suspense and surprise, and on the juxtaposition of levels that is the essence of both humor and discovery. But like any good theatre, knowing the plot doesn't ruin the performance.

Within this setting, three different kinds of things take place. First, there are presentations by the trainer, providing information and philosophical analysis, distinctions and definitions, and charts of different levels of experience and kinds of knowing. Second, there is "sharing" and questioning by participants. Participants are encouraged, but not required, to share what is happening to them, their realizations about their lives, their problems. Finally, there are "processes," exercises in imagination that may be done in an altered state of consciousness, usually sitting in a chair or lying on the floor with eyes closed.

All three of these activities—the sharing and the processes as well as the presentations—are designed to bring various areas or levels of unconsciousness into clearer relief. These areas fall into four categories:

1) Mind structures, or the "organizing principles" of Mind
2) Mind traps
3) Life programs
4) Repressed incidents of a traumatic character.

The first two categories are generated by the Mind state *as such*—indeed, they *define* the Mind state—and they relate to all persons who are in the Mind state. The contents of the third and fourth categories vary from individual to individual. Only the fourth category is unconscious in the Freudian sense of being blocked from awareness. The first three categories are usually not blocked, but are unconscious in the sense of never having been examined.

1) The first category—Mind structures, or the organizing principles of Mind—includes the nature and design function of the Mind, the manner in which ego is generated, the mechanisms that reinforce positionality in all its forms. These mechanisms provide the conditions under which any specific Mind content operates. That is, any Mind content whatever will serve the structure and design function of the Mind: it will be used to further survival. Any Mind content whatever will be used to make the Mind right and others wrong; to dominate and avoid being dominated; to justify the Mind and invalidate others.

Mind structures are thus not composed of specific belief systems, attitudes, or points of view. Rather, Mind structures govern *all* belief systems, attitudes, and points of view that arise in the Mind state; all such things must conform to the Mind structures. These structures govern the way in which men believe what they believe and know what they know. They define where one is "coming from" vis à vis belief and knowledge. That is, in the Mind state, one is coming from survival, domination, perpetuation of positionality; and will use belief, knowledge, attitudes, points of view on behalf of such aims. One will not live to know, but will know to live.

In a fundamental sense, the principles of Mind define the structure of one's world. This is why the training is so often, and so aptly, called philosophical. During the training, the trainee's philosophical context, the organizing structure of life in the Mind state, is displayed. He sees his way of knowing (his epistemology), his way of being (his ontology), and his morality as skewed toward positionality and domination, toward the survival of the Mind state.

2) Secondly, there are what might be called "traps of the Mind state." Among the most important of these are *resentment, regret* and *righteousness,* which were treated earlier, particularly in the discussion of the self-image merchants Napoleon Hill and Maxwell Maltz. Although insufficiently basic to be themselves organizing principles of Mind, these traps define contextual *styles of operation* engendered by Mind structures regardless of specific content. Any person who is in the Mind state will tend to operate in life in a righteous, regretful and resentful style. These traps deter escape from the Mind state, and deflect attack on it. The training relates them explicitly to the organizing

structures, demonstrating how righteousness, regret and resentment reinforce positionality. Although abandoning the traps does not in itself destroy the Mind structure, it weakens its defenses.

3) Thirdly, there are "life programs," as in the case of the misunderstood genius discussed earlier. Each person has such life programs, or "stories," which determine how his or her life is lived. These consist in specific unconscious contents on the level of belief systems, identifications, fantasies, emotions. A life program differs from a Mind structure or Mind trap in that it defines the *specific content* of an individual life rather than the conditions under which all life in the Mind state occurs. Yet this specific content, whatever it is, is still controlled by and operates in terms of the design function of the Mind and is protected by the Mind traps.

4) Finally, there is specific repressed material in the Freudian sense: unconscious contents that had once been conscious and that were blocked from awareness traumatically. Such individual traumas act on particular Minds in accordance with the generating principles and traps that apply to all Minds, and also in accordance with individual life programs.

The purpose of uncovering these four areas and levels of unconsciousness is not simply to inform, but to put participants in a position to observe the Mind, and to become aware of its power and mechanical nature. A remarkable thing begins to occur when the trainee begins to examine the unexamined, and becomes aware, experientially, of these areas: part of their power evaporates. In the act of observing Mind, the individual expands beyond Mind, and becomes more open to experience and life. The temptation to belief, for instance, dramatically diminishes: one is now so aware of unconscious commitments and their imprisoning effects that one is less tempted deliberately to add further commitment to the baggage. Thus, a transformed individual is unlikely to become a "true believer."

To the extent that consciousness in these four areas does pierce through the "wiring" of the Mind, to that extent the power of the past over the individual is removed, bringing him to the state of transformation—or of "completion"—with regard to his own past. This is the state of here and now.

To achieve such a state of completion, all four areas may need to be dealt with. Yet it is, in Werner's view, *much* more empowering to deal with the first category than the second, the second than the third, the third than the fourth. The key fault of much of psychotherapy, and also of most disciplines in the self-help movement—Maltz and Hill, Mind Dynamics, Scientology, and such—has been to be preoccupied with the third and fourth categories, particularly with the fourth. Preoccupation with these last two categories—and with explanations in terms of them—can jam the individual further into the Mind system. Therein, he can achieve explanation but not mastery. Preoccupation with explanation—and with the content, as opposed to the context, of life—elevates the environment and belittles the individual in order to service the mental machinery. Explanation *alone* gives no power. Mastery, as Werner puts it, comes from realizing one's *philosophical* context—which operates chiefly on the first and second levels—and transcending one's attachments and circumstances.

The *est* training presents and examines the ideas and assumptions that I have described. By discussing them in this way, in a chapter of a book, I may have given the misleading impression that the training aims chiefly to convey information. It has to be emphasized again that the training aims to enable transformation to occur, not to convey information. The information presented provides only a multilevel commentary that intensifies the experience leading to transformation. The actual presentation of the training thus has a kind of spiral structure. The individual trainee begins at the edge of the spiral, where he immediately encounters all the content of the training; as he goes through succeeding layers of the spiral, that same information is conveyed again and again—holographically, as it were—more and more intensely, and more and more experientially. By the time he reaches the center of the spiral, the center of the cyclone, the eye of the hurricane, the initial content has become contextual.

The training is about sixty hours in length, and is held on two successive weekends. The four days of the training begin at nine in the morning and continue until late at night. These sessions usually take place in a hotel ballroom. The training usually ends between midnight and 2:00 A.M., and has been known occasionally to last until five in the morning.

The first day of the training is the most conceptual, least experiential of the four. For it has to begin at the level where people ordinarily operate, and where trainees themselves initially find themselves: at the level of concepts. This starting point, as the trainer quickly demonstrates, itself defines the chief issue of the training. The trainees begin to confront conceptual systems as things that devastatingly limit and shape not only the content but also the quality of their lives. They also begin to confront the whole issue of conceptuality itself.

To present the issue starkly, the trainer raises the question of how life's problems may be dealt with. His answer seems simple: all one needs to do is to tell the truth about them! What prevents people from telling the truth about their problems? They are imprisoned in their concepts, and thus never even confront their problems. Rather, they fit what is so into their preexisting conceptual frameworks. The difficulty is twofold. First, any concept, by its very nature, being a symbol for experience rather than experience itself, can serve to cut one off from experience. Second, the concepts are contained in a Mind system the function of which is to perpetuate all aspects of itself, including its concept-contents, *regardless of experience*. As a result, one tends to settle in life for a form of conceptualized nonexperience. The issue, then, is to break through the concepts, or "hidden barriers," *which are self-imposed* and which stand in the way of telling the truth about problems.

The trainer illustrates these suggestions with practical examples, which the trainees themselves offer him. Here is a more abstract, but simple and clear illustration of the kind of point that is being made. Consider the following nine circles:

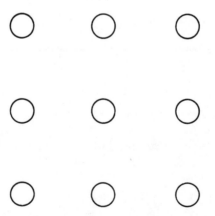

The problem is to connect the circles with four straight lines without lifting one's pencil or pen from the paper. Most people find this problem inordinately difficult. A typical attempt to solve it may look like this:

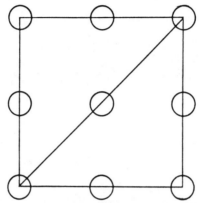

The individual who produced this attempt vowed that it was impossible to connect the circles with fewer than *five* straight lines.

In fact, however, the solution is simple, and goes as follows:

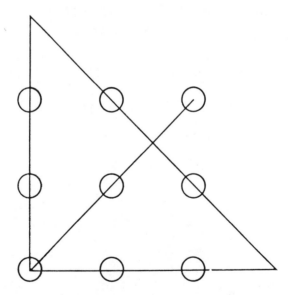

What prevents people from seeing this obvious solution is that they create—no one else does it; it is not in the directions!—an invisible barrier around the circles. I have drawn in a dotted line to show this "invisible barrier."

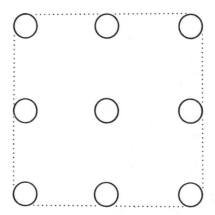

In effect, people form what Werner calls a "concept" about this problem—the concept of a box—which creates an invisible barrier preventing them from dealing effectively with it. Once one achieves a position "at cause" vis à vis the problems of life, one is no longer imprisoned by such barriers, but gains immense imagination and power. One can then expand into the space created by removing the barriers.

Suppose the problem to be changed somewhat. Suppose we are asked to connect the circles with *three* lines!

Here is a solution:

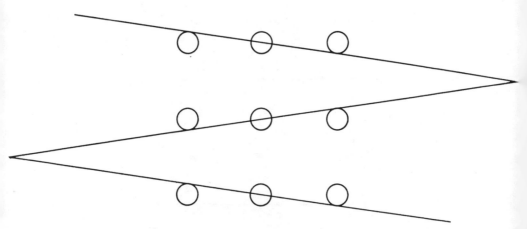

Many people—even those who managed to solve the first problem—will be unable to reach this solution because they have created a *different* invisible barrier: they suppose that the *circles* are *points*. And indeed, one could not connect nine such points with three straight lines. But with circles it is easy.

Take yet another example. Suppose the problem is to connect those circles with *one* straight line! Impossible? Hardly. All one needs is a very *very* large pencil or brush wide enough to cover all nine circles at once. For who said that the pencil or pen to be used must be one of ordinary size? That limitation too was a self-imposed, self-created barrier to the solution of the problem.[4]

To illustrate further what is involved in confronting and telling the truth about life's problems, the trainer makes use of a "cycle of existence" that is due to the French existentialist philosopher Jean-Paul Sartre.[5] All existence, on this account, can be categorized under *being*, *doing*, and *having*. As an individual goes through life, he comes from *being*, a state of creativity, through *doingness*, activity, to *havingness*.

Untransformed life, life in the Mind state, as Werner sees it, is lived backward: life in the Mind state is the attempt to go from having to doing to being—and to define one's being or identity in terms of what one has or does. As a result, one becomes imprisoned in having-ness, which shapes doingness, and prevents one from achieving any longer the creativity of being. One becomes limited by what one possesses, including, especially, patterns of behavior, points of view, and systems of self-identification and presentation. One is indeed *possessed* by things. Life becomes circumscribed by self-created but seemingly intractable problems. "Things are in the saddle and ride mankind." One is the victim of circumstances: the past, the environment, relationships, behavior patterns. One is under the influence of everything one has gone through, done or achieved. For example: one selects a specialty, and then goes about trying to be the sort of man who goes with the subject he has chosen to specialize in. Or one marries a husband, and then goes about trying to be the sort of woman who would be married to that sort of man. To live this way is to live backward. Rather than achieving satisfaction from life, one becomes the slave of life. Love, health, happiness, and full self-expression are forfeit. The Mind state, by its nature, works to perpetuate rather than to solve problems.

As Werner sees the matter, an environment, an econiche, in which the truth is being told is one where one proceeds from being to doing to having—and then to being again—without becoming "stuck" in any part of the cycle. A transformed individual is one who can tell the truth; and a transformed environment is one where the truth can be told.

The aim of the training is thus to effect transformation by restoring the natural flow: to allow a trainee to *be* apart from doing or having —and to allow his doingness and havingness to flow effortlessly from his being.

How can one achieve such a result? The trainer proceeds to show that the usual answer to life's problems—change—is futile. Change looks like this:

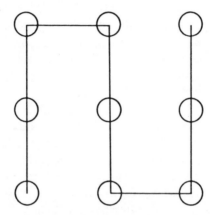

This does not solve the problem; it is just a different way of failing to solve the problem. The way to deal with a problem is to transcend it by *recontextualizing* it, i.e., by seeing it within a different context, as was done in the successful solutions of the nine circle problem. Just as one cuts oneself off from experience and from life—and from the truth about things—by false conceptualizing, so by re-creating in experience the offending condition or problem, one begins to tell the truth about it. When one looks at the nine circle problem outside of one's original concepts about it, and tells the truth about it, one sees that the circles are circles, *not* points, and that there is no barrier around the circles preventing the lines of one's solution from extending into that space. The problem disappears.

Here the trainer introduces a principle which can be compared with the Scientology principle of duplication. He suggests that as soon as one has re-created or duplicated one's problem or condition—that is, has told the truth about it—one is again in a state of being, as opposed to having, with regard to it.

Having introduced the *concept* of experiencing, the trainer remarks on the difference between conceptualizing and experiencing. And then he begins a series of processes and a presentation called "The Anatomy of an Experience," so as to initiate trainees into the *experience* of experiencing. For example, a body process is presented to enable the trainee to relate to his or her own body experientially rather than conceptually. "Tiredness" is, for instance, relatively conceptual—whereas "a tingling in the left forearm, four inches below the shoulder" or "a numb feeling in the lower right leg" is relatively experiential. It is not only bodily sensations that are dealt with. Emotions, such as "annoyance," and attitudes, such as "frustration," are also treated experientially. Although any rendering of experience into language is, inevitably, conceptual, the trainee learns to attend more closely to experience, and to allow it to penetrate concepts. A way to make a condition vanish—by taking the concept out of it and experiencing it—is then demonstrated by a simple technique of making a headache disappear through deconceptualizing it and "experiencing it out."

Each trainee is asked to bring to the second day a statement of an unwanted persisting condition or problem in life. On the morning of the second day, the trainer goes over these in detail, only to find that trainees persist in conceptualizing. Their statements of their own unwanted problems remain narrative rather than experiential. Indeed, they appear to be virtually unable to state their problems experientially.

Eventually, after recasting their unwanted problems in experiential terms, trainees are led through the "Truth Process," a powerful exercise during which many of them do experience the disappearance of the problems on which they chose to work. The second part of this second day is devoted to the "Danger Process," the aim of which is twofold: to experience one's own position, and to experience the fear—arising from relationships with others—that drives one to retain it.

The third day of the training, beginning on the second weekend, is directed to the question of the nature of reality. During the latter part of this day, two processes in "active imagination" are presented, both designed to rehabilitate the powers of the imagination, the "subjective universes," and experiential realities of the participants. One of these also provides a technique for retrieving suppressed memories and traumatic incidents.

The fourth day opens with a lengthy discussion entitled "The

Anatomy of the Mind," which is in effect the cornerstone of the training. Within the context of the training, this discussion has a powerful
effect: it stuns participants; by its end many of them are in a state akin
to horror. For the way has been well prepared; by now they are able to
take something not merely conceptually but to experience it. Like
Wilmer in *The Maltese Falcon*, the Mind has been set up. It is the fall
guy. So trainees experience what many merely believed before: that
the Mind is a machine, and that—to the extent to which they have
identified with their Minds—they themselves are machines. There is
no help for them—no hope. At this point in the training, as Werner
puts it, they "hit bottom." Their very clothes exude the stench of con-
gested thought.

As this lecture-discussion takes its relentless course, trainees
apply it experientially to their lives, and to their experiences in the
training itself. They observe the machines that are their Minds "going
off." They notice that their "reasons," and indeed even their objections to the data and to the initial agreements governing the training,
may be seen as mechanical, rigid, and mindless Mind-machine reactions. They observe that the heroism in their lives is as mechanical as
is their victimization. At some point in this process, most trainees
realize that they are not their Minds or their positions, but have falsely
identified with them, thus creating ego. At that point they transcend
their Minds. Their Minds are blown. The siege is ended.

The training is, however, not yet over. Just after trainees have
experienced the absence of choice and the extent of mechanicalness in
their lives, a process is introduced to give them the opportunity to experience choice and responsibility.

The next step is to identify the *chief* choice in life: one can stay
stuck in the position one is in—when that position produces being
right and making others wrong. Or one can "get off it"—not once for
all, but over and over again—and enjoy satisfaction, wholeness,
aliveness. The choice is absolute: the cost of righteousness and positionality is aliveness. One either identifies with Mind, and orients
oneself toward righteousness and domination; or one transcends Mind
and gives up the "hunger and thirst after righteousness" and all, in
terms of domination and survival, that is associated with it.

The training, now moving to a close, turns to "The Anatomy of
the Self." As Werner puts it: "You can experience Self only after you
have transcended Mind. And the way to transcend Mind is to experience it directly. On the fourth day of the training you have a direct
experience of your own Mind, which is akin to seeing the back of your

eyeballs with your own eyes." Werner's understanding of Self was indicated earlier. Self is without position; it is space. It is without content; it is context, or matrix—that which has no form or process or content or position but gives rise to them. This is who one really is.

Finally, the trainer turns the attention of the group to the problems of communication, power, sex, love, and relationships, and shows the implications of what has been presented for each of these. He now approaches these issues from the view of Self rather than Mind. After an encounter with the new questions about human communication and relationships opened by the Self, the training ends.

THE MORALITY OF TRANSFORMATION
At the heart of the *est* training, and of Werner's perspective, there lies a distinctive morality. The key to it lies in the notions of responsibility and appropriateness, and in the contrast: being at cause/being at effect.

Most morality—irresponsible morality—comes from the Mind state, and is oriented toward the defense of a position. Generated in the attempt to assert power over others, to control and dominate them, to make them predictable, it is really a form of politics.

Responsibility, by contrast, comes from the Self. When one is not identified with some position that must be defended and held blameless, then one may choose to be responsible for all the positions, forms, contents, and circumstances that arise in the matrix of life. Right action is contextually determined behavior; wrong action is determined by position, by concepts.

Responsibility, in Werner's sense, begins with the willingness to come from the context of being at cause. This means, mechanistically, being willing to deal with any situation from and with the point of view, whether at the moment realized or not, that one is the source of it. As understood here, responsibility is not fault, praise, blame, shame, or guilt, and includes no judgments or evaluations of good and bad, right and wrong, or better and worse.

To be responsible for a situation does not mean that one *did* it. Responsibility, which is a way of experiencing life, is a level of abstraction that transcends "I did it," which claims a territory, as well as "I didn't do it," and "Somebody did it to me," both of which defend positions. Responsibility precludes equally the position of the victim and of the hero.

The responsible person does not blame his circumstances on

external forces and other persons. Without resentment, he is not interested in revenge. He exemplifies the philosopher Nietzsche's sentiment: "To be unable to take one's own enemies, accidents and misdeeds seriously for long—that is the sign of strong and rich natures." The responsible person does not hunger and thirst after righteousness. No matter where he starts, he comes to be strong: for the abandonment of positionality and resentment is empowering. Yet his purpose is not to strengthen his own position, but rather to heighten, through his own contribution, the aliveness of the matrix.

How is this done? Simply by being appropriate.

What is it to be appropriate?

To be appropriate, to act appropriately, is to do what is fitting or suitable to a situation.

The situation is, however, in flux or change from moment to moment. Thus what is appropriate to one moment is not necessarily appropriate to the next moment. How then is one to do what is appropriate?

To be appropriate, to follow the Tao, one must be in the here and now. Appropriateness is a readiness for the situation as it really is, and not as one might wish it to be. Appropriateness thus has to do with creation and is indeed always creative. It is creative even when it creates nothing—for it is sometimes appropriate to create nothing. To be able to refrain from creating precisely when one is in a position to create is itself creative. This is true control.

Yet one cannot create with regard to what *was* appropriate or fitting, but only with regard to what is now, from moment to moment, fitting. To carry over "standards of appropriateness" or "conventions" or "proprieties" from one moment to another is to fail to complete one moment and to set up a barrier to experiencing the next moment. This is to become stuck in a form or position. What is appropriate is to *have* completed and always to be beginning anew— from and as cause. Any "standard of appropriateness" is thus a recipe for a lie.

Appropriateness cannot be gauged or measured in terms of necessary and sufficient conditions. For the latter only exist in the realms of doing and having, while the former exists in the realm of being.

Appropriateness, the Tao, the way, is revealed as unconsciousness is removed. As one begins to experience life, one's behavior effortlessly becomes more and more appropriate just in the process of living itself.

Appropriateness in a situation and control of a situation without force or domination are thus identical. For appropriate action is not doing anything: it is neither submitting nor resisting—nor "doing nothing." It is just being there. Although often misunderstood, this principle was understood by some writers in ancient China, where the Taoist writers advocated *wu wei*, nonaction. As the writer of the *Huai Nan Tzu* explains:[6]

> Some may maintain that the person who acts in the spirit of *wu wei* is one who is serene and does not speak, or one who meditates and does not move. . . . Such an interpretation of *wu wei* I cannot admit. The configuration of the earth causes water to flow eastward, nevertheless man must open channels for it to run in canals. Cereal plants sprout in spring, nevertheless it is necessary to add human labor in order to induce them to grow and mature. . . . *What is meant . . . by* wu wei *is that no personal prejudice (or self-will) interferes with the universal Tao, and that no desires and obsessions lead the true course of techniques astray.*

Personal prejudice and self-will, in Werner's view, stem from automaticity and positionality. Thus to act appropriately, to act in the spirit of *wu wei*, is to act without automaticity and positionality.

The verb form "to appropriate" can be understood similarly. To appropriate is to take over something as one's own. To appropriate each moment as one's own is to be at cause.

The morality of the Mind state, by contrast, is irresponsible. The irresponsible person sees himself, and comes to his experience of life, as a heroic victim—of circumstances, people, things, events. The misunderstood genius discussed earlier illustrates the condition. Preoccupied with the wrongs he supposes others to have done to him, his life is dominated by feelings of resentment and fantasies of revenge. Denied the opportunity to act out his resentments, to exact revenge, he lives not in the here and now but in a world of fantasy—set sometimes in heaven, sometimes in some future utopia—where and when "justice" will one day be meted out. At the same time, his own life story, the story of the injustices done to him, becomes all-significant. The whole fabric of his judgments and feelings depends upon its significance.

If one is not responsible, then one *must* be the victim, and someone else, some evil one, must have done it to one. Such an approach settles all moral issues, assuming as it does that the side that is battling what it designates as evil is itself good. Hence good already exists, and does not need to be sought, invented, debated. Rather, the decision about what is evil saves one from needing to make any choices about good. Thus does irresponsibility give rise to values.

This distinction between the transformed and the untransformed, between the responsible and the irresponsible, between those at cause and those at effect, is only sketched briefly here. When fully set out, it has profound implications for the history of morality and religion, and for all questions of social reform. Attitudes to programs of social reform, for instance, will differ, depending on whether one is "coming from" a position at cause or a position at effect. Social reform for a responsible individual will differ from social reform for one who is not. At effect, action is fundamentally reaction. One's chief idea of social reform may be to *get* somebody and to punish him. You are righteous; the man in power is evil; you displace him from power and punish him. Such is the scenario of social reform.

In weaning people from this viewpoint—and from such values—Werner combats those elements of our culture and institutions that are characteristic of the Mind state, and thereby comes into conflict with all defenders of the Mind state. This brings up the question of the social ramifications of transformation.

SOCIAL TRANSFORMATION
A transformed individual is one who can tell the truth; and a transformed environment is one where the truth can be told. Although the *est* training provides a temporary econiche in which mutations of consciousness are fostered, in which transformation on an individual level can take place, the training by itself is not intended to solve the problem of the ecology of consciousness.

For the relationships and institutions in which individual transformation must manifest itself are contextual, and thus either create space or restrict it. When untransformed, families and institutions manifest the Mind state; they generate survival orientation and positionality. *They restrict.*

Hence the environment to which transformed individuals return after an experience like the *est* training is usually not one where the truth can be told. It is a restrictive econiche that is deadly dangerous to transformation, having been created by individuals in the Mind state to foster the Mind state.

Werner Erhard has spoken bluntly of this environment: "The

world as it is, in an untransformed state, is evil. When using the word 'evil,' I do not mean what is ordinarily meant. What I mean by 'evil' is the selling or trading of aliveness for survival. Virtually every existing institution is like this. Government and education, for example, fail to do their jobs; but they are very good at justifying and perpetuating themselves, and dominating others. Like the individuals who created and who sustain them, they *come from* the Mind state, from survival. Instead of being an activity to generate a healthy community life, politics becomes an end in itself. Nationalism, which increases positionality, is an *epistemological* disaster.

"People who have the experience of transformation consequently have little room in which to express it. They are validated almost not at all. The world is not friendly to the experience that your life works, that you are capable of having relationships that are meaningful and nurturing. There is, on the other hand, plenty of room to be slick and clever and successful. The world is truly friendly to that. Such a world is an unhealthy space for transformation. Transformation *must* appear ultimately threatening to the Mind state. Thus to express transformation into an untransformed relationship or institution is automatically to generate survival behavior from the affected relationship or institution. Yet the transformed state, the state of Self, is a naturally expressive and expansive state. A transformed individual demands a transformed relationship because only in such a context can he naturally express his transformed individuality. Similarly, transformed relationships or families demand transformed institutions and organizations in which to manifest and express *their* transformation.

"You cannot foster transformation by retreating from life to some twentieth-century version of a cave. In fact, the historic retreat of the enlightened to the cave simply manifests the hostility of the environment to transformation. When the untransformed environment provides an inadequate or restrictive space for the transformed individual, he will not be readily able to expand into it. Or he may rapidly reach the limit of the space. When that happens, there is the danger that he will evolve back against himself in weird variations. This is essentially what is involved in the retreat to the cave, and in most monastic and world-denying endeavors. Some of these variations are beautiful to watch; but they represent a terrible waste."

Thus, in Werner's account, an effective siege on Mind cannot be directed only to the individual, but must be directed to the social environment too. Hence the larger *est* program has a revolutionary goal: to create the conditions—the space, the context—in the larger environment to foster transformation at each level: individual, family-relational, organizational-institutional, and cultural-societal.

How do survival orientation and positionality manifest themselves in institutions? And how can they be combated?

Simply to raise these questions is to identify an immense program of research and experimentation aimed at exposing those social, economic, environmental, cultural, psychological, and philosophical conditions that best further transformation. So far, work on this program has only begun. In the course of building a series of programs to supplement the *est* training—a communication workshop, the series of courses on "Making Relationships Work," the *est* graduate program, and others—Werner has identified various institutional mechanisms wherein positionality manifests itself. In two particular institutions, he has been combating positionality directly, in an intensive and intimate way. These two institutions—his own family, to which we shall turn in the next chapter, and the *est* organization, which has acquired a reputation for crack efficiency—are ongoing experiments in search of an answer to the question of the ecology of transformation. Among the mechanisms that foster positionality in families and institutions are lack of full communication; pretense (which is a socially sanctioned form of lying); unacknowledged mistakes; and uncorrectability. The result is "ritual behavior," which "goes through the motions," but is not "on purpose." This creates effort, struggle, red tape, complexity, work that fails to produce satisfaction.

A simple example, from my own experience in education, illustrates what happens where these mechanisms are at work in a practical situation. Each year, in one of my philosophy classes, I show a beautiful motion picture whose theme plays an important part in my lectures. A projectionist on the university staff is given the time and place of the screening. Every year something goes wrong with the film equipment: the soundtrack is inaudible; the projector does not work properly; the film is torn. Last year, for instance, the extension cord with which the projector was provided was too short. The only way to hook up the machine was to take the projector so far to the rear of the room that the image was many times the size of the screen. The only supply of extension cords was a fifteen-minute walk away, on the other side of the campus.

The man who set up that projector was going through the motions in Werner's sense. He was not "on purpose"; he had no *intention* on what he was doing. He was not *doing* what he was doing.

A commercial movie theatre that operated that way would have had to close. But at the university it was . . . "a small matter." Why is it not corrected? Every year, I go over the requirements for the film with the audio-visual department; I stress the film's importance, and do whatever I am permitted to do myself. When, after the incident with the short extension cord, I complained about the workman, I was told that he was *just doing his job* —when that was precisely what he was *not* doing. My colleagues were baffled at my "preoccupation" with so "insignificant" an incident. The administration was not interested in hearing about it. I was viewed as one lacking a sense of proportion. The pretense was that everything was as it should be and was working well. It almost seemed as if the whole institution—a state institution—were set up to go through the motions, and to frustrate attempts to do otherwise. Everyone seemed to be afraid of being unmasked, of being exposed, of being found at fault. It was not an environment that would tolerate the telling of the truth.

Everyone has many stories like that. For many people, that is the story of one's life. Almost everybody these days has a *post-office* story that goes like this. For the past eighteen months, virtually every time my regular postman has had a day off, my mail has been delivered to a different address a mile away. I have gone as far as I can in the post-office hierarchy to correct the matter. When I asked the man at the top to help me to solve the problem, he told me—these are his words— "It is not my job to solve your problem; it is my job only to defend the post office." I was told that if I knew of the terrible problems of the post office I would not be so concerned with *minor* problems. If I didn't like it . . . I could write my congressman.

No wonder everyone at the university and at the post office seems tired. When the environment is one into which one cannot express oneself, into which one cannot communicate, and which cannot be corrected—one gets tired. Going through the motions takes the sweetness out of life. Such an environment is not nurturing.

Individuals who spend their lives merely going through the motions—how tiring that seems!—will seek out for employment and other protection institutions that tend to tolerate going through the motions—where there is "no pressure." As that happens, such an institution becomes more and more tolerant of going through the motions. As an institution, it stops working; it is no longer on purpose:

the institution survives, but its purpose—whether education or delivering the mail—becomes increasingly secondary.

From the vantage point of the irresponsible, going through the motions in life—i.e., just getting by in the face of obstacles—is good; and any attempt to prevent this is evil or authoritarian. "Better working conditions," for example, may be seen as conditions that make it easier to go through the motions, to get by. One sees oneself as oppressed, in which case to do one's job purposively would be the work of a sucker. You would just be helping *them*, those whom you see as oppressive.

I have deliberately selected "minor problems" to illustrate this discussion. For in charting his own perspective on social revolution, Werner Erhard does not see such problems as minor. His family, the *est* training, and the *est* organization are organized so as to frustrate unconscious going-through-the-motions behavior in minute detail; so as to elicit full communication; so as to implement immediate correction. When comparatively minor problems of correction and communication cannot be handled effectively, Werner sees no prospect of successfully pursuing more ambitious aims, such as the "hunger project," which aims to create a context in which death by starvation will be eliminated from the earth within twenty years.

Without going into the details of the operation of the *est* organization, two examples illustrate behavior light-years distant from that of the audio-visual operator and the post office.

Both examples were given to me by Randy McNamara. Randy took the Mind Dynamics course from Werner in April 1971; he began to assist him a month later, joined the *est* staff, and eventually became an *est* trainer.

"As long as I have known him," Randy told me, "Werner has been concerned with details. This used to drive me crazy. In the summer of 1971, we were giving seminars at a house in the Marina, in San Francisco. When we'd get done with the seminar, he would get out a rake to rake the shag rug in the living room. The assistants would rake the rug in one direction; when that was done, they had to rake it in the other direction. There were also about sixty pillows, each of which had an exact place in the room. A pillow could not be off by two inches. And it wasn't legitimate to ask what two inches mattered to a pillow. You got to be enlightened from Werner's handling of pillows: you either did it *exactly* or you didn't get to assist Werner with pillows anymore."

Randy described another example of attention to detail in communication.

"You know," Randy said to me, shaking his head, "people will just not answer your questions. They will do anything to avoid answering your questions. But Werner always gets answered exactly the question that he wants answered.

"He knows that if you do your job wrong and fail to acknowledge it, you will dramatize it. You will get tired, or get a cold, or a headache, or be bitchy to someone. You will make more and bigger mistakes until you make one so dramatic that you get called on the carpet and perhaps even fired. So if I ever did anything wrong—and in the beginning I rarely did anything right—Werner would correct me as soon as he found out.

"Sometimes he'd find my mistakes in the middle of the night while he was still working and I was sleeping," Randy said, smiling. "The phone would ring at three in the morning and the voice at the other end would say, 'Randy, hold on for Werner.' And then Werner would come on. He would say, 'Randy, this and this happened. Did you do that?' I would come up with some airy-fairy explanation or justification for what had happened. He would then repeat, 'Randy, I said *did you do that?*' I would say, 'Werner, I don't really recall it very well.' He'd say, 'Good, recall it.' I'd say, 'Werner, it was a long time ago.' He'd say, 'Good, what happened?' I'd say, 'Werner, you know there were a lot of things happening then. I don't remember it.'

"At that point he would just pound the desk. I could hear it. He was using a speaker-phone. And then I got off it. I got that I did it, gave up my reasons, and simply acknowledged responsibility for what I had done. The next thing would be that he would say, 'Thank you, Randy, good night.' As soon as he got the acknowledgment from you that you had done it, then he was off it.

"Don't misunderstand me," Randy said. "If he telephoned and I said, 'No, I absolutely did not do that,' then he would immediately thank me and the matter would be at an end. He wasn't trying to get me—or anyone—to take the blame for anything. He is aware that people make errors. He just knew that if we failed to acknowledge our errors we would harm either ourselves or the organization. He took responsibility for everything we did do, didn't do, or might do."

This instant correction—the *est* people call it "support"—appears to explain the energy around them. Whereas going through the motions is exhausting, real work—work with intention—is not.

And incidentally, Confucius "would not sit on his mat unless it was straight" (*Analects*, X, 9).

Werner assumes that transformation—whether attained through *est* or in some other program—will have a radical effect on society, as it is mediated by transformed individuals through transformed relationships and transformated organizations and institutions. Existing institutions—in education, law, medicine, government—will then start to work. The manner in which people relate to each other and to the world will be regrounded. And humankind will, in the process, be transfigured.

Meanwhile, Werner does not see social reform as potentially effective. Replacing one group of leaders by another group is in his view futile if neither of the groups, nor the institutions in which they operate, are able to function on purpose.

As he put it to me, "I am a sort of revolutionary. I have a strange ambition, though. I don't want any statues. I don't want any ordinary monuments. *What I want is for the world to work. That's* the monument I want. There's egomania for you! The organizing principle of *est* is: 'Get the world to do what it is doing.' I want to create a context in which government, education, families are nurturing. I want to enable, to empower, the institutions of man.

"This is not revolution in any ordinary sense of the word. Ordinary revolution is concerned with social change. It involves resistance. One revolts against something. Whereas a true revolution *transcends* what one was previously either resisting or submitting to. In this sense I am revolutionary.

"Social transformation doesn't argue against social change. Radicalism and resistance produce obvious values. But after a while, social change chases its own tail. Social change just produces social change. After most ordinary revolutions, after most social change, the world still doesn't work. For the world to work you must have social transformation, which creates the space for effective social change.

"Thus I have no political or social ideology. I have no idea about where you ought to be going, what your goal should be. The information that can transform where you are going is to know where you are *coming from*—from survival and positionality. You transform where your life goes by experiencing where it is coming from, rather than by having an attachment to how it's going to turn out."

The social aspect of Werner's account of transformation answers a recurrent criticism of the consciousness movement: that it leads to narcissism, preoccupation with self at the expense of political and social responsibility.

It is perhaps odd that the charge of political and social irresponsibility should ever have been leveled at the consciousness movement—even to that part of it where the commitment to share transformation with others is not as explicit as is Werner's. It is no accident that many leaders among political activists in the sixties now participate actively in the consciousness movement. Moreover, the various movements toward individual and social liberation, including women's liberation and gay liberation, rely heavily on consciousness and awareness techniques borrowed from the human potential and transformational storehouses in order to implement their goals. The same people participated in the sixties, in California and elsewhere, in the creation of the political protest against the war, in the ecology movement, and in the consciousness movement. These movements are not antagonistic but complementary. The assumption that they are antagonistic is a projection from the old consciousness against which they are *all* rebelling.

In part, of course, the charge of narcissism has to do with a verbal misunderstanding. Some writers have been led astray by a technical use of the word "self." "Self," as used by Werner, has nothing to do with "selfish"; it has no connection to the accidents of individual biography or history, personal appearance, achievement or possession. There is nothing narcissistic about attempting to transcend those things in life that lead people to narcissism.

This is not a new issue; and perhaps Hermann Hesse put the matter best. "The intellectual content of Buddha's teaching," Hesse wrote, "is only half his work. . . . A training, a spiritual self-training of the highest order, was accomplished . . . a training about which unthinking people who talk about 'quietism' and 'Hindu dreaminess' and the like . . . have no conception. . . . Instead Buddha accomplished a training of himself and his pupils, exercised a discipline, set up a goal, and produced results before which even the genuine heroes of European action can only feel awe."[7]

PART IV Completion

To redeem those who lived in the past and to re-create all 'it was' into a 'thus I willed it'—that alone should I call redemption.
 —*Friedrich Nietzsche*

TWELVE One Big Family

I didn't go to the moon, I went much further—for time is the longest distance between two places.
—Tennessee Williams

MEANWHILE IN PHILADELPHIA. HARD TIMES
The pile of photographs had been pushed to one side of the dining-room table at Joe and Dorothy Rosenberg's house in Plymouth Meeting. Joan and Harry Rosenberg, Werner's sister and one of his brothers, and Pat Campbell, his first wife, had come in to join us. It was early evening now. In a while we were to go out to dinner. Dorothy had served tea, and the conversation had turned to that long twelve-year period following Werner's disappearance. What happened, I asked Pat, after she realized that Werner and Ellen had gone?

"It was the first of June, 1960, by then," Pat answered, very matter-of-factly, "so the first thing I did was to contact my landlord and tell him that I had no money and wouldn't be able to pay the rent. He was the one who told me about welfare. I didn't want to do it, but in those days there were no day-care centers, and I had no place to put the children. I was certainly not going to put the responsibility on our families.

"I waited a month before I told my parents that Werner had left,"

Pat said. "Then I had them over for dinner one Sunday and told them. They were shocked, and my father began to rant and rave. They asked why I hadn't told them earlier, and I said for the simple reason of what just went on. I didn't need all that excitement. I didn't tell my sister that Werner was gone until the following October.

"When Werner left," Pat said, "I did only what I legally had to do. When I went on welfare I had to notify the police that he was missing. I couldn't see any point to going after him. I knew that he was alive and well, and would return one day."

Joe and Dorothy, however, had asked Jim Clauson, Dorothy's brother, to make inquiries. Jim learned of a restaurant where Werner had been going during the months prior to his departure. When Jim went there, the waiter, John Croft, denied knowing anything of Werner's whereabouts. Jim took him by the coat collar, and said to him, "If I ever find out that you knew where he was and didn't tell me, I'll come back and throttle you." Jim had come close to tracing Werner: Croft was the only person in Philadelphia with whom Werner kept in touch during those years. He knew how to contact Werner, and kept him informed about the family's health and well-being.

I asked Pat how she supported herself and the children. "Well, at first there was welfare. My father and mother chipped in, and bought clothes for the children. Dorothy came every Tuesday night and always insisted on leaving a twenty-dollar bill in the cookie jar. After a while I started to earn money sewing. I made clothing, I was a dressmaker. I did that at home when the children were small. When I started doing that, I of course went off welfare. And after I remarried in 1965 there were no more financial worries."

Joe touched Pat's arm to interrupt. "She was incredibly strong," he said. "She just kept everything going, almost as if nothing had happened." Dorothy nodded agreement.

What about the family, I asked, how did they react? The immediate family, Pat replied, was drawn together. "I was closer to Mother than ever," Pat said, referring to her mother-in-law, Dorothy. "Dorothy telephoned me every day, and came over to see us once a week. My four children and Werner's brothers and sister all grew up together. It was one big family."

"Yes," Dorothy interjected. "At one point I thought of building an addition on the house, and moving everybody in here."

"I lived in Hatboro for two years after Werner left," Pat said. "Then I moved to Norristown, where I was closer to my family and to Dorothy and Joe and their children."

"That was the immediate family," Joe said. "Things weren't so good with the bigger family. The family was torn by rumor and gossip. My brother Al and I remained on good terms, but no one else. Everybody was enemies for a long time."

Pat nodded agreement. "The family seemed to fall apart. There were no more get-togethers with the Rosenberg and Clauson families. No more social events and dinners at Uncle Al's." Pat smiled at her mother-in-law. "Dorothy had something to do with that. She put together a convincing story about how Al and Edith, Werner's uncle and aunt, had helped him to leave and knew where he was. She thought that Jim Clauson had something to do with it too—and Norm Danoff, Werner's cousin in Los Angeles. They resented the accusation. Deep down, I did not believe that they did that. I was so fond of them. But I was caught in the middle, and didn't say much. Until a few years ago, Uncle Al believed that I thought he had helped Werner to get away."

Dorothy lifted her eyebrows disapprovingly, and rose to take the teapot back to the kitchen. I asked Pat when she accepted the idea that Werner was gone for good. "It wasn't until after Christmas, seven months after he left," she replied. "I was sure that he would be back at Christmastime. We couldn't imagine a holiday going by without his being in touch with us. For the longest time, I didn't think that it was a permanent break."

At first, she explained, she told the children only that Werner was away, later that he was out West. As they grew older, she gave them more details of his departure.

"I was clear about what he was doing," Pat said. "I knew that he was getting it together, and would return one day. But it's hard to explain that to children."

Eventually, despairing of his return, Pat got a divorce on grounds of desertion; the original marriage was annulled in the Episcopal Church.

The worst casualty of Werner's leaving, Pat added, was Dorothy, who plummeted into a twelve-year-long depression. Joe shook his head in irritation.

"When my poor wife became distraught," Joe said, "I thought she was going to go out of her mind. I tried to get her to go to a psychiatrist. I told her that only one thing would save her: 'Hang the crepe on the door and say he is dead.' But she insisted that he was alive. She kept his photograph on her dresser all those years. That son of mine wouldn't even put a dime in the phone to call her to say he was fine and that she shouldn't worry about him!"

Dorothy nodded wistfully as she brought in a new pot of tea. "I thought I would die in those years. Something went out of me. I almost forgot I was here. To recall that period is painful for me. Even while I am talking about it the pangs come up again. They are definitely physical sensations. I had constant headaches all those years. And I began to drink a lot. I caught that just in time; I could have become an alcoholic. My house went to pot! You should have seen it! My kids really suffered."

Harry Rosenberg, Werner's brother, had been sitting quietly, rummaging through the photographs. At this point he looked up. "My mother was in a terrible place during those years," he said. "After Werner left she like died. She got terribly, terribly depressed. She broke. The house would get wrecked. As the years went by I just assumed that home would be in a state of upset—even when things were good. Just around the corner there was always another upset. I would try to talk my mother out of it; Joan would get into an argument with her. And Nathan would flee upstairs to his room.

"She used to cry," Harry continued. "It was like wailing. It came from deep down in her gut, from the very bottom of her stomach. It was anguish.

"My mother is very disciplined," Harry reflected. "There is a parameter within which she operates. Werner's departure had invalidated her whole life, everything around which she had built her life.

"I unconsciously blamed Werner for her state of mind," Harry went on. "Consciously, I had no animosity toward him. I was only ten when he left, and I had good memories of him. But he was constantly on my mind, all through those twelve years. Where he is? What's happening? I kept asking these questions over and over."

And so those years dragged—and went speeding—by. Reminders of Werner remained everywhere: his old lacrosse sticks stood in the attic, his books were scattered in Pat's home and in Joe and Dorothy's too, his two younger brothers grew into his old clothes, his hand-me-downs. His photograph remained on Dorothy's dresser.

As those years passed, Joan and Harry went to college, and left home. Nathan went to the Air Force Academy. Pat remarried; the marriage was unhappy, and in September 1972 she filed for divorce.

By October 1972, Werner had been gone for nearly twelve and a half years. Joe and Dorothy were both sixty-two years old. Pat was thirty-seven. Joan, Harry, and Nathan were, respectively, twenty-four, twenty-two, and twenty. Clare, Lynn, Jack, and Debbie— Werner and Pat's children—were respectively, eighteen, seventeen, thirteen, and twelve. Over these years non-being lay thick.

THE PRODIGAL SON RETURNS

During its first year, from October 1971 to October 1972, the *est* training was an astonishing success, spreading from San Francisco, to Los Angeles, to Aspen, and then to Hawaii. Six thousand persons were trained. As he led those trainings, and the seminars that followed them, Werner continued to share with trainees and graduates the details of his own past, and his relationships with Ellen and with his parents and family. Philadelphia began to loom larger and larger on the horizon.

When he had cleared up his relationship with Ellen, he turned to Dorothy and Joe again. When he first began to speak of them, he still spoke from his old position. I recall how he talked of them during my own training, in April 1972. He spoke of Dorothy, in particular, as the embodiment of self-righteousness.

The *est* training, however, has a way of leading people to relinquish their positions. Werner's positionality toward his family had already been undermined by his years of studying and practicing disciplines; the emotion, the feeling against his family, had long vanished. His remorse and guilt over deserting them was by now also nearly gone. "I am certain," he has said, "that *est* came about by my completing the pattern of blaming my mother for my life. Handling one's past by completing it goes hand in hand with the transformation experience." All that was left was the narrative account of his old position. As he articulated that position and shared it with his trainees, the righteousness in it became apparent, and he dropped it. As he put it to me, "It wasn't just the trainees that got off it. I too got off it." He was ready to return.

The first *est* training in New York City was scheduled for the last two weekends of October 1972, and Werner was to lead it. On Monday afternoon, October 23, the day following the first weekend of the training, he picked up the telephone in his hotel room in New York City and dialed his uncle, Jim Clauson, his mother's brother, with whom he had had no contact for twelve and a half years.

"Werner didn't tell me where he was," Jim told me. "He said only that he was in New York City and would be back in a week. He made an appointment to come to see me the following Tuesday. But I couldn't be sure about it. I didn't know whether it was just a sudden urge on his part to call. I was afraid he might change his mind and that we would never hear from him again. So I didn't tell anyone except my wife, Kitty. I swore her to secrecy."

Three days later, on Thursday, October 26, Jim got an unexpected call from Joan Rosenberg. Joan told me about this. She and

Harry, so Joan explained to me, had been talking for months about going in search of Werner, and she had discussed this also with Pat. "Harry and I had saved some money that summer," Joan said, "and we were talking about going to California the following year to look for Werner. We had never been out West, but we were sure that he must be there. I had written a letter to my cousins there (Norm Danoff and Don Clauson), and I had it in my handbag to put it in the mail. But I wasn't satisfied, and I couldn't get Werner out of my mind; so I decided to call Jim Clauson, who had done some FBI work, and who works for the government, and ask his advice. I said, 'Uncle Jimmy, I know you'll think I'm crazy, but Harry and I have been talking and we'd like to hire a private detective to find Jack. Have you ever heard anything about him? Do you think this is a good idea?' Jim said, 'Now, Joan, why would you call me today to ask me that question?' I said that I had just been thinking about it. He repeated, 'I know, but why did you pick *today* to call me?' I repeated that it was just on my mind that day. Finally he asked how I would feel if Werner did come back, and how my mother and father would feel. I told him of course that we'd all be delighted. Then he said, 'Joan, I wouldn't do anything for a while. Why don't you just cool it? Think about it for a while. Meanwhile, don't worry about anything.' When Jim said that, I knew that something was going on. I said nothing to my mother, because I didn't want her to get excited."

"That call was strange," Jim told me. "I hadn't talked to Joan about Werner for years. Suddenly, just a few days after he had called me, there she was with this request.

"On the following Tuesday, just as he had promised, Werner did come to my office in Philadelphia," Jim said. "We went over the whole story. He wanted to know about Joe and Dorothy's health, whether it would be too much of a shock, what would happen if he came home. Werner wanted my advice about the best way to contact the family without causing more upset than necessary. I cautioned him, from my police experience, that I couldn't be certain that Pat wouldn't press charges against him. He said he was prepared to face any such eventuality. So I asked him to let me call Dorothy and Joe and to say that I had heard from him, without saying that he was there then. Dorothy answered the telephone. I told her I had heard from Werner and that he was coming to see me in a few hours. I asked her how she wanted to handle it. 'What do you mean, "handle it"?', she exclaimed. 'Just bring him home!' "

Dorothy told me of that phone call. "I was in the tub upstairs at home," she said. "I was getting ready to go to work. I had to grab a towel and tear downstairs to the phone. Jim asked me whether I had a minute. I said that I didn't, that in fact I was running late. And then he just said it. He said, 'Jack has just got in touch with me.' I couldn't believe it. I told him to bring Werner over to the restaurant where I was working. It was like a whole new world opened up."

Jim brought Werner back on the train from his office to his home in northeast Philadelphia, so that he could get his car for the drive to the suburbs. Werner was able to see Jim's wife, Kitty, briefly, and then the two men drove over to the restaurant where Dorothy was working.

Meanwhile, Dorothy left a note for Joe, saying, simply, "Jackie's back. Come over to the restaurant." Joan told me about this. "When I arrived home from work, my father had just got home, and had got my mother's note. He looked like it was Christmas and every other special day that you can think of. He said, 'You'll never believe what has happened!' He was so excited. We went over to the restaurant. Werner and Jim had just arrived, and were sitting with Mother, at a table, in a back room. That restaurant is a series of train cars. They had gone into an empty car at the back."

"When Werner walked in," Dorothy added, "it was very shocking to me. First I just went all to pieces. Then all I could do was to keep looking at him. He looked different. He couldn't take his eyes off me either. He was probably thinking, 'a different mother,' too."

Joan described their reunion to me. "We walked into the restaurant, and there he was. I no longer had a visual image of what he looked like. But I recognized him immediately. I knew that he was my brother. He got up and hugged and kissed my father, and they both cried. Then I went over and hugged and kissed him. It was unbelievable. An instant later, it was just like he had always been there."

After a time they left the restaurant, and returned home to Plymouth Meeting. "It gives me a chill to recall that time we met," Joe told me. "Dorothy cried continuously for hours. After we came home from the restaurant, she sat with Werner in the kitchen. They were facing each other, and she was crying so much. I motioned to him to hold her close."

Werner spent the night at his parents' home, and left the following morning for California, promising to return in two weeks. He asked that they arrange for him to see Pat. They tried, unsuccessfully, to reach Harry in Philadelphia. They then telephoned Nathan at the Air Force Academy, in Colorado.

"I was lying in bed," Nathan told me, "and the orderly came down to my room at about seven in the morning and knocked on the door to tell me that I had a long-distance telephone call. Immediately I thought something must be wrong. So I rushed down and picked up the phone, heard Joan crying, and was sure that my father must be ill. And then she started to laugh and said, 'Guess what's happened? Jack has come home!' I started crying too."

The reaction of Harry and Nathan Rosenberg to their brother's return was both interesting and revealing. I talked with Harry in San Francisco, where he has worked for *est* since 1973. He has served as manager of the graduate division, and also as manager of the San Francisco center. He is now Werner's personal assistant. Prior to Werner's return, he had studied engineering, and then English literature, at Drexel and Temple universities. When Werner returned in late October 1972, Harry was living with some friends in a warehouse in downtown Philadelphia. He was leading, as he put it to me, "a long-haired hippie existence." An aspiring writer, he was "heavily into Oriental religions and the consciousness movement." He was preparing to write a psychological novel about Werner's departure and its consequences for the family.

"We had just had the telephone disconnected because we hadn't paid the bill," Harry told me. "One of the guys I was living with had called his parents' house that night, and was told that Joan had been calling there to try to get in touch with me about something important. I can remember leaving the warehouse and walking down the street to the phone booth. You know, I had the feeling that Werner was back! I called home, but couldn't reach anybody. So I walked back to the warehouse, and that was it for that evening. The next day, after school, I went to my parents' house. When I heard that Werner had already been there, just a few hours before, I was really annoyed that no one had come down to get me. But I was excited too. My mother was like a contented hen. My father was relieved. And it was something big for Joan to handle. I was full of anticipation about what his return could mean for all of us.

"On the day that he was due back in town, I got what was for me dressed up. I put on cleaned and pressed corduroy Levi's, and a good sweater and shirt, and my good boots. I was going to live at home while Werner was there. My father had gone to pick him up at the Chestnut Hill train station. Werner was coming in from New York City.

"I remember the way he came in. He came through the back

door. He came up and gave me a hug and kissed me, and said 'Hi, Harry' in a booming voice. I was dumbfounded. He didn't fit my expectations at all. For one thing, I expected him to be taller. I had remembered him from a time when he was big and I was a small boy.

"Werner was going to stay in the room that Nathan and I used to share. We took up his luggage, and told him where he could leave things. He was going to be staying for four days.

"When we came downstairs, my father was making up dishes, delicatessen-type things, cold cuts and pickles. We sat down together in the dining room to eat these. The atmosphere was very light. Werner asked me what I was doing, what I was studying.

"He was fascinating to watch. I observed the way he related to my mother, and later to the other people who came in. I wanted to get some insight into his relationship with them. This was important to me, since I didn't really know him at all.

"For instance, I watched him relate to my sister Joan. He had got to name her when she was born, and he had a special relationship with her before he ever left. I remember being a little jealous at the attention he gave her.

"I had never seen anybody operate that way before. He was very straightforward. There wasn't any shit to what he did. It took a lot to do that, to go back after thirteen years, and to be able just to be there. Those three days with Werner were definitely enlightening for me. They changed my life."

Harry grinned. "It's hard to explain this. You know, a conversation with Werner in it is completely different from the other conversations that I had had all my life. For instance, Werner and my father got to talking about religion. My father was telling Werner about his religious experience, and Werner was giving it right back, but from a different place. Some people get embarrassed when somebody starts talking about religion. But Werner wasn't embarrassed. He was very clear, and it was uplifting just to be around him in that conversation. Werner didn't make my father wrong for his position. He supported it, and also gave my father another point of view with regard to it. He told Joe about a religious experience that *he* had had. When he was living in San Francisco, on the water, he had gotten up one night, and was walking in the living room, and the moon was out over the bay, and he just felt two hands pushing him down to his knees.

"Werner had already talked to my mother and dad, and to Joan, about why he had left. But after we were finished eating, and came back into the living room, he started to talk about this again. He gave us the main events of his life during those years when he was away, why he left, what he was doing. He told us about *est*. He described how he had changed his name on the plane, that he had been in Saint Louis, and had stolen a car. He talked about it as if he weren't talking about himself—there was so little of him involved in that old story.

"At one point in the conversation," Harry said, smiling, "he told us that he wasn't really there. He said, 'You're creating my being here.' You know, we hadn't taken the training yet! But I got it anyway! I looked over at him, and something happened just then. My experience changed. Something physiological changed too. It was a high—a strange high. I didn't understand what he was talking about, but at some level I got it.

"We continued talking that first night until very late. At two in the morning my father and mother went to bed, and Joan and I stayed up with Werner for a while longer. Joan asked him why he came home. And he replied, 'I came here because I didn't go to the place next door.' It was a Zen type answer. I laughed, and Joan got a little upset about it.

"When I came home from school the next day," Harry went on, "Pat had arrived, and Werner was sitting with her, Joan, and my mother. Pat was definitely reserved, very wary. It was as if she had said to herself that that was the way to be in that situation. Her wariness kept being broken down, however; it kept having the rug pulled out from underneath it by the way Werner handled himself. He told her, for example, that he wouldn't do anything with the children without clearing it with her first. He kept just taking things out from underneath any position that she operated from."

Pat told me of this first encounter. "I was uneasy at the first meeting," she said. "Werner had at first suggested to Joe and Dorothy that we meet someplace else, at a hotel, for example. And I wish we had, so that we could have talked better. Everyone was right there, listening, wanting to know just what was going on, what was being said. But it doesn't matter.

"When he walked in it was," Pat said, "as if he had never gone away. He was a little heavier. Other than that he looked the same. Even though I had assumed that he would be successful and happy when he did come home, I had expected him to look older.

"I didn't hear from him what I wanted to hear—that everything was going to go back to the way that it had been. He told me that he was still with Ellen. I had suppressed my love for him during all those

years, and it was quite a surprise to me to find that I was still very
much in love with him. So I was very uncomfortable when I saw him.

"I kept myself under control throughout the visit. It wasn't until
I walked out the door to get in the car that I broke down and cried. He
was talking and my mind was going and I just couldn't say anything. I
was just too filled up, and I wanted to get into the car and go."

Among the many things about which Werner and Pat came to an
understanding was finances. Werner and Pat agreed, for example, that
he would immediately repay to Pat's and his own parents, with interest, everything that they had contributed toward the support of the
family during the years that he had been away. And he would immediately begin again to support their children and to pay for their
educations.

That night Dorothy and Joe gave a party at the house for the
larger family, and Nathan arrived home from the Air Force Academy.
At that party, Harry again watched everyone closely, to see how different people reacted to Werner, and he to them. Some of those who
came were quite relaxed. Werner's cousin Helene Feinberg came in
and said, "Well, *Werner*, what's new?", a line that made everyone in
the room laugh. Others were reserved or uneasy at first. Werner was
different with different people, Harry told me. "Werner took responsibility for the pictures that people had of him, and took them into account. At first I saw this as phony, that rather than maintaining the
same position with everyone, he was different with different people.
He was whatever way the situation called for. I was struck by the way
he and my Uncle Al interacted. The two of them kidded each other,
and there was a knowingness in their kidding. I got that my Uncle Al
knew Werner. With him, Werner didn't have to play from a position.
It was a good-natured gathering. There was a fire in the fireplace.
People were enjoying themselves. And there was a tremendous sense
of relief in the whole family, not just the immediate family. Werner's
absence had affected everybody."

As I talked with them about this meeting, each member of the
family emphasized to me Werner's attempt to communicate with
them.

"Werner just told us to ask him anything we liked," his Aunt
Edith told me. "He promised to tell us the answer, no matter what we
asked. That was nice. And it cleared up so much."

"When Werner returned," Dorothy observed, "he communicated openly with us. While it was difficult to rehash the past, he was
completely open to hear what every member of the family had to say

and to answer each of our questions fully. He said he was responsible for his past action or lack of it, and he corrected what was correctable. At first we didn't understand when he did not justify or try to explain or give reasons. Instead of doing that, he just communicated clearly and acknowledged his responsibility, so that each of us within the family could satisfy ourselves regarding the past and did not have to carry it around with us any further."

"Yes," said Joe. "Everything was now out in the open. He'd say to me, 'Just ask, Dad, and if I can tell you, I'll tell you.' There were to be no 'withholds' anymore."

"After I watched Werner communicating with my family for a while," Harry told me, "I relaxed. I became proud of the way that he was behaving. Nathan and I had both invited girl friends to the party, and they got really interested in Werner too. People would just cluster around him. As he talked about what he was doing, I felt prouder and prouder. I felt proud that all these people were sitting there listening to him and that he was my brother. The way that he communicated to people was just different.

"Later that night," Harry paused and smiled, "I got very upset at Mother. I went through the house arguing with her, and then slammed the back door and went outside. I was crying as I went down the driveway. When I hit the street, Werner was walking right next to me. He had followed me out. He asked me what happened, and we talked, and then he wanted to know what I wanted to do now. I decided to go back in.

"But I remained outside for a few minutes, because I had been crying. I had gotten something about my mother, and about my relationship with her, about the whole of it. And it wasn't complete for me at all. I went to the back of the yard, and was standing there. Joan came out to talk with me, and was giving me agreement about the position I had been in when I walked out of the house. Except that I wasn't in that position anymore. Whenever Werner talked to me, I moved to another place, you know? My consciousness expanded.

"At that point Werner came out again. Joan said something to him about Mother. Werner replied that I wasn't upset by that anymore. And then Werner turned to her and said, 'Water's wet, rocks are hard, and Mother's Mother.' I'll never forget that moment. Joan shot around and said, 'Oh, no she isn't!' She thought for a moment that for Werner to say that meant that he didn't care. She was upset by his not being involved in the soap opera. But when Werner said that I got my consciousness raised.

"Everything changed after that. I got cleaned up and went back into the party. I felt embarrassed about having left, but I was willing to have that be there. The party went on and I enjoyed myself. My mother's behavior didn't bother me anymore. I had already learned from Werner how to 'make space.'

"I got some more of it the next day." Harry grinned. "My mother had asked me to sweep the leaves off the back patio. I was bitching about that, and Werner came out, picked up a broom, and started helping. He showed me where he was at about doing things exactly. 'If you are going to do it, do it exactly,' he said to me, 'and do it completely.' I got that that is what he was doing now with the family too. I got something more about his way of communicating then too. There was nothing added to it. He meant exactly what he said, nothing more, nothing less. To have that in an environment where something was always added to any communication was truly refreshing."

Werner had already spoken to me of his behavior on returning to his family.

"What I did essentially," Werner said, "was to let them discharge all the things that hadn't been said over the past thirteen years. They could see that I was handling the matter in an unusual way, and I talked straightforwardly about *why* I was able to handle it. People would ask me, for example, whether I felt guilty. I would answer them in *est* ways."

Werner's father, Joe Rosenberg, told me of his own astonishment at Werner's behavior on his return. "I said it can't be," Joe said. "He is open. He doesn't hide anything. You know, he's telling the truth. He's a different Jack. Here's what I get. He went away as one character, and came back as another character—an open, honest, healthy character. He just completely turned around."

Werner agreed with Pat that he would return to Philadelphia again on January 15, and would see their four children then. Meanwhile they would be in touch by phone. Nathan was the first to telephone Werner, just a few days after their meeting in Philadelphia.

"I had gone back to the Air Force Academy after that party," Nathan told me. "I was really feeling low, and wanted to leave the place. So I telephoned Werner to say, 'I'm getting out of this place.' He said, 'Well, that's okay.' So I was immediately a little leery: What did he mean, 'okay'? Then he said, 'You know it's going to be the same way anyplace else.' And I said, 'Yeah, but I don't like it here.' He replied, 'Okay, and you aren't going to like it anyplace else.' Then I said, "What I'll do is to quit here and go to Harvard.' So he said, 'You aren't going to like it at Harvard either.'

"At that point I started to get a lump in my throat, and I didn't know what the hell was going on. So I said, 'Well then I'll quit and just come to work with you.' He said, 'You won't like that either.' With that, I started to cry. Then I said, 'Then I might just as well kill myself.' And he said, 'Well that's great, but you know what? You're going to die and then you'll come back again and you won't like that either!"

"At that point," Nathan continued, "everything just snapped. I was in a booth in a phone room at the Academy. There were about five phone booths in there, and somebody went walking by just then. I was sitting there with huge tears running down my face.

"When Werner heard me moan, he said, 'Now if you'll just take a hold of that, it will make you free.' And I looked, and I got it. There was a transformation of my life right there. I started smiling, the same guy went by the phone booth again, and this time I had a huge grin on my face. He gave me a very puzzled look."

A week later, Nathan flew from Colorado to San Francisco to spend Thanksgiving with his brother. He was the first to gain some idea of Werner's success with *est*, and of his growing influence. On the thirtieth of November, Joe and Dorothy, and Jim Clauson, also flew to San Francisco to attend the "Love" experience, a huge *est* meeting with four thousand people attending, held in the Masonic Auditorium on California Street. "When we were taken down front," Joe told me, "I didn't know what was going on. There was an empty stage, and the place was filled with thousands of people. Suddenly the lights dimmed, and someone said: 'Ladies and Gentlemen, Werner Erhard.' You know, I couldn't believe it. The roar that went up! That's the first time I heard him speak. I was in shock. I had no idea he was doing anything like this. I had never seen anything like this before!"

That evening, Werner talked with the assembled *est* graduates about love. Toward the end of his talk, he told again how he had left his family, and then announced that he had now gone back to find his parents. He said that he would like to share them with everyone, and brought Joe and Dorothy to the stage—to a standing ovation.

This time, Joe and Dorothy were able to stay in San Francisco for only a day. That was long enough for them to meet Ellen and their three grandchildren, Celeste, Adair, and St. John.

"I couldn't speak to Ellen the day that we met her and the children at the hotel in San Francisco," Dorothy told me. "It just wasn't there for me to do that. She sat with us at the event, in the auditorium, and I was very uneasy being with her. But I couldn't deny those children. They were so pleased to have grandparents!"

During the next several weeks, Werner contacted those of his relatives who now lived in California: his grandmother Clauson, his Aunt Ethel, his cousin Don Clauson, and others. He invited his cousin Norman Danoff, now an advertising executive in Los Angeles, to attend a special Guest Seminar there.

"He telephoned me one night around eleven o'clock," Norm told me. "We had a pleasant chat, and he remarked that he had heard that I was into meditation. He told me about *est*, and invited my wife Julie and me to attend the next Guest Seminar, at the Coconut Grove! *The Coconut Grove!* I wasn't really impressed: I thought it was just Werner treating everybody to drinks again. But we went, arrived at the Coconut Grove, and discovered that he had reserved the whole place! And it was free. At that point I was impressed.

"Then we heard Werner do his number. I am in advertising and as we left that night I said to Julie, 'Honey, you have just heard one of the greatest presenters you will ever see. He would make the greatest advertising man in the world.' That son of a bitch was good. Damn good. The audience was just going bananas.

"At the break we went up to see him. We invited him to have a drink with us afterward. When we finally reached him through the crush afterward, Julie remarked to him that people treated him like a god. He just laughed. Then I asked him whether God drinks. And he laughed again and said, 'Yes, God drinks. He also screws.' "

Meanwhile, in Philadelphia, Werner's return was still being kept secret from his and Pat's children. Just before Christmas, Clare, the eldest, guessed that he had returned. The younger three were not told about the return until a few days prior to his next visit, on January 15.

"After Christmas," Clare told me, "the three other children and I sat down at the table with Mom, and she told us about Dad's return. I thought that all the children would be thrilled, but they were very cool, and the younger ones—Jack and Debbie—weren't sure that they wanted to see him. Mom told us that it would be a good idea to see him, and then to make up our minds. I felt hurt and angry that some of them reacted like that. Yet I was glad that they weren't acting *too* excited, because I wanted to be careful not to hurt Mom's feelings. I was thrilled that he was back.

"We all went to see him at my grandparents' house. When we arrived, we didn't expect him to be there yet, but all the kids shoved me in the door first, just in case. He *was* there already. Just then he came around the corner.

"I started to get upset, and ran up to Joan's bedroom. I hadn't even said 'hello' yet. And there he was, kissing and hugging the other kids. Joan came up to me, and told me that it would be okay, and that I should go down to him. So I did.

"Everybody talked together for a while," Clare continued. "Then we went into the den—Mom, Dad, and us four kids—to be alone.

"The kids went over to the other side of the room, as if to be as far away from him as possible. But I sat down right next to him, and I felt for a while as if we were on a panel or talk show. Everybody was waiting for me to start the talk, and to handle it all with him. I didn't talk angrily with him, but I remember feeling angry when I talked about why he had left. I asked why he had left, and what he was doing now, and why he had returned. With every answer that he gave, I had another question.

"When I asked him why he came back, he said, 'Because I'm at a point where I can take responsibility for that.' I didn't know what that meant, and I told him so. Then he said, 'I'm at a point in my life where everything that I have done in the past is all right with me. So now, for the first time, I can take responsibility for what I have done.' When he put responsibility together with being all right, I got what he meant.

"But you know"—Clare beamed—"I didn't really care why he left. I felt that I was expected to get back at him, so that he would know that he had been bad.

"The other kids still weren't saying anything, so we decided to go back into the living room. Just as everyone was leaving the den, I touched him on the knee and asked him to wait a minute so that I could talk to him by myself. After the kids went out, Mom noticed that we were still there, and she shut the door and went out. I sat down in his lap then and told him how excited I was that he was back. I told him that I wanted to be very careful that Mom never got her feelings hurt, because I really loved her too. I told him how thrilled I was that he was back, and that I really loved him.

"By the end of that evening, all the kids had lightened up, and nobody wanted to leave. After sat down to eat, we were just like a family, and it was okay again. We stayed there with him until two or three in the morning."

Harry Rosenberg also told me about Werner's encounter with his children. "Their initial reaction to him," he said, "was much like my own. When they came in the door to the house, it was like they were going in front of the firing squad. They weren't frightened, but there was a lot of anticipation and some misery in their faces. There were a lot of questions to be answered.

"Pat was good about it," Harry said. "She was clear that she was wary, but she did not lay her own wariness on the kids. Their wariness was their own. Pat would get her remarks in, but it was clear that they were her own. Werner showed them all a lot of love and affection. Everyone wanted to sit next to him at dinner. By the end of the evening they were just hanging all around him. I have the picture of their all being in his arms. And they cried.

"You could see some jealousies popping up when he would turn his attention from one to the other. Werner did with them exactly what he had done with us. He told them what he did. He came clean with them. By the time they were ready to leave the house that night, the matter was no longer an issue for them. You could tell in the way that Werner spoke that he had felt incomplete without his family, and that he was truly glad to be back. It was clear that a part of his life had been missing, and that he wasn't getting full nourishment out of life with his family missing. He also explained that he had come back then because he was now able to handle it.

"But it never really looked like Werner was handling it," Harry concluded. "It just got handled."

A few weeks later, Werner returned again to the East Coast to lead a Guest Seminar in New York City. Most of the family went up to New York to hear him—uncles, aunts, parents, brother and sister. Clare was the only one of the children to attend, the others being still in school. "We went into that hotel," Clare told me, "and there were so many people waiting to hear him. Then he was introduced, and came onto the stage, and everybody stood up and started clapping. I realized then that my father was an important man, and I started crying."

In March, Dorothy, Joan, Harry, Clare, and Jim and Kitty Clauson went to New York City to take the training. "Werner cautioned us," Joan told me, "that we would go through the whole spectrum of emotions during the training. He said that we had to agree to finish it, that that was the only thing that he asked of us. He said we would hate him, and love him, during the course of the training."

Toward the end of the first weekend, Dorothy was asked to leave the training because she insisted on keeping her eyes open during one of the processes. She decided to return—and to keep the "agreements"—for the second weekend.

And she *got* the training. A few months afterward, as she told me, "I was sitting at Edith's house playing cards. I said to myself,

'What is is; and what ain't, ain't. Ellen is somebody's daughter. She is a mother. And she isn't a devil.' I got off it right there. I stopped carrying around all that resentment. I began to get along with her. If I hadn't taken the training I would never have been able to speak with her. That's when I started to get rid of a lot of my narrow-minded positions."

Dorothy also spent part of the summer of 1973 in San Francisco, where she took the *est* "consulting program," a one-to-one application of *est* techniques that is ordinarily available only to staff members. "By now the transformation in Dorothy was really beginning to show," Pat told me. "Before going out that summer, she had told me that she wouldn't stay with Ellen. When she got back, after having been through the consulting program, everything was suddenly all right with her about Ellen."

"I looked at Dorothy then," Joe told me, and saw the end of her misery. You can see the change in her. It's amazing. When I look at her now I could cry with joy."

The house in Plymouth Meeting became tranquil. "When I used to go home for the holidays," Nathan had told me, "my mother and my father, and my mother and Joan would always be fighting. Since they took the training, there has been peace and quiet at home. Now it's a pleasure to return."

Between 1973 and 1975, virtually every member of the wider family, including even Pat's parents and Ellen's mother, took the training. Most of them traveled to San Francisco to visit Werner, and participate in *est* events and seminars either in California or in Philadelphia and New York.

Joe Rosenberg was the last of the immediate family to take the training. "I was the doubter," he told me, "I kept saying to myself that that son of mine can't be that great. Finally I took it, and I see now how it changes people's lives. It is frightening to me that my son could do something that tremendous."

Any remaining doubters in the family were converted by the children. "My younger brother Jack and I went to our grandparents Fry," Clare told me. "We talked to them about the training, and about going through Rolfing, and all the things that we had done. Jackie and I had my grandfather—he is seventy-five years old—down on the floor, showing him what would happen to him if he got Rolfed. He was laughing and having a great time. He and my grandmother really wanted to take the training, you could tell. When they finally did enroll and take it, that opened the space for everyone else on that side of the family to take it too."

"Pat's parents, Mr. and Mrs. Fry, really love Werner, and support him," Joan told me. "He still calls them 'Mom' and 'Dad.' Their only problem initially was with Ellen. They had never met her, and they had all kinds of pictures and stories about who she was and what she represented. That wasn't resolved until Pat and Ellen themselves became friends."

THANKSGIVING: ONE FAMILY
By Thanksgiving Day 1974, two years after Werner's initial return to Philadelphia, there was no question but that one big, happy, and reunited family had been created. There was one loose end: Ellen and Pat had not yet met again. They had not seen each other since that afternoon in 1959 when they had confronted each other for the first time.

A grand reunion and three-day family meeting was arranged for Thanksgiving Day 1974. Werner and Ellen and their children were to fly in for the occasion, and Pat and Ellen were to meet.

I found Ellen and Pat together in the *est* Central office building, on California Street, in San Francisco, where they were both at work. Pat now works in Werner's office, and Ellen was in for the day to assist. I asked them about that Thanksgiving meeting, and about their relationship.

"The children had all gone out to California and had met Ellen before I did," Pat told me. "I had to get Werner handled first; then things could be all right with Ellen too. I had come to terms with her existence. So by Thanksgiving 1974 the only thing that remained was for me to meet her again. She had been back to Philadelphia before that—she had come in for Dorothy and Joe's fortieth wedding anniversary in 1973, and had met most of the family then, but I hadn't been able to be present. I still had reservations about her. Particularly with the kids out in California a lot, and with her being more or less in charge of them while they were there. At first I didn't want them to be with her. But by the second summer it got to be okay with me for her to be there, and for that to be the relationship that Werner wanted.

"When she walked in, at that Thanksgiving meeting, I guess we were both uneasy," Pat said, smiling. "Neither of us knew what to say. So we just started talking, and everything turned out to be great. You wouldn't have known that anything had taken place. She is the one person in my life of whom I can say that I went through all the emotions—from pure hatred to loving her."

"Pat and I are friends now," Ellen confirmed. "We were both nervous when we met. And we are a great deal alike.

"It's hard, I know," Ellen reflected, "for people to accept that our relationship is the way it is, and that it works. That we should have a good relationship conflicts with some people's pictures about what *should* happen. It doesn't fit the conventional pictures, and therefore some people, I suppose, find it threatening.

"If I had been in Pat's position," Ellen continued, looking very serious, "I don't know whether I could have gone through that. Pat's behavior toward me, and the way that the whole family behaved, really earned my admiration and respect. They did what needed to be done, and that was that. So the new relationship with the family formed gradually, and it is now superb. It all could have been blown so easily. It is a kind of fairy tale."

The Thanksgiving meeting, the two women told me, was carefully organized so as to draw each part of the larger family into the core group. The day after Thanksgiving, Al and Edith Rosenberg gave a party for the Rosenberg side of the family; on Saturday night Dorothy gave a party for the Clausons. Sunday night, Pat's parents joined the group. But most of the time was reserved for the core family group to be together.

This group—Joe and Dorothy, Werner, Joan, Harry, Nathan, Pat, Ellen and the seven children—gathered together in a circle, in the large den behind the living room at the house in Plymouth Meeting. Joan had already told me how the meeting began.

"Werner told us," Joan said, "that problems occur in families because the people in them are in mystery about one another. When you are really clear about me, you don't have a problem—whatever way it is. He said we were going to tell the truth, to allow everybody to know exactly where the others in the room were.

"So we each shared. Even the little kids came in—Celeste, and Adair, and even St. John. They got to meet everyone, and to say where they were too. Each of us said where we were in life; and if we had any problem with any other person in the room, we could communicate that, and clean it up right then and there, so that the family could start working. For the first time, I got to know those people that I had grown up with.

"Werner shared about where he was in life. When he did that, I experienced who he was; and the instant I got who he was, I got who I was. The past disappeared, and all that was left was *now*. Prior to that"—Joan smiled—"I had had some doubts about Werner and the training. I knew that he did good things, but I still thought that it was a rip-off. I fantasized that Werner was laughing behind the scenes at the idiots who paid for the training. I remember once that Jack Rafferty told me, 'Joan, you don't get it. You don't know who Werner is.' I thought then, 'Oh, sure Jack, you work for him.' But at Thanksgiving I got it. Werner said then that his purpose in life is to have people's lives work, and that he made an agreement with God to do that—and that everyone has that agreement with God. And he had broken that agreement. There was so much sincerity and truth and love when Werner told us about this. It was just so for him. The room was still. You could hear a pin drop. That's the first time I heard him say that. And I got it.

"The space really opened up at the Thanksgiving meeting for my mother too. My mother is now my best friend. And it was not like that before. There is now nothing that I couldn't tell her. I have no withholds from her."

Joan beamed. "That is when my family actually started. The love had been there before, but was held down by all sorts of messy things. The messy stuff was brought out into the open, and communicated, during the meeting. Afterward, all that was left was the love."

Clare added to Joan's account. "It got a little uncomfortable for me," she said. "All these deep dark secrets were coming out. Dad seemed always to know just what was going on with anybody in the room. He didn't let any of us get away with anything. If there was something there, it got said.

"We began to get that we are a family," Clare said, "and that we had to allow a lot of space for it to be there and to participate in it. We realized how great our family was, and that we all contributed to what it could be.

"Since then, there haven't been many problems in the family. We get together a lot now, and talk about things, whereas we used to fight a lot.

"The room got very high," Clare said. "A lot of love and communication came from the sharing. I thought that the roof was going to come off the house. It was the way the training is on the fourth night. Everybody became really quiet, listening and interested."

"It is incredible," Joe Rosenberg told me, shaking his head. "There is no longer anything hidden between any of us. I'm not ashamed to tell Werner what I feel like, and he's not ashamed of telling me what he did and didn't do. The relationship is so great that all the other wonderful things that Werner has done are as nothing compared to this. If Werner never did anything else, or never does another thing, he has pulled this family together like nothing in the world could."

THIRTEEN On an Airplane Flying East

For most mortals personality may signify the greatest of blessings: it is the tragedy of tragedies for the metaphysician that he cannot ever entirely overcome his own individuality.
   —Hermann Keyserling

I don't have any personal history. One day I found out that personal history was no longer necessary for me and, like drinking, I dropped it.
   —Don Juan, Journey to Ixtlan

PUPPETS PLAYING OUT INSTRUCTIONS

In his lectures on *The Politics of the Family*, psychiatrist R. D. Laing reports how each generation molds the one that follows. We enact, "unbeknown to ourselves, a shadow play, as images of images of images . . . of the dead, who have in their turn embodied and enacted such dramas projected upon them, and induced in them, by those before them."[1] We are all, Laing suggests, puppets playing out instructions, projections, machinelike programs, patterns. We are wholly dependent on, prisoners and victims of, our individual pasts.

While Werner Erhard does not contest what Laing writes, insofar as it does apply to the lives of most people, he makes a remarkable claim. "At all times," he says, "and under all circumstances, we have the power to transform the quality of our lives." Like Castaneda's Don Juan, Werner denies that he continues to be the living ghost of his own or his parents' past, denies that he is the victim or effect of what he has been or been taught, of what has happened to him. Rather, he claims to have completed his own past, and his relationships with people in his past.

Thus Werner makes an extraordinary claim to freedom. If what he says is correct, the story of his life, his "soap opera," as he calls it, is—despite its great interest—the least important thing about him as he is today. To concentrate on his past to understand how he got to where he is today—or where he may be tomorrow—is to miss what he has to say.

To the psychologist such as Laing, or Freud, or for that matter to most philosophers of empiricist stripe who believe that a man is the sum of his bodily sensations, Werner's claim to be free of a past that he has completed may sound preposterous. To the man of "character," Werner's notion may also come as an affront: it may be supposed that any reliable man finds his character or "identity" and sticks to it. In the good old days, nobody worried about rigidity of character; it was supposed to be rigid. You could not count on someone who was flexible. Change of character, change of values, were supposed to be desirable only for the wicked.[2]

In this view, one has enough freedom to bear full blame for one's faults, but not enough to be able to reform. Jean-Paul Sartre speaks of the supposition that "one never seeks but that which one has already found. . . . One never becomes other than what one already was," and of the precautions by which we imprison a man in what he is, as if we lived in perpetual fear that he might escape from it, that he might break away and suddenly elude his condition.[3] Werner's claim also affronts "common sense," the common sense for instance of Johann Nestroy, when he wrote: "I believed the worst about everybody, including myself, and I was but seldom mistaken."

In Werner's view, such common sense, as well as the philosophical empiricism that is a part of it, serves to reduce consciousness and awareness, serves to keep men and women in a waking sleep, serves to retard the creation of value. His own role he sees precisely as an intrusion into, a deliberate affront to, such areas of unconsciousness, and to the spiritual nihilism and defeatism that attend them.

WITH DIGNITY, AND WITHOUT RIGHTEOUSNESS

It was now just a year since my first trip to Philadelphia to meet Joe and Dorothy Rosenberg. I was on my way to Philadelphia again. This time Werner was with me. We sat together in the lounge of the jet.

The occasion was a special one. Werner was on his way to lead the first *est* training to be given in Philadelphia. And his mother, Dorothy, had been in charge of organizing it. The Philadelphia center had not yet been set up by *est;* and all the arrangements, including the registration of the trainees, had been made through a temporary telephone installation in Joe and Dorothy's living room in Plymouth Meeting.

"The transformation in my mother has been spectacular," Werner confirmed to me. "During those years when I was away she became old. On my return she was haggard; she was no longer the beauty that she had been as a young woman. But in the last several years even her beauty has returned.

"But that is the least of it. My mother had never been popular with my father's side of the family. She always suspected that somebody was up to something. And although she was usually right, that got to be a pain in the neck. In the last several years, however, that too has altered. The whole family has begun to feel her warmth. Not that it wasn't there before: it just was not expressed before."

I asked Werner about his own relationship with Dorothy. He grinned. "To put it in the most modest terms," he replied, "my mother and I have now worked ourselves *up* to a ground zero in our relationship. We had gone far down into minus; and we have now at least come up to zero.

"Most of what goes on between us is the simple expression of affection, with little form to it. My mother has played well, and has avoided form. She has for the most part taken the forms that are not directly related to me: she goes to seminars, for example, but I am not there. And she has organized this training for me to lead. She has given up her righteousness, but has maintained her dignity. Her behavior throughout has been totally appropriate.

"The potential in our relationship is still not expressed," Werner said. "And it may never be expressed. It may indeed be more difficult to express than it is worth. The important things are, first, that the past no longer controls either of us in the development of our relationship. And second, our relationship truly is expanding. My mother is one of comparatively few people with whom I feel that I truly can play at the highest level. She has intention."

YOU CAN'T GO WEST FOREVER

As our plane cruised over the Rockies, the sky became sparklingly clear. Werner was standing on the far side of the cabin, peering out the window, trying to locate Aspen.

"My relationship with Dorothy is expanding now," he said when he returned to his seat. "That is the only important thing about *any* relationship. In fact, there are only two games in life. One is to expand—to participate, and play wholeheartedly. The other is to contract. There is no such thing as holding still.

"The secret—as to whether you will contract or expand, in your relationships and in life—has to do with your relationships with your parents. Until you complete your relationships with them, you have little ability to expand. Indeed, you can do little more than act out or dramatize the limitations in your relationships with them.

"The reason why this is not more keenly perceived has to do with *change*. People mistake change for expansion. In fact, however, change is usually a manifestation of contraction. For change is simply a variation on a theme; and the theme is some unconscious pattern in your relationship with your parents. Thus change is the reenactment of, a variation on, some limited pattern. Such change produces no satisfaction in life, not even when it is undertaken precisely to obtain greater satisfaction.

"Much of my life is the story of such *utterly futile* change. I fled from Philadelphia westward to Saint Louis. I fled Saint Louis for California and the Northwest. I wandered from one discipline to another trying to change myself—from self-image psychology and psycho-cybernetics to human potential and encounter; to Zen, Subud, and Scientology.

"Of course good things can come out of change: these moves and changes benefited me in obvious ways, as it turned out. In the register of pluses and minuses, they were pluses. But pluses don't produce satisfaction. No amount of pluses can add up to make you whole. Quite the contrary, these changes in my life circumstances were expressions not of my satisfaction in life, but of my lack of it. I was never satisfied where I was, no matter how good it became; and thus I constantly sought to change—within narrowly defined limits. These changes only dramatized my inability to create satisfaction in my life from where I was.

"If I wasn't happy where I was—and I never was—I thought that I could always change or move on. I could always go west. That is the story of most people, perhaps especially in America: they don't like it where they are; they move or change; and then they make the same mess all over again—just as I did. Their pasts become their futures. People make the same mess over and over again because they carry with them, wherever they go, whatever they do, the patterns and dramatizations stemming from the lack of completion in their relationships with their parents.

"But you can't go west forever.

"Not, at any rate, if you want satisfaction. To be satisfied, to expand, *you must first be where you are, and do what you're doing*—no matter where you are and no matter what you are doing.

"Transformation produces this kind of state; and you can't be transformed without completing your relationships with your parents.

"This doesn't mean that transformed people don't change. To the contrary, when you are transformed, and are *coming from* satisfaction—that is, when you are coming to your experience of the world from a state of being satisfied—then you *can* change. And that is different from *having to* change. Now you have a true choice. You can go west, east, or stay where you are. Whatever change occurs, occurs in the context of transformation, and thus occurs in the direction of expansion, workability, and aliveness. Transformation recontextualizes change."

FORGIVENESS

It was early evening now. For the past hour Werner had been writing. As he finished his work, he turned to me again.

"There is something I've left out of this story," Werner said. "After my experience of transformation, there was no doubt that I would return to Philadelphia to attempt to correct what I had done there, and to complete my relationships with my parents, and with Pat and our children.

"But that doesn't mean that they had to take me back! No one would have blamed them if they had refused to have anything to do with me. Many people would say that that would be the 'right' thing for them to do. My parents are obviously very big people, if for no other reason than for having made space in their lives for me after my having been gone, and out of contact, for nearly thirteen years.

"Not only did they make space for me. They gave me the ultimate gift a parent has for his children. They expanded their own aliveness, and they allowed me to participate in their lives while they were doing that. My mother and father, each in his or her own way, used the experience of the *est* training to expand his or her experience of love, happiness, health, and self-expression. And thereby they assisted me to become complete in my relationships with them.

"I'm not talking here about forgiveness," Werner added. "You can of course say that my parents and I have forgiven each other, but that doesn't capture what happened. People often don't understand what is involved in forgiving. They think that if somebody does something wrong, and you forgive him, that is like saying that it was all right to do it that time—but don't dare to do it again. But life doesn't work that way; and it's stupid or hypocritical to forgive someone on that basis. If somebody does something, you can bet that he or she will do it again.

"That is why I prefer to talk about 'making space' and 'completion.' To the extent that forgiveness is involved, it is more like *self*-forgiving and self-acceptance. When you forgive yourself for something, you have to create the space for that thing to exist. For whatever you resist, and fail to make space for, will indeed manifest itself in you.

"Self-forgiving, and self-accepting, is an essential part of completing relationships. If there is something about your past that you are ashamed of, or guilty about—if there is something in it that you are hanging onto—if there is something there that you are using to burden another person—that will prevent you from completing your relationships.

"In order to transcend *having to be* any particular type of person, you have to make it all right with yourself to be that type of person. The moment when you really experience that you have created yourself being whatever way you are, at the same moment you will never have to be that way again.

"This self-forgiving, self-acceptance, goes hand in hand with forgiving others, making space for others, completing your relationships with others. You cannot complete a relationship with any person whom you do not admire and respect *as he or she is, and as he or she is not*—rather than the way you think she is or would like her to be. What I told Joan that night outside the house in Plymouth Meeting is accurate: 'Rocks are hard, water's wet, and Mother's Mother.' Love for a person is acceptance of him or her the way he is and the way he is not.

"So long as you do not know who you really are, this will be difficult. To complete a relationship, you may have to give up a lot of things to which you may be attached. You may have to give up your resentments, your anger, your upset, your annoyance, your desire to punish. You have not been assigned the job of evaluating your parents, and you will have to give up making them wrong. You will have to give up resisting their domination, and be prepared to have it appear that they win and you lose.

"Thus the only cause for not admiring and respecting someone is something *within yourself*, something that you are unwilling to create. You cannot forgive anyone else until you have forgiven yourself. Once you know who you really are, you can complete all your relationships. By giving myself the space to be bad, by forgiving myself, I created the possibility, for the first time in my life, truly to be good. As soon as I could accept myself, I could accept my parents. That is why I seemed 'different' when I returned to Philadelphia.

"The only way to deal with the future," Werner said, looking out the window at the Philadelphia skyline, which had just come into view as the plane began to descend, "is to put yourself in a space where you are functioning effectively *now*. My past used to have me. By taking responsibility for it—as those years of disciplines and the particular experience that generated *est* enabled me to do—I got to get my past. Now I no longer am my past; now I have my past, and it does not have me. My past is now my past. It isn't sticking into my present and my future. Now I have the space to come from the Self, to generate my own experience, here and now.

"I don't have to encounter my past in others either—since my parents and my whole family have also taken responsibility for all of it. Our relationship with one another is so great because we can, *all* of us, expand."

We rose to return to our seats in the main cabin. "It is written in the Bible," Werner Erhard recalled, "that a prophet is not without honor save in his own country, and in his own home. I cannot tell you what incredible support it is, and what a beautiful place it is to come from, when one has made it with one's own family, in one's own home."

"And in one's own city," I added, as the pilot announced our landing in Philadelphia.

Epilogue

It is perhaps not surprising that stories about gurus are devoted chiefly to their trials and enlightenment, and pass hurriedly over what happened "after" the moment of transformation. For it is all so irrelevant. There is, for instance, the gruesome Indian tale of the hero king Vikramaditya and his long night of adventure in the graveyard, carrying the corpses of his own selves. Finally he passes the macabre test and the "veil of ignorance" is lifted. At this point the Hindu storytellers know enough to end their tale, adding only that "during the following years . . . his earthly life was enlarged in virtue and glory." Similarly, David Stacton's Zen story *Segaki* is devoted to the trials, tribulations, and eventual enlightenment of the medieval monk Muchaku. In the last chapter, almost as an afterthought, we learn that "in the course of time, somewhat to his surprise, he became a National Teacher."

This book follows in this tradition. My purpose in writing it was threefold. First, I wanted to tell the story—the *essential* story—of Werner Erhard, the story of his education and transformation, and the completion of his relationship with his family. It is an extraordinary and moving tale, and so distinctively American as to have veritable documentary power. Second, I wanted to give an account, in the setting of an individual life, of the chief disciplines Werner encountered in his long years of searching prior to creating *est*. These are, I believe, an important part of the American story today; yet they are unfamiliar to many readers; and there has been, hitherto, little context or background in which they could be intelligently discussed or evaluated. This book takes a step toward making them more accessible, and tries to do so without mystification. Third, I have tried to give a preliminary literary statement of the fundamental presuppositions, theoretical and practical, behind Werner's own perspective, as it has been embodied, in oral form, in the *est* training and educational program. I have *not* tried in this book to tell the story of *est*. That is a subject for another book, to be told in the perspective of another decade.

Yet many readers will want something more: they will want to know *what happened*. A success story is after all mythic too. And Werner allowed for this when he said, describing the aftermath of his experience of transformation: "It was all over for Werner Erhard. Yet now, for the first time, I could use that particular personality, Werner Erhard, as a means of expression." What happened afterward—up to the present moment—is the story of the deployment and self-expression of that curious and composite personality, Jack Rosenberg/Werner Erhard.

Werner's first, and perhaps major, form of self-expression is, of course, the *est* training itself. I am thinking not of its commercial success, but of its impact on the 150,000 persons who have so far graduated from it. For many of them it has been, as Ron Baldwin said earlier of Werner, "*the* irreversible experience" of their lives. Perhaps this justifies Werner's striking claim that he has, through the medium of the *est* training, been "privileged to be profoundly intimate with more people than anyone in history."

Language is a medium of intimacy; and in his impact on the language of this decade, Werner has also affected the sensibility of the wider community. People often remark on the ease with which one can identify an *est* graduate, and explain how this is due to the *est* jargon, the network of terms—space, relationship, responsibility, appropriate, agreement, barrier, communication, acknowledge, aliveness, contextualize, get it, re-create, intention, Mind machinery, source, support, victim, and so on—that arise in the *est* training, and which many graduates continue to use afterward. The dictionary defines *jargon* as "unintelligible words, gibberish, barbarous or debased language." In this sense, *est* terminology is hardly jargon; and it is hardly limited any longer to *est* graduates. Language does not simply express thought; it also molds it. Metaphor determines the space one inhabits and creates a way of seeing the world and its inhabitants, a sensibility. In adopting a form of expression, one's patterns of thinking, style, attitudes and reactions, experience of life, may be altered. *est* terminology thus serves as a deliberate tool for consciousness raising and context creation, and constitutes an invasion, by *est*, into the wider community.

The standard *est* training is not the only vehicle for Werner's perspective. In addition to the training and the graduate seminar program, which are now offered regularly in twenty cities, there are the six-day course, the communication workshop, the relationship series, the teen and children's trainings, and others. Prison trainings have been offered to prisoners in San Quentin state prison, and in Leavenworth, Lompoc, and Alderson federal prisons; and negotiations are under way on the federal level to give the *est* training routinely to persons who are about to be released from prison. The aim of each of these programs, although they are implemented in different circumstances, is the same: to effect transformation on a personal, relational and institutional level, to expose positionality and the damaging effect it has on human lives, and to turn individuals away from being the victims of the circumstances in their lives, thereby producing happier, more loving, and more responsible people.

With The Hunger Project, founded in 1977, Werner extends this aim beyond individuals and institutions to the whole world community. This project, at once the most promising and most bewildering of Werner's inventions, is dedicated to exposing the *assumptions* that prevent a solution to the problems of world hunger (here, as always, Werner's basic conviction is that ideas, not conditions, defeat human aspirations), and eradicating death by starvation within twenty years. It is not designed to feed anyone; it is not a food-shipment or charity program. It is intended, rather, to transform defeatist public opinion throughout the world that permits widespread starvation to continue. Although the project is only one year old, it has had a promising beginning. At its very start, in September 1977, a writer for the *Colorado Statesman* came away puzzled by Werner's first Hunger Project presentation. "It is difficult to believe," he wrote, "that 1,700 tickets could be sold at $6 apiece for a discussion of the problems of world hunger and starvation. Certainly no Colorado politician has that kind of clout with his constituency." Colorado was, however, only the start. Within two months, some 36,000 persons across the country attended Werner's presentations on world hunger; and over 200,000 persons have now enlisted in the Project. Werner, meanwhile, is working in regular consultation with statesmen and politicians both in America and abroad to devise ways to implement the Project; and he has been nominated to membership in the Club of Rome, an exclusive and informal international organization founded in 1968. Often described as an "invisible college," the Club's members are convinced that traditional institutions are unable any longer to cope with the complex economic, political, and social problems confronting mankind. Their aim is to foster understanding of the scope of problems and to promote new initiatives.

Another of Werner's personal projects—after completing his relationship with Ellen, and with Joe and Dorothy, Pat, and their families—has been to complete his relationship with his *spiritual* ancestors. He has traveled extensively in the Orient, particularly in India, the Himalayas, and Japan, in search of spiritual leaders from whom he could learn, and to sponsor visits by them to America. "My approach," he has said, "is one of wanting to get the universal from the Eastern tradition, rather than wanting to get the *Eastern* from the Eastern tradition. I would like to make space for a true transformation of society that is not limited by any one of those disciplines and traditions and that includes them all." To further this aim, *est* has sponsored visits and presentations in America by Swami Muktananda and also by His Holiness the Gyalwa Karmapa, one of the chief religious leaders of Tibet.

When Werner visited the Karmapa, in Sikkim, His Holiness told him about the ancient prophecies of Padma Sambhava, Guru Rimpoche, who brought Buddhism to Tibet. Padma Sambhava prophesied that the Dharma—the Buddhist teachings and knowledge of enlightenment—would go to the West "when iron birds fly and horses have wheels." It was also prophesied that, in this future time of stress and turmoil, people would no longer be able to pursue enlightenment by traditional means requiring long periods of withdrawal from the world. Instead, there would be created a method equal to the greater stress and accelerated pace of society, so that what had previously taken years of practice could be achieved much more quickly. "So it feels to me," the Karmapa said to Werner, "very much as if you have come home."

At one point in their travels in the United States, Swami Muktananda and the Karmapa met—at a conference in Ann Arbor, Michigan. Swami Muktananda turned to the Karmapa. "Werner," he said, "is a yogi who hides his knowledge."

Appendix & Notes

Appendix
A PHILOSOPHER'S EVALUATION OF THE est TRAINING

Much discussion and evaluation of the *est* training has been published in the last several years. Both euphoric praise and damning criticism of it leave something to be desired. Neither is very informative; and both reactions may be connected with the "right/wrong game" that is discredited in the course of the training itself. One cannot tell from excitement alone whether an individual just had a good time at the training or actually experienced transformation. In negative responses, silly carping can be lumped together indiscriminately with insightful observations.

There is, however, no reason why the *est* training cannot be evaluated in a relatively responsible way. This appendix aims to do some consciousness raising about the whole issue of evaluating a training.

First, there is the *consumer question* as to whether good value is received for the sum paid (at present $300). The question applies whether the trainee took the training for enlightenment, therapy, improved relationships, to be "with it," for the theatre of it all, for entertainment, to meet people, whatever.

The answer appears to be favorable. *est*'s policy has been to have satisfied customers, satisfied with what they got, whatever they got. Thus *est* has always refunded the cost of the training to anyone who withdraws from it. Moreover, the growth in the number of graduates of the training has taken place entirely by word of mouth on the part of the people who have taken the training: *est* has never advertised. Finally, *est*'s financial statement shows that most receipts are poured back into the enterprise for development and expansion, and to support such enterprises as The Hunger Project.

Another question is the *question of danger*. Can the *est* training harm a participant? Four independent surveys of *est* graduates have been commissioned by *est* to assess results of the training and deliberately to seek evidence of possible harm. No evidence of harm has been found. The first of these, a modest survey prepared by Behaviordyne, Inc., an independent research group, on the basis of the California Psychological Inventory (CPI), was published in Abstract form in May 1973. The results were wholly favorable. A more elaborate survey, referred to as "The *est* Outcome Study," was conducted, with 1,400 *est* graduates participating, during the following year, and was authored by Robert Ornstein and Charles Swencionis, of the University of California, San Francisco, medical center; Arthur Deikman, M.D., and Ralph Morris, M.D. The results, in the words of Ornstein and Swencionis, "support the view that *est* is not harmful." A third study was prepared in 1976 by sociologists Earl Babbie, of the University of Hawaii, and Donald Stone, of the University of California, Berkeley.[1] The Babbie-Stone study concludes that *est* graduates are strongly favorable in their reports of benefits from the training "in a wide variety of life conditions," and that these benefits do not diminish over time.

A fourth study, prepared in 1977 by Professor J. Herbert Hamsher, of Temple University, in Philadelphia, surveyed 242 mental health professional workers—psychiatrists, psychologists, and social workers—who are graduates of the *est* training and who have worked with 1,739 patients who have graduated from the training. The therapists surveyed rated the impact of the training on their personal lives, on their ability to do therapy, and on their patients, in an overwhelmingly positive way. Sixty-eight percent of those therapists surveyed also reported applying *est* processes in their own work.

The Hamsher study also searched for evidence of possible harm from the training. From a sample of 163 persons who had been hospitalized prior to the training, it was discovered that 119 had no hospitalizations after the training; 33 had fewer hospitalizations than before; 11 had the same number; and no one had more hospitalizations than before.

The Hamsher study also examined psychiatric emergencies following the training. In twenty-six cases reported, patients were rated by their therapists as slightly improved in functioning after the emergency as compared to their prior level of functioning.

The therapists studied by Hamsher advised that those patients with neuroses, character disorders, and addictive personalities could take the training profitably without serious risk of harm; but that compensated psychotics should not take the training.

A recent study by Glass, Kirsch, and Parris appears to relate to this last recommendation. Glass and his associates report seven cases of persons who suffered serious disturbances following the training.[2] These authors carefully point out that these case reports do *not* establish any cause and effect relationship between *est* and a psychotic episode. On the contrary, Glass has stated in an interview that "we don't know if more people become psychotic after *est* than after riding on the F train."[3] A reading of the *"est* Outcome Study" suggests that there is a lower incidence of psychotic episodes for people who have taken the training than for those who have not.

The view that *est* is not harmful is also supported by the existence of many medical and psychiatric professionals on the *est* Advisory Board. These include Philip R. Lee, professor of Social Medicine and former chancellor of the University of California, San Francisco; and Dr. Helen Nahm, former Dean of the School of Nursing of the University of California, San Francisco. Four of the *est* trainers or trainer candidates also have medical or psychological qualifications. In any case, *est* attempts to screen out disturbed persons prior to accepting their applications; and even persons in ordinary therapy may take the training only with the knowledge of their therapists.

Another question is the *question of results*. Does the *est* training work? Is it effective? This question needs to be analyzed. *On whose terms* does it work? 1) On terms accepted by independent investigators? 2) Or in *est*'s own internal terms?

The first question has been investigated in a preliminary and favorable way by the Behaviordyne report, the Outcome study, and the Babbie-Stone study. The second question does not appear to have been researched.

The Behaviordyne report, as could be expected from its use of the California Psychological Inventory Test, focused on *improved self-image*. Both males and females started out above average in this area, yet the survey still showed improvement—and improvement that increases with time. Three months after taking the *est* training, a male is "less anxious and dependent. He shows less guilt and fewer fears; with a lessening of psychophysiologic reactions." For females, the report states, one may "say the same as for the males, plus some additional changes such as a greater sense of self, more ambition coupled with an increased demand upon self."

The Outcome study focused more on issues of "health and well-being." Respondents reported "strong positive health and well-being changes since taking the *est* Standard Training, especially in the areas of psychological health and well-being and those illnesses with a large psychosomatic component."[4]

While results such as these are interesting, they are not entirely to the point. For the terms in which the independent investigators were working are different from *est*'s own terms. *est* does not claim to produce changes in self-image or in health; it aims to enable a *transformation* in one's ability to experience living. It may be difficult to measure this: as Werner himself put it, commenting on this research, "The real value of *est* is found in the transformation of the quality of graduates' experience, which is difficult, if not impossible, to measure in the commonplace scientific sense."

A more informative behavioral survey would, then, need to identify those manifestations that are emphasized in the *est* training. These might include responsibility; freedom from resentment, righteousness and domination; the ability to "be here now" without being controlled by memories or images from the past; the lack of positionality implicit in being able to "get off" one position after the other. While such behavior is not tantamount to enlightenment or transformation, it is on the *est* view more representative of transformed being. While "improved self-image" may be related to such behavior, it plays no role in, and to some extent conflicts theoretically with, the *est* training, which aims at the transcendence of ego images.

The most important kind of research that needs to be done on the *est* training, however, has little to do with behavioral surveys. Although *est* is *all about* nonconceptual experience, that does not prevent it from itself being a theoretical system memorialized in concepts. The examination of theoretical conceptual systems has today reached a rather refined level, and the *est* system has as yet gone unexamined on such a level. Such an examination would assist in clarifying key *est* notions, such as enlightenment and transformation, Mind, Self, and responsibility, and in refining the understanding of such things as levels of knowing and experiencing. This book is itself a halting first step in this direction, taking as it does a living philosophy which is being formulated and communicated entirely orally, and attempting to render it partially in literary form.

Such an examination would also permit the *est* position to be compared and contrasted with other disciplines and traditions. At the moment it is hard to do this. For example, Werner's use of "Self" *seems* to be developing in a direction different from some Oriental notions with which many persons have compared *est* in the past. Without a systematic conceptual and theoretical investigation, however, it is difficult to determine whether and to what extent this is indeed so.

Although Werner deplores the way in which individuals use concepts to cut themselves off from experience, thus impoverishing their lives, he is neither anticonceptual nor anti-intellectual in the way in which some persons in the human potential movement have appeared to be from time to time. Rather, he has argued that conceptualizing is inevitable. In that case, one would need to "take responsibility" for it. It would be most responsible for *est* to assume the task of pioneering research on the theory and concepts that it has itself injected into the world. These are at the moment still a rampant restless sea of metaphor.

Such research would contribute to the investigation of the core theory and techniques of the training. One area that needs clarifying is the treatment of determinism in Werner's thinking and in the *est* training, wherein the Mind is represented as being determined, and the Self as being free. If Mind is taken to refer to the entire human "biocomputer," then there appears to be a disagreement between Carl Rogers and Werner: Rogers sees an area for indeterminism within the biocomputer, and Werner does not. As I indicated in the third *Intersection*, I believe that current research in these areas, as represented for example by Popper and Eccles, would corroborate Rogers's position.[5]

The principle of re-creation, which is a variant of the Scientology principle of duplication, also needs to be examined. Werner contends that the force in *any condition in life*, if fully re-created in experience, will disappear. This is a truly cosmic principle, more abstract than the related theory of anamnesis and abreaction in Freud. This principle applies not only to headaches and minor aches and pains (processes for dealing with which are presented in the training). If correct, it applies to *anything whatever*, not just to minor problems. It provides a recipe for the destruction of matter by consciousness. Werner himself contrasts this principle with the principle of the conservation of energy. Such a striking general claim should most certainly be tested. Meanwhile, apparent success or failure of techniques founded on this prin-

ciple in the context of the *est* training itself does not suffice for purposes of testing. The training is not a test situation, and within it only
very general guidelines are laid down for re-creating experience. In
the *est* graduate seminars, and in the *est* consulting program, a rather
more detailed technology is worked out. Even here, however, the
theory and technique remain programmatic.

What would happen, for instance, if a condition that someone
had attempted to re-create experientially did *not* vanish?

When that happens, a choice appears: either to abandon the principle of re-creation; *or* to say that the person in this instance simply
failed sufficiently to re-create the condition. At this point in the development of *est* theory, it would perhaps be reasonable to take the
second alternative. But at what point does one cease to put the onus on
the person who is attempting an experiential re-creation and instead
fault the principle of re-creation itself? Here is the point where a good
program stands in danger of being turned into a bad *belief*. The principle could become an impregnable belief. In this case, it would be the
belief that, whatever actually happens, if something *were* sufficiently
re-created in experience, then it *would* vanish. Such a belief may be
maintained whether or not anything ever does vanish. It may be maintained in the face of any experience whatever, and thus is intrinsically
nonscientific.

This kind of difficulty in testing is by no means unique to *est*'s
principle of re-creation; such difficulties are endemic in scientific research. Philosophers and methodologists sometimes call such principles *metaphysical research programs*. They express ways of seeing the
world that suggest ways of exploring it. Such programs have played a
vital role in the history of science and medicine, and have sponsored
some important research—and some rank nonsense. The difficulty in
them, which distinguishes them from scientific statements, is that
they are largely immune to experimental falsification.

It might seem that it would be an advantage for a theory to be
immune to falsification, but this is not so. Potential falsification is the
very essence of scientific enterprise, and the question that scientists
ask of a new theory—"Under what conditions would this theory be
false?"—is itself like an *est* process: it detaches the questioner from the
theory that he is examining; it places him in a point of view outside the
positionality of the theory itself; such a question is intrinsically enlightening.

It is important in this connection to distinguish between a verification and a falsification of a theory. A verification, or validation, is

simply a positive instance. Thus for "all planets move in ellipses," a verification would be an example of a planet that does move in an ellipse.

A falsification is a negative instance. Thus for "all planets move in ellipses," a falsification would be an example of a planet that fails to move in an ellipse. Falsifying examples are obviously more important than verifying examples: whereas a single verifying example comes nowhere near proving a theory, a single falsifying example may suffice to refute it.

So the theory that, say, "all planets move in ellipses" is scientific in character because one can ask and answer, in advance, the question of what conditions would render it false. One knows what is at stake. The scientist can *specify in advance* that the theory would be refuted, and thus abandoned, in case a planet that does not move elliptically were discovered.

Verifying, or validating, instances, by contrast, are less enlightening. While any scientific theory can of course be verified, so can any other theory, including metaphysics and pseudoscience. Positive instances are cheap and easy to come by; and a positive instance, in and of itself, tells almost nothing about the truth of a theory.

Metaphysical research programs can be verified or validated, but not falsified. Take some important examples:

1) "For every event there is a cause."
2) "For every disease there is a cure."
3) "All bodily changes are due to physical causes."
4) "All mental changes are due to physiological causes."
5) "There exists a philosopher's stone, a stone that turns base metal into gold."
6) "There exists a fountain of youth."

Each of the principles cited has played an important role in the history of science. The first four are still, although controversial, part of contemporary science. The fifth, although no longer believed to be true, played an important role in the development of chemistry. The last principle, also no longer accepted, inspired some of the great voyages of exploration.

Each can potentially be verified or validated. One may find a cause for some event, a cure for some disease, a physical cause for some bodily change, a physiological cause for some mental change. And one may—if one is *very* lucky—find a philosopher's stone or a fountain of youth.

But under what circumstances would these principles be refuted? It is hard to specify potential falsifiers of such principles in advance.

Suppose that one is investigating an event and can find no cause. Will one reject the principle that every event has a cause? Probably not; instead one will go on looking, for *there is no way to tell* when one has found an event without a cause. Seeming exceptions will be treated as evidence only of ignorance. The same applies to the second principle: if one is investigating a disease and can find no cure for it, one may well not abandon the principle that there is a cure for every disease. There is no way to specify in advance what circumstances would force one to give up the search. The other examples may be treated similarly. Since such statements, although closely connected with science, are not themselves scientific, are not themselves refutable, it is easy to turn them into dogmas.

This brings us back to the principle of re-creation—the contention that any condition that is experientially re-created vanishes. Under what specified experimental circumstances would one be prepared to abandon this principle?

Although there are at the moment many examples of apparent verifications, or validations, of this principle, there have so far been no serious attempts to refute it. Until such an attempt is made, the theory is untested; it is a metaphysical research program and not a scientific theory.

Thus *est* needs to sponsor attempts to specify the conditions under which this theory and its associated techniques and processes work—and those conditions, if any, under which they do not work. Such research, whether or not ultimately successful, would be bound to be enlightening.

If, after such testing, this core *est* theory and technique were refuted, that would by no means invalidate the training or such results of the training as have been attested by the Behaviordyne, Outcome, Babbie-Stone, and Hamsher studies. The training would remain a way to benefit health and well-being, to improve self-image, and even to effect transformation.

In conclusion, it seems to me that one may take either what I call a "minimal view" or a "maximal view" of the *est* training.

According to the minimal interpretation, the *est* training does work in the sense that it is highly effective in rapidly producing results agreed to be beneficial: it improves self-image and benefits health and well-being; it decreases righteousness and positionality; it takes people out of the self-destructive role of victim and into a more responsible and creative stance in their lives—*whatever the explanation*. It produces such results, as a matter of practice, whether or not the *est* theory is correct.

A maximal interpretation, on the other hand, would contend not only that the training is effective in the respects just suggested, but that it is also theoretically sound in all particulars.

Werner Erhard himself does not take the maximal interpretation. He advocates the theory of the *est* training in a conjectural and nonpositional way as an effective way of looking at the world and dealing with experience. He is interested in finding out how well his theories stand up to scientific test, but he is not attached to their truth, and is absolutely opposed to their being turned into a belief system. Thus the interpretation held by Werner himself presumably lies somewhere between the minimal and maximal interpretations. Until further research is done, that is a good place to rest.

Notes

Introduction
Epigraph. George Santayana on William James in "The Genteel Tradition in American Philosophy," delivered to the Philosophical Union of the University of California on August 25, 1911. Printed in *Winds of Doctrine* (London: J. M. Dent, 1912), p. 204.
1. op. cit.
  Epigraph to Part I Nigel Dennis, *Cards of Identity* (London: Weidenfeld & Nicolson, 1955).
  Chapter 1 Epigraph. Sigmund Freud, *The Interpretation of Dreams*, in *The Basic Writings of Sigmund Freud* (New York: Modern Library, 1935), p. 308.
  Chapter 2 Epigraph. C. G. Jung, "Psychological Aspects of the Mother Archetype," *Collected Works*, vol. 9, paragraph 172.
  Chapter 3 Epigraph. Erik H. Erikson, *Young Man Luther* (New York: W. W. Norton & Co., Inc., 1958), pp. 261ff.
  Chapter 4 Epigraph. *The Real Mother Goose* (New York: Rand McNally, 1936). Epigraph: Tennessee Williams: *The Glass Menagerie*.
1. R. D. Laing, *The Politics of the Family* (Toronto: Canadian Broadcasting Corporation, 1969), p. 30.
2. D. M. MacKinnon, "Moral Objections," *Objections to Christian Belief* (New York: J. B. Lippincott, 1964), esp. pp. 23ff.
3. David Stacton, *Segaki* (London: Faber and Faber Ltd., 1958), p. 13.
  Chapter 5 Epigraph. Søren Kierkegaard, *The Journals (1834–1842)*, in *A Kierkegaard Anthology*, ed. Robert Bretall (Princeton: Princeton University Press, 1951), p. 1.
1. Daniel J. Boorstin, *The Americans: The Democratic Experience* (New York: Vintage Books, 1974), pp. 666–67.

2. 16th edition, Saint Louis, 1954.

3. For such processes, see Robert Masters and Jean Houston, *Mind Games* (New York: Delta, 1972); Roberto Assagioli, *Psychosynthesis* (New York: Viking, 1965); and the publications of the Psychosynthesis Research Foundation.

4. Maxwell Maltz, *Five Minutes to Happiness* (New York: Grosset and Dunlap, 1962), p. 11.

5. See *The Cybernetics of Cybernetics*, ed. Heinz von Foerster (Urbana: Biological Computer Laboratory, University of Illinois, 1974); and Norbert Wiener, *Cybernetics* (Cambridge: M.I.T. Press, 1948), p. 11.

6. See *Encyclopaedia Britannica*, Chicago, 1973, vol. 11, pp. 995–97; and *Encyclopedia Americana*, International Edition, New York, 1973, vol. 14, pp. 679–82.

7. James Esdaile, *Mesmerism in India* (London: Longman, Brown, Green, & Longmans, 1846).

8. Ronald E. Schor, "Hypnosis and the Concept of the Generalized Reality-Orientation," *American Journal of Psychotherapy*, 13, 1959, pp. 582–602. Reprinted in *Altered States of Consciousness*, ed. Charles T. Tart (New York: Doubleday, 1972).

9. Meanwhile, see Tart's anthology, op. cit., and his *States of Consciousness* (New York: E. P. Dutton & Co., Inc., 1975), and Daniel Goleman, *The Varieties of Meditative Experience* (New York: E. P. Dutton, 1977). For an account of Mesmer himself, see Stefan Zweig, *Mental Healers* (New York: Viking Press, 1932).

    Chapter 6   Epigraph. *General Introduction to Psychoanalysis*, chapter 27.

1. The name "human potential" was given to the movement by George Leonard and Michael Murphy. See Leonard's article, "Human Potential and the Failure of Nerve," *AHP Newsletter*, August 1977.

2. For studies of the seminal influence of Gestalt psychology, see W. W. Bartley, III, *Wittgenstein* (New York: J. B. Lippincott & Co., 1973); and W. W. Bartley, III, "Theory of Language and Philosophy of Science as Instruments of Educational Reform: Wittgenstein and Popper as Austrian Schoolteachers," *Methodological and Historical Essays in the Natural and Social Sciences*, ed. Robert S. Cohen and Marx W. Wartofsky, *Boston Studies in the Philosophy of Science*, vol. 14 (Dordrecht: Reidel, 1974).

3. *Psychotherapy and Personality Change*, eds. Carl R. Rogers and Rosalind F. Dymond (Chicago: University of Chicago Press, 1954), p. 345; and Carl R. Rogers, *Client-Centered Therapy* (Boston: Houghton Mifflin Company, 1951).

4. Carl R. Rogers, "In Retrospect: Forty-Six Years," *American Psychologist*, February 1974, vol. 29, pp. 115–23.

5. See his *Toward a Psychology of Being* (Princeton: Van Nostrand, 1968); and his *Motivation and Personality* (New York: Harper & Row, 1970).

6. Quoted in Richard J. Lowry, *A. H. Maslow: An Intellectual Portrait* (Monterey, California: Brooks/Cole Publishing Company, 1973), p. 91.

7. See Rogers's paper, "Learning to Be Free," in Carl R. Rogers and Barry Stevens, *Person to Person: The Problem of Being Human; A New Trend in Psychology* (Lafayette, California: Real People Press, 1967), pp. 47–66. See also Carl R. Rogers, *Carl Rogers on Encounter Groups* (New York: Harper & Row, 1970).

8. Carl R. Rogers, *Carl Rogers on Encounter Groups* (New York: Harper & Row, 1970).

9. See Gardner Murphy and Robert O. Ballou, *William James on Psychical Research* (New York: Viking Press, 1960), esp. pp. 8–12.

10. It was to become important to Werner and *est* in 1975, when *est* was accused of practicing psychology without certification by the Hawaii Board of Psychologists. The matter was referred to the Office of Consumer Protection, which has not acted in the matter on the grounds that no clear definition exists of the meaning of the key words in the relevant legislation.

11. Richard Farson, "Carl Rogers, Quiet Revolutionary," *Education*, 95, Winter 1974, pp. 197–203.

12. One goal of the *est* training is to bring the trainee fully to confront determinism—and then to transcend it.

13. I owe this image to Sir Karl Popper, to whom my understanding of determinism is much indebted. See his *The Self and Its Brain* (with Sir John Eccles) (Berlin: Springer Verlag, 1977). See also Sir Karl Popper, *Objective Knowledge* (London: Oxford University Press, 1972). See my paper "The Philosophy of Karl Popper, Part II: Quantum Mechanics, Probability, Indeterminism, The Mind-Body Problem," *Philosophia*, Israel, 1977.

14. P. S. Laplace, *A Philosophical Essay on Probabilities* (1819) (New York: Dover, 1951), pp. 4–5.

15. I borrow this metaphor from Popper, *Of Clouds and Clocks: An Approach to the Problem of Rationality and the Freedom of Man*, Arthur Holly Compton Memorial Lecture, Washington University, Saint Louis, 1965, published by Washington University in 1966; reprinted in *Objective Knowledge*, op. cit.

16. Rogers, "Retrospect," op. cit.

17. Rogers, "Learning to Be Free," op. cit., p. 47.

18. Sir Karl Popper, "Indeterminism in Quantum Physics and in Classical Physics," *British Journal for the Philosophy of Science*, 1950–1951, pp. 117–33 and 173–95.

19. See D. M. MacKay, *Brain and Conscious Experience*, ed. Sir John Eccles (New York, 1966), and Sir Karl Popper, *The Poverty of Historicism* (Boston: Beacon Press, 1957). See also the bibliography of Popper's writings in Popper's autobiography, *Unended Quest* (London: Fontana, 1976). See Alan M. Munn, *Free Will and Determinism* (London: MacGibbon & Kee, 1960). See also Arthur Koestler: *Janus* (London: Hutchison, 1978), chapter 12.

20. Rogers, "Retrospect," op. cit. See also Abraham H. Maslow, *The Farther Reaches of Human Nature* (New York: Viking Press, 1972).

21. On this whole matter see Arthur J. Deikman, "Deautomatization and the Mystic Experience," *Altered States of Consciousness*, op. cit., pp. 25–46.

   Chapter 7

1. William James, *The Varieties of Religious Experience*, lecture 8, et passim.

2. Watts did not *turn* to Zen after giving up his Episcopal priesthood. He had in fact been interested in Zen, and in other forms of Oriental thought, since he was a youth, and had published extensively about them. Among his many books, see *The Legacy of Asia and Western Man: Study of the Middle Way* (1937); *The Spirit of Zen: A Way of Life, Work and Art in the Far East* (1936); *The Meaning of Happiness: The Quest for Freedom of the Spirit in Modern Psychology and the Wisdom of the East* (New York: Harper, 1940); *Outline of Zen Buddhism* (Golden Vista Press, 1932); *Zen Buddhism: A New Outline and Introduction* (Perkins, 1947); *Supreme Identity: An Essay on Oriental Metaphysics and the Christian Religion* (New York: Pantheon, 1950); *The Way of Zen* (New York: Pantheon, 1957); *This Is It and Other Essays on Zen and Spiritual Experience* (New York: Pantheon,

1960); *Psychotherapy East and West* (New York: Pantheon, 1961); *The Book: On the Taboo against Knowing Who You Are* (New York: Pantheon, 1966); *In My Own Way: An Autobiography, 1915–1965* (New York: Pantheon, 1972).

3. This story is adapted from "A Cup of Tea," *Zen Flesh, Zen Bones,* ed. Paul Reps (Penguin Books, 1971), p. 17.

4. Koji Sato, *The Zen Life,* with photographs by Sosei Kuzunishi (Kyoto: Weatherhill, 1972).

5. *The Three Pillars of Zen,* ed. Philip Kapleau (Boston: Beacon Press, 1967), pp. 42–43.

6. See Koji Sato, "Zen from a Personological Viewpoint," *Psychologia,* 1968, 11, pp. 3–24, which has a valuable bibliography on these matters. See also Koji Sato, "How to Get Zen Enlightenment—on Master Ishiguro's Five-Days' Intensive Course for Its Attainment," *Psychologia,* 1959, 2, pp. 107–13; Heinrich Dumoulin, "Methods and Aims of Buddhist Meditation—Satipatthana and Zen," *Psychologia,* 1962, 5, pp. 175–80; Thomas Hora, "Tao, Zen and Existential Psychotherapy," *Psychologia,* 1958, 2, pp. 236–42.

7. One evening in June 1967, Werner was sitting in his car, in the parking lot in front of his apartment in Sausalito, counseling a member of his staff who was deeply distraught over a number of personal problems. A security officer disturbed them; Werner became very angry; and the officer filed charges of assault against him. All charges were later dismissed by the court.

Chapter 8

1. Santayana, "The Genteel Tradition in American Philosophy," op. cit., p. 205.

2. These books are all published by the American Saint Hill Organization, Los Angeles.

3. Christopher Evans, *Cults of Unreason* (New York: Delta, 1973).

4. Martin Gardner, *Fads and Fallacies in the Name of Science* (New York: Dover, 1957).

5. L. Ron Hubbard, *Scientology 8–8008* (Los Angeles: The American Saint Hill Organization, 1967), pp. 35–36.

6. A detailed description of Mind Dynamics procedures may be found in Jess Stearn, *The Power of Alpha-Thinking—Miracle of the Mind* (New York: William Morrow and Co., 1976).

7. See José Silva and Philip Miele, *The Silva Mind Control Method* (New York: Simon and Schuster, 1977). See also Masters and Houston, *Mind Games,* op. cit., and Jerome L. Singer, *Imagery and Daydream Methods in Psychotherapy and Behavior Modification* (New York: Academic Press, 1974).

Epigraphs to Part III Quoted in R. H. Blyth, "Zen and Zen Classics," vol. IV, *Mumonkan* (The Hokuseido Press, 1966), p. 175. Hermann Hesse, *Siddhartha* (New York: New Directions Paperback, 1951), pp. 101–2.

Chapter 9 Epigraph. Bassui Tokusho Roshi is quoted in *The Three Pillars of Zen,* op. cit., pp. 176–77.

1. Available from *est,* an educational corporation, 1976.

Chapter 10 Epigraph. From "Schopenhauer als Erzieher," in Nietzsche's *Werke* (Leipzig: Naumann, 1906), II, pp. 263–64.

1. Ludwig Wittgenstein, *Tractatus Logico-Philosophicus* (London: Routledge and Kegan Paul, 1922), proposition 6.54. See also Gershon Weiler, *Mauthner's Critique of Language* (Cambridge: Cambridge University Press, 1970), and Gershon Weiler, "On

Fritz Mauthner's Critique of Language," *Mind*, 67 (1958), pp. 80– 87, for Mauthner's use of the image of the ladder.

2. Sextus Empiricus, *Against the Logicians*, II, 481, trans. R. G. Bury (Cambridge: Harvard University Press, 1935), p. 489. The image of a fishnet is sometimes used in a similar way, as in Chuang-tzu, as quoted in Ben-Ami Scharfstein, "Salvation by Paradox: On Zen and Zen-Like Thought," *Journal of Chinese Philosophy*, 3, 1976, pp. 209– 34. See also Frederic Spiegelberg, *Living Religions of the World* (Englewood Cliffs, N. J.: Prentice-Hall, Inc., 1956), p. 167.

3. Werner Erhard, *If God Had Meant Man to Fly, He Would Have Given Him Wings* (San Francisco, 1973).

4. See Erik H. Erikson, *Childhood and Society* (New York: W. W. Norton & Co., Inc., 1950); Erik H. Erikson, *Young Man Luther* (New York: W. W. Norton & Co., Inc., 1958); Erik H. Erikson, *Gandhi's Truth* (New York: W. W. Norton & Co., Inc, 1969).

5. Allen Wheelis, *The Quest for Identity* (New York: W. W. Norton & Co., Inc., 1958), p. 41.

6. Søren Kierkegaard, *The Point of View for My Work as an Author* (1848), published posthumously in 1859.

7. See W. W. Bartley, III, *The Retreat to Commitment* (New York: Alfred A. Knopf, Inc., 1962), pp. 6– 7.

8. Friedrich Waismann, "How I See Philosophy," *Contemporary British Philosophy*, ed. H. D. Lewis (New York: The Macmillan Company, 1956), pp. 447– 90, and John Wisdom, *Philosophy and Psychoanalysis* (Oxford: Basil Blackwell, 1953), p. 274.

9. Hermann Keyserling, *Travel Diary of a Philosopher* (New York: Harcourt, Brace and Co., 1925), vol. I, p. 16, and vol. II, pp. 366– 67. See also Hermann Hesse, *My Belief* (New York: Farrar, Straus & Giroux, 1974), pp. 367– 68.

10. Homer, *Odyssey*, iv, 354– 569.

11. See W. W. Bartley, III, *Morality and Religion* (London: Macmillan and Co., Ltd 1971), pp. 56– 59.

12. William James, "Pragmatism. A New Name for Some Old Ways of Thinking," Lecture VI, New York, 1907. Reprinted in William James, *Essays in Pragmatism* (New York: Hafner Library of Classics, 1954), as "Pragmatism's Conception of Truth," p. 159.

13. H. G. Baynes, *Analytical Psychology and the English Mind* (London: Methuen and Company, 1950), pp. 61– 75.

14. See W. W. Bartley, III, "The Philosophy of Karl Popper, Part II," op. cit. See also Sir Karl Popper, *The Self and Its Brain*, op. cit., p. 14. For the view that something cannot come from nothing—that there is nothing new under the sun, or *ex nihilo nihil fit*—see *Ecclesiastes* 1:9, and Epicurus, *Letter to Herodotus;* and Lucretius, *De Rerum Natura*.

15. See W. W. Bartley, III, *The Retreat to Commitment*, op. cit., p. 140 et passim, and "Rationality versus the Theory of Rationality," *The Critical Approach to Science and Philosophy*, ed. Mario Bunge (New York: The Free Press, 1964). In the nonjustificational theory of rationality and criticism developed in these publications, I attack blind commitment or attachment to belief systems and ideologies and show— contrary to common philosophical supposition—that there is no theoretical excuse for such commitment.

Chapter 11 Epigraph. Friedrich Nietzsche, *Ecce Homo,* translated by Walter Kaufmann (New York: Vintage, 1967), p. 227.

1. Luke Rhinehart, *The Book of est* (New York: Holt, Rinehart, Winston, 1976).
2. Werner Erhard and Victor Gioscia, "The *est* Standard Training," *Biosciences Communications,* vol. 3, 1977, p. 112. See also Werner Erhard, Gilbert Guerin, and Robert Shaw, "The Mind's Dedication to Survival," *Journal of Individual Psychology,* 31, May 1975.
3. The training is, however, occasionally done in a nonarduous format, as for instance in prison trainings, without any apparent diminution of its effectiveness.
4. I owe this example to Dr. James Fadiman.
5. In *Being and Nothingness,* Sartre writes: " 'Having,' 'doing,' and 'being' are the cardinal categories of human reality. Under them are subsumed all types of human conduct" (New York: Washington Square Press, 1956), p. 557.
6. As quoted in Joseph Needham, *Science and Civilisation in China,* vol. II (Cambridge: Cambridge University Press, 1969), pp. 68–69.
7. Hermann Hesse, "The Speeches of Buddha," *My Belief,* op. cit., p. 383.

Epigraph to Part IV Friedrich Nietzsche, *Thus Spoke Zarathustra,* trans. Walter Kaufmann (New York: Viking Press, 1966), Part II, section 20, p. 139.

Chapter 12 Epigraph. Tennessee Williams, *The Glass Menagerie.*

Chapter 13 Epigraphs. Hermann Keyserling, *Travel Diary of a Philosopher,* op. cit., vol. I, p. 15; and Carlos Castaneda, *Journey to Ixtlan* (New York: Simon and Schuster, 1972), p. 29.

1. R. D. Laing, *The Politics of the Family* (Toronto: Canadian Broadcasting Corporation, 1969), p. 11.
2. See Allen Wheelis, *The Quest for Identity,* op. cit., pp. 17–18.
3. J.-P. Sartre, Selections, *Existentialism from Dostoevsky to Sartre,* ed. Walter Kaufmann (New York: Meridian Books, 1956), pp. 256, 274–75.

Appendix

1. Earl Babbie and Donald Stone, "An Evaluation of the *est* Experience by a National Sample of Graduates," Portions presented at the annual meeting of the American Psychiatric Association, Miami Beach, May 13, 1976.
2. Leonard L. Glass, Michael A. Kirsch, and Frederick N. Parris, "Psychiatric Disturbances Associated with Erhard Seminars Training: I. A Report of Cases," *American Journal of Psychiatry,* March 1977, pp. 245–47.
3. Interview reported in the *New York Times,* April 24, 1977. The Babbie-Stone report states that the incidence of psychotic episodes after the training is approximately 0.8 percent, "less than the number of people having episodes in college classrooms or just walking the street."
4. Letter to Graduates of the *est* Training, March 15, 1976. The results of this study are recorded in Robert Ornstein, Charles Swencionis, Arthur Deikman, Ralph Morris, "A Self-Report Survey. Preliminary Study of Participants in Erhard Seminars Training," March 21, 1975.
5. See Popper's work, as cited above. Also see his *Conjectures and Refutations* (New York: Harper Torchbook, 1968), especially chapters 12, 13, and 14.

Acknowledgments

Acknowledgments

For their assistance in the preparation of this book I want to thank, first of all, Werner Erhard himself, and the members of his family with whom I talked: Ellen Erhard, Pat Campbell, Joe and Dorothy Rosenberg, Al and Edith Rosenberg, Bessie Clauson, Ethel Clauson Cohen, Marjorie Wittingham, Sam and Helene Feinberg, Don Clauson, Mary Ellen Clauson, James Clauson, Kitty Clauson, Norm and Julie Danoff, Harry Rosenberg, Nathan Rosenberg, Joan Rosenberg, Clare Erhard, Lynn Erhard, Jack Erhard, Debbie Erhard, Celeste Erhard, Adair Erhard, St. John Erhard.

Every reader of this book will appreciate the openness of Werner's immediate family, their willingness to permit their privacy to be invaded in order that an accurate account of Werner's life might be presented.

Next I want to thank Don Cox, president and chairman of the board of directors of *est*, an educational corporation. It was his idea that this book be written, and that I write it. I am much indebted to him.

I want to thank the members of the *est* Public Information Office, in particular, Brian Van der Horst, Morty Lefkoe, Suzanne Wexler, Robert Alman, Barbara Blackstone, Linda Esposito, Mike Orgill, John Poppy, and Neal Rogin.

It is a pleasure to thank the *est* trainers and trainer candidates for interviews, and for permission to sit in on Trainers' days. My thanks go to Randy McNamara, Charlene Afremow, Phyllis Allen, Ron Browning, Ron Bynum, Landon Carter, Stewart Esposito, Tony Freedley, Vic Gioscia, Hal Isen, Jerry Joiner, Ted Long, Neil Mahoney, and Laurel Scheaf.

I am happy to thank the members of Werner's personal staff and office for their understanding and support of my project, and for their patience: Gonneke Spits, Marianne Andrascik, Diane Behling, José Bouchot, Lin Carter, William Clements, Roger Dillan, Nathan Fierman, Raz Ingrasci, Steve Jaber, Locke McCorkle, Maxine Mandel, Pat Peters, Jack Rafferty, Koko Sakai, and Pat Stimson.

I owe a special debt of thanks to *est* executives Rich Aikman, Elaine Cronin, Vincent Drucker, Gary Grace, John McMillan, Marcia Martin, and Howard Sherman.

I also want to thank Robert Dunnet, Harry Margolis, and the members of their law firm.

To Janice Wilcox, who was my research assistant, I owe a special expression of thanks, as I do to Tracy Stanfield, Sylvia Douglas, and Barb Otto, who typed drafts of the manuscript. I am particularly grateful to Norissa Leger and Francine Kohn, who typed the final manuscript. To Susan Stowens and Nancy Stillwell, who typed transcripts, I am also very grateful.

I express my thanks also to Ken Anbender, Ron and Shirley Baldwin, Elvina H. Bartley, Marie Cantlon, Clayton Carlson, Richard Carlson, Dianne Cox, Robert Culver, Rick Cunningham, Barbara Downes, Wendy Drucker, Lester W. Eckman, Alexander Everett, James Fadiman, Liz Ferris, Jo Fielder, Phyllis Ford, Robert W. Fuller, Betty Fuller, Sharon Geiger, Brian Gomes da Costa, Jay Greenberg, Samuel Gruen, Dub Leigh, William McCain, Peter Monk, David Norris, Charles Rosen, Bernard Roth, Sarah Rush, Camilla Sherman, Henry Tooke, Hugh Van Dusen, Charles P. West, Madeleine Wilkinson. Carol Wright is to be thanked for her illustration to chapter 11.

I am particularly indebted to my friend Stephen Kresge, who read the successive drafts of this manuscript, criticized it line by line, and made many suggestions that importantly improved the book; and to Vic Gioscia, who gave the penultimate draft a searching and brilliant reading. Any unity the book may have is due to these two friends. I am also indebted to Donovan Bess and to George Leonard, who gave extremely helpful readings of the manuscript.

I express my thanks also to these others who read and commented on the manuscript: Byron Callas, Robert Curtis, Nancy Fouchee, Helen Gilhooly, Norman Horowitz, Clayton Jones, Kate Lloyd, Frank M. Robinson, Ed Rosenfeld, Marcia Seligson, and Wendy Van der Horst.

I am grateful to the publisher, Jane West, and am especially indebted to the editor, Carol Southern, for her superb work on the manuscript.

I am obliged to the staffs of the following libraries, where I did research in connection with this book: The California State University, Hayward; The University of California, Berkeley; Stanford University; The University of London.

About the Author

WILLIAM WARREN BARTLEY, III, is Professor of Philosophy at California State University, Hayward. From 1967 to 1973 he taught at the University of Pittsburgh, where he was Professor of Philosophy and of History and Philosophy of Science. His previous appointments include the Warburg Institute of the University of London; The London School of Economics and Political Science; the University of California (Berkeley and San Diego); and Gonville and Caius College, Cambridge University.

Born in Pittsburgh, he graduated from Harvard College, and received his doctorate in Logic and Scientific Method at the London School of Economics. He has been Editorial Chairman of the *Harvard Crimson*, and a reporter on the Night City Staff of the *Boston Globe*.

Professor Bartley is the author of *Lewis Carroll's Symbolic Logic, Wittgenstein, Morality and Religion* and *The Retreat to Commitment*. He is a contributor to the *Times Literary Supplement*, the *New York Review of Books*, the *Scientific American, Commentary, Encounter*, and many other journals. He is known both for his historical researches and for his contributions to the theoretical foundations of philosophy, where he has developed the theory of rationality and solved Goodman's paradox.

He has held research fellowships from the United States Educational Commission in the United Kingdom, the American Council of Learned Societies, the University of California Institute for the Humanities, the Danforth Foundation, and other bodies. He is a member of the Board of Directors of the *Philosophical Forum*, and of the Werner Erhard Charitable Foundation; and is a member of the Advisory Board of *est*, an educational company, Ltd.